Issues in the Contemporary Politics of Sub-Saharan Africa

The Dynamics of Struggle and Resistance

Graham Harrison
Department of Politics
University of Sheffield

First published 2002 by
PALGRAVE MACMILLAN
Houndmills, Basingstoke, Hampshire RG21 6XS and
175 Fifth Avenue, New York, N.Y. 10010
Companies and representatives throughout the world

PALGRAVE MACMILLAN is the new global academic imprint of the
Palgrave Macmillan division of St Martin's Press, LLC and Palgrave
Macmillan Ltd. Macmillan® is a registered trademark in the United
States, United Kingdom and other countries. Palgrave is a registered
trademark in the European Union and other countries.

ISBN 0–333–78635–1 hardback
ISBN 0–333–98725–X paperback

This book is printed on paper suitable for recycling and
made from fully managed and sustained forest sources.

A catalogue record for this book is available from the British Library.

Library of Congress Cataloging-in-Publication Data

Harrison, Graham, 1968–
    Issues in the contemporary politics of Sub-Saharan Africa: the
    dynamics of struggle and resistance/Graham Harrison.
        p. cm.
    Includes bibliographical references and index.
    ISBN 0–333–78635–1
    1. Democratization – Africa, Sub-Saharan. 2. Peasantry – Africa,
Sub-Saharan – Political activity. 3. Rural poor – Africa, Sub-Saharan –
Political activity. 4. Rural development – Africa, Sub-Saharan. 5. Africa,
Sub-Saharan – Politics and government – 1960– I. Title.

JQ1879.A15 H34 2002
320.967–dc21

                                                                    2001058054

10 9 8 7 6 5 4 3 2 1
11 10 09 08 07 06 05 04 03 02

Printed and bound in Great Britain by
Antony Rowe, Chippenham and Eastbourne

Contents

Acknowledgements

This book is a product of five years teaching African politics, and the time provided to me to write by Tony Payne during my first year at the University of Sheffield.

I would like to thank Alison Howson at Palgrave for her support and flexibility during the book's preparation. External readers' comments on the project were also very helpful.

Thanks also to Jane, Jack and Lydia for too many reasons to mention.

This book is dedicated to Carlos Cardoso – Mozambican journalist assassinated in November 2000 – and the struggles he pursued.

List of Abbreviations

AICAJU	Cashew Industrial Association (Mozambique)
ANC	African National Congress
CCM	Communist Party of Tanzania (*Chama cha Mapinduzi*)
CDR	Committee for the Defence of the Revolution (Burkina Faso)
CMEA	Council for Mutual Economic Assistance
CZI	Confederation of Zimbabwean Industries
DRC	Democratic Republic of Congo
ESAP	Economic and Social Adjustment Programme
FORD	Forum for the Restoration of Democracy
FRELIMO	Mozambique Liberation Front
GEAR	Growth Employment and Redistribution Programme
HIPC	Highly Indebted Poor Country
IFI	international finance institution
IMF	International Monetary Fund
LIPAD	Patriotic League for Development (Burkina Faso)
MDC	Movement for Democratic Change
MMD	Movement for Multiparty Democracy
MOP	mode of production
MOSOP	Movement for the Survival of the Ogoni People (Nigeria)
NGO	non-governmental organization
NLC	Nigeria Labour Congress
NPC	Northern People's Congress (Nigeria)
NPN	National Party of Nigeria
NRM/A	National Resistance Movement/Army (Uganda)
NRP	National Republican Party (Nigeria)
ONUMOZ	United Nations Operation in Mozambique
PAMSCAD	Programme for the Amelioration of the Social Consequences of Adjustment
PDP	Popular Development Programme (Burkina Faso)
PNDC	Provisional National Defence Council (Ghana)
PRE	National Reconstruction Programme
quango	quasi-autonomous non-governmental organization
Renamo	Mozambique National Resistance
RPA	Rome Peace Agreement (Mozambique)

SAL	Structural Adjustment Loan
SAP	Structural Adjustment Programme
SDP	Social Democratic Party (Nigeria)
SINTIC	Cashew Workers Union (Mozambique)
SWAPO	South West Africa People's Organization
TANU	Tanzania African National Union
UDI	Unilateral Declaration of Independence
UN	United Nations
UNDP	United Nations Development Programme
UNECA	United Nations Economic Commission for Africa
UNIP	United National Independence Party (Zambia)
WAI	War Against Indiscipline (Nigeria)
WENELA	Witwatersrand Native Labour Authority
ZANU	Zimbabwe African National Union
ZAPU	Zimbabwe African People's Union
ZCTU	Zimbabwe Congress of Trade Unions

Map: Contemporary Africa

1
Introducing Political Struggle as Contemporary African Politics

Politics are thought and fought.

(Therborn, 2001: 87)

History is as much about Mandelas as it is about Malans.

(Allen, 1999: 470)

What do we mean when we speak of 'African politics?' Simple answers to this question would be foolhardy (Young, 1999), but much useful discussion has revolved around the concepts and issues which are central to the asking of this question. My aim in this book is to outline a conceptualization of political struggle and demonstrate the enduring importance of struggle in any understanding of African politics. This is not to say that 'struggle is everything'; certainly there is much empirical material to demonstrate the salience of political disengagement, Machiavellian strategies of power-seeking and the intermixing of political actions/strategies in particular local contexts. But, because there is a striking decline in academic attention paid to struggle, I justify this more parochial contribution as making a worthy point: it would be wrong to abandon a concept of political struggle when discussing how to answer the grand question that commences this book.

By paying particular attention to political struggle, the book offers a different 'angle' on the political analysis of a continent which is principally represented as a place of repression, authoritarianism and generalized decline. A great deal of the existing work on African politics has outlined and analysed the ways in which African societies have been the theatres for dictatorships, conflicts and poverty. There are obvious empirical reasons for this focus, and this book does not try to deny the dire situation that much of Africa faces. But the general impression left by this literature does violence to Africa's image. It produces images of passivity, helplessness and incompetence. It also produces images of innate violence and malice. We will return to the question of representation shortly, but it is important to note here that the general image evoked by these notions is misleading because it ignores the capacity of African societies and social groups to innovate, resist, challenge and elaborate new ideals of liberation in the face of the dire forces that produce the orthodox images of Africa. The message is not one of naive optimism, and far less of diagnostic-style programme building, charting 'a way forward' for a particular country or, more heroically, an entire continent. Rather, the point is clearly to argue that all forms of oppression produce their own seeds of resistance and all structures of inequality yield struggles for transformation. A genuinely measured analysis of African politics must take adequate conceptual account of the diversity of African agencies (collective and individual) based in dynamics of resistance.

This book will maintain a focus on popular struggle for this reason. It begins by analysing the tensions and contradictions that form the politics of *peasant* farmers in Africa because peasant farmers are both the most populous class in Africa and constitute those who are, by and large, the most remote from the centres of state power. Subsequently we will look at two key contemporary processes in Africa, *structural adjustment* and *democratization*, paying particular attention to struggles and political action. This is followed by an analysis of other forms of political action and struggle embedded in the elaboration of collective *political identities*, forged along the lines of work, migration or age. The next chapter takes three country *case studies* to illustrate the importance of struggle to postcolonial historiography. The concluding chapter takes a more reflective perspective, considering the prospects of an *ideal* of struggle. The rest of this chapter will deal with issues of methodology: how to analyse struggle, how to conceptualize 'African politics' and what boundaries to establish in the analysis of political struggle.

Analysing political struggle

Any analysis of political struggle must necessarily (but with varying degrees of explicitness) involve a normative component. The notion of struggle necessarily projects an ideal, or an end point which evokes an ideal situation or state of affairs, that is a condition in which a certain kind of struggle is no longer necessary. This ideal cannot be anything but normatively constructed, that is based on notions of what *should* be. Researchers might demur from making these normative positions clear, perhaps because – as with many liberal writers – they consider them self-evident and universal, but they always exist within the logic of an argument (e.g. see Jones's (2000) analysis of relativism). Normative postures can create problems, however, as implicit norms can easily appear as prejudices in the eyes of the reader. For this reason, I will be explicit about the normative framework of this book.

The book takes as its starting point the centrality of capitalism as a social system which has generated contradictions, forms of oppression and processes of exploitation. These phenomena take specific historical forms in different African societies: there is no universal 'base' upon which then to place forms of struggle as effects of the system. However, there are important generic characteristics to these phenomena: exploitation, oppression, and contradiction are hardly intrinsically capitalist phenomena, but there are specific forms of exploitation which derive from the fact that they occur within a capitalist global political economy. Responses to these phenomena, while not complying to some form of 'logic' demanded by an economic process, can hardly be seen as disengaged from the former's capitalist form. Furthermore, recognition of the centrality of capitalism and its political economy does not necessarily impute some specific functionalism to our analytical methodology. What it *does* do is privilege an integrated set of processes which give our understanding of struggle a particular content based in class relations, popular claims on social surplus and the relation between accumulation and notions of social justice. These points will be returned to later, but let us first relate the political economy of capitalism to our region of interest. There are four key features to capitalism's historical impact on sub-Saharan Africa which allow us to locate sub-Saharan Africa within the combined and uneven development (Rosenburg, 1996) of the world system.

Colonialism

It is debatable whether colonialism was an expression of the desire of European capital to expand its accumulation or a political rivalry between nation-states (see, for example, Freund, 1988). European powers certainly displaced their capitalist rivalries into the conquest of African territory, embodied most clearly in the Treaty of Berlin (1884) which constituted a 'handshake over new African boundaries at

European conference tables' (Freund, 1988: 90). Because capitalism is best understood as a form of society, not just an economy, it seems something of a false dichotomy to disentangle a supposed political and economic aspect to the colonial moment. From this perspective, we can discern two key effects of colonialism on African societies.

The creation of a national economy

National economies were constructed by European states and their colonial state progeny. From the late 1800s, and particularly in the 1920s, European capital was invested in infrastructural development (Iliffe, 1996: 212; White, 1993) such as ports, dams, telegraph systems and railways. These investments constituted the sinews through which broader social change took place. Colonial states imposed (via compulsory cropping) and regulated (via marketing boards and the imposition of taxes) the integration of African farmers into global markets, a process we will detail as peasantization in the following chapter. New working classes emerged at the ports and in the homes of European elites as cooks, servants, gardeners and guards. Some farmers – including lineage chiefs – became small-scale capitalists. Trading classes, often based on older patterns of trade, grew: in East Africa immigrant Asian communities became merchants and later owners of industries, as did Levantine communities in West Africa. There is a wealth of historiography detailing the complexities and variations of these processes (some of the best being: Cooper, 1987; Kitching, 1980; Brett, 1973; Mamdani, 1976), but for our purposes here it is important to recognize that colonialism ushered in a quickening pace of class formation (Sender and Smith, 1986), associated with direct foreign investment (private and public) and the development of capitalist markets, heavily regulated by colonial states. All of this took place within the boundaries of nation-states, which brings us to the second key feature of colonialism.

The creation of a nation-state

Before colonialism, Africa's political geography was very fluid and varied. The orthodox distinction offered to understand pre-colonial political geography is between centralized and segmented societies, but this obscures as much as it reveals as pre-colonial states expanded and retracted and patterns of trade and migration often linked individual societies. Colonialism imposed an alien political geography on Africa, based on absolute distinct borders and sovereign states. These states were made in the image of colonizing European powers, not with reference to African social realities. Despite some valid criticism, Alavi's (1972) metaphor of the overdeveloped state seems to encapsulate the initial construction of nation-states in Africa: states which derived their characteristics from Europe rather than Africa which existed 'over' or above African society.

The apparatus of the state prosecuted and reflected the prevalent *violence* of colonialism (contrary to images of a *pax colonia*): a police force, chieftaincy, military, networks of informants, all designed to enforce colonial domination. Economic instruments were designed to extract resources from Africans and to facilitate the expansion of foreign capital. In time, some states would begin to elaborate forms of economic nationalism which conflicted with the model of colonial state as a handmaiden for the metropole; this was most clear in those colonial states where significant numbers of European settler farmers emerged (Berman and Lonsdale, 1991; Smith, 1991; Arrighi, 1966; Pankhurst, 1995). The colonial nation-state also established a central and enduring contradiction: the aspiration to create a nation with a fairly homogenous citizenry in a social landscape defined by ethnic plurality and systems of migration and cultural intercourse which often violated the boundaries drawn up in Berlin (Davidson, 1992).

Economic integration

African societies have been integrated into broader economic systems for as long as any other region of the world. Trans-Saharan trade has connected Africa to Europe since classical times; Indian Ocean and Atlantic trade systems involving slaves, cloth, ivory, guns and so on, developed and changed over centuries (Alpers, 1975; Blackburn, 1997). Colonialism provided a political infrastructure that *intensified* economic integration and more strictly *linked* it to the economy of the colonial power. African colonial economies were the ultimate captured market. The establishment of states as authoritarian regulating instruments also facilitated new forms of investment and the development of an industrial base in some colonies (for example Nigeria and Kenya).

Colonialism established a more rigorous integration of Africa into flows of world trade and investment. In terms of investment, African colonies became the recipients of capital from the colonizing power. With respect to trade, almost all of Africa came to export a small number of unprocessed (primary) crops or minerals to the West (and mainly the colonial power), for example cotton, coffee, cocoa, sugar, copper and oils. As economies grew, colonies imported more European manufactured goods and technologies. Thus, colonialism established an *international division of labour* which has proved remarkably durable: African states became exporters of primary commodities and importers of manufactured (secondary) goods. This division of labour remains today, with many African economies relying on one or two primary commodities for 80 per cent or more of their export revenue.

But integration was, and is, far from even, both between and within African states. Within states, coastal areas, cities and mineral-rich regions received what economic benefits colonialism had to offer. In states with a European settler class, some rural areas – those with European farms, high rainfall and relatively productive soils – received the lion's share of infrastructural development, relegating other rural areas to poverty as 'reserves'. One can see the legacy of this in contemporary South Africa or Zimbabwe, where a geography of 'commercial farming areas' and 'reserves' persists. Regional inequalities have generated and reinforced ethnic rivalries within African states, a stark example being Nigeria and the perceived 'northern domination' of the Hausa Fulani over the more economically developed 'Igbo' or 'Yoruba' regions to the south (see Chapter 6). Although there is no one-on-one correspondence between ethnic and economic geography, one can also see the interplay of regional differentiation and ethnic politics in Zimbabwe (Shona-Ndebele), or Kenya (Kikuyu dominance in the 'white' highlands). In West Africa, older Atlantic networks created coastal elites which were consolidated during colonialism, creating divisions between the coast and 'up country'. This is a key part of any explanation of conflict in Sierra Leone or Angola, for example, where Creole elites have dominated inland societies, the former often seeing the latter as less developed. Another example of differential integration into the world economy and its divisive effects might be Uganda's north–south division (Doom and Vlassenroot, 1999).

Imperialism

Imperialism, in its broadest sense, means the employment of state power to shore up or project economic power outside its own national boundaries. In respect to Africa, this draws our attention to a postcolonial history of external intervention and power projection, perhaps only matched in its erosive effects on state sovereignty by America's bullying of Central America since the late 1800s. For this reason, a term with common currency in the 1970s was *neo-colonialism*, connoting a substantial continuity from the colonial period, a kind of 'show' or 'flag' independence. One can see this enduring external influence from the ex-colonial power most clearly in francophone Africa, where the central and west African franc zones tied postcolonial economies to France, and where the French Foreign Legion maintained a presence, even taking action to promote or prevent changes of regime (Cruise O'Brien, 1991; Luckham, 1982). In anglophone states, British forces provided military training, either at Sandhurst or *in situ*, for example in Zimbabwe and Kenya.

More broadly, postcolonial elites – very much the product of the colonial period – looked outwards to their relations with the West as much as to their relations with their own citizens (Clapham, 1996). This produced what Jackson and Rosberg (1982) call 'quasi states': states in which a degree of sovereignty is only realized through external support and the mutual recognition of state sovereignty within the state system. *Internal* sovereignty – that is, sovereignty over a national citizenry – can be quite meagre, even in situations of powerful external support and recognition. Foreign transnational companies also promoted this 'extroverted' (Bayart, 1993, 2000) world view in postcolonial elites through corruption, or more specifically the payment of high-ranking officials to maintain an advantageous business environment (Moody Stuart, 1997).

The most significant development in Africa's experience of imperialism was the growing interest of the two Cold War superpowers in certain parts of Africa (Halliday, 1989). In general, superpower rivalry was only intense where significant geopolitical conflicts emerged, most importantly in the Horn of Africa (Luckham and Bekele, 1984; Petras and Morley, 1984) and in southern Africa (Anstee, 1996; Stockwell, 1978; Brittain, 1998; Hanlon, 1986; Minter, 1988, 1991; Nesbitt, 1988; Wright, 1997), and most violently in Ethiopia and Angola. The Cold War exacerbated conflicts as protagonists were supported, mainly militarily, by one or other of the superpower rivals, to immense human cost (something for which neither victor nor loser in the Cold War is willing to consider responsibility). More broadly, the Cold War imposed a dualizing ideological framework on Africa: postcolonial states were either to be aligned with the West or the Soviet Union, or displayed tendencies of 'falling' into one camp or another. It was resistance against this external dichotomy that led Julius Nyerere to be a strong proponent of the Non Aligned Movement. For others, notably Joseph Mobutu, this external environment constituted the rules of his 'game' of extroversion: he would play up the communist danger in order to win favour with his American backers. He was himself on the CIA payroll before his coming to power in 1965, creating a difficult relationship between superpower patron and regionally powerful client state that was to endure for another thirty years (Schatzberg, 1990; Schraeder, 1996). This example highlights that extroversion can be a strategy actively pursued by African elites, the key to Bayart's understanding of the term. The interaction of external imposition with internal co-option can only be fully understood by looking at concrete historical examples.

State and class

The politics of African postcolonial states cannot simply be understood by looking at the influence of global political economy: this would be to simplify African politics and reproduce images of African societies solely as passive and victimized. African postcolonial societies are complex and divided, much like anywhere else in the world. One key 'internal' social relation is that between political power and economic accumulation. At independence, postcolonial societies contained a class of capitalists which did not enjoy class rule in the sense that we generally understand in developed capitalist societies (Charney, 1987). With the significant exception of immigrant merchant classes (Asian in East Africa and Levantine in West Africa), and because of the late and brief colonial period and the baroque rules and regulations colonial states imposed to restrict indigenous bourgeoisies, African capitalists constituted very much an *aspirant* class, not possessing the social domination afforded by a pervasive ownership of private property. Capitalist classes varied significantly between states: different relations to the state; activity in different sectors of the economy; different ethnic or racial composition and so on (Iliffe, 1983; Kennedy, 1988). But, in many countries a key component of emerging postcolonial politics was the forging of a unity of political (state) and economic power. The exact form of this unity was, again, varied: capitalist classes might 'capture' the state, as in Côte d'Ivoire (Rapley, 1994); they might be substantially created and regulated by the state, as in Zambia (Baylies and Szeftel, 1982); or the state might develop a strong parasitic tendency, 'milking' a bourgeoisie of its surplus (MacGaffey, 1994). But underlying this complex relation – partly complementary, partly antagonistic – was (and is) the employment of political power directly to promote accumulation. Control of the state has become so central to accumulation that political struggle has taken on a keenness that reflects competition not only for office but also for business: to be out of the political loop is to face economic marginalization as well: a loss of export licence, a failure to win public contracts, a lack of support from public authorities in legal matters and so on. To gain office is to have the ability to employ patronage and violence to shore up one's business, spread property among one's family and clients, and to enrich oneself through basic theft from the state coffers.

This powerful relationship, quite different from the contemporaneous theorizations of the relative autonomy of the state in the West, led academics to conceive of a bewildering mixture of terms for the ruling elites: bureaucratic bourgeoisies, petty bourgeoisies, state classes and so on (Shivji, 1978; Saul, 1974). Rather than engaging with these terms – most of which confuse as much as enlighten – we should note some of the effects of the unity of political and economic power because these effects contribute significantly to the way African people experienced political power after independence.

- *Corruption*. Much of the corruption in postcolonial states was essentially a series of strategies of private enrichment and accumulation from office, as described above. The levels of corruption varied significantly from state to state (Harrison, 1999a), but in the sense described above, we can see corruption as accumulation and enrichment through the state.
- *Authoritarianism*. Political power became so central to accumulation that political and high-ranking bureaucratic office became keenly contested. Ruling elites were very unwilling to open state power to rival factions, or to the population in general. This dynamic contributed to the collapse of multipartyism (Munslow, 1983; Cohen and Goulbourne, 1991), the continuity of succession within a particular clique and the violence of many changes of power as rival factions struggled for office.
- States and *extra-economic coercion*. State power was employed not just to regulate capitalist activity but to *promote* it, in partisan or semi-licit fashion, on behalf of particular factions that had control of the state and often employed the threat or practice of coercion. As such, the state employed violence or bureaucratic fiat in order to extract surplus from the labouring masses. Mamdani identifies this process as key to class struggle in Uganda (1983; 1987). As we shall see in the next chapter, some states developed tendencies to act as large-scale capitalists, using state companies and marketing boards to extract surplus from peasants, underpinned by interventions into peasants' modes of livelihood.
- The unity of political and economic power was not a stable or harmonious relation. *Contradictions* between accumulation and political power abounded as factions fought over patronage, and states

extracted such high rent from their citizenry that peasants (Chapter 2), traders and others bypassed the state altogether. As the spoils of office declined, politics became less stable and more contradictory (Allen, 1995). In other words, the state–class relation was not a structural-functionalist component of capitalist modernization: the struggle for office and the consumptive proclivities of ruling elites could constrain capitalist accumulation as much as promote it (Boone, 1994: 164).

In sum, the key historical components of Africa's modern interaction with global capitalism are: colonialism, global economic integration along the lines of the international division of labour, the rise of superpower rivalry in the Third World, and the unity of economic and political power. With the partial exception of the Cold War, these historical processes allow us to understand the importance of capitalism in determining African states' political trajectories since the late 1800s. This is not a narrative of 'capitalist logic' derived from an economic model, but a specific political economy generated historically. But how does this inform our understanding of struggle and political action?

Structure and struggle

The section above narrates a quite severe set of inauspicious historical [*non-favorable*] processes for any notion of struggle; in fact, it seems hard to imagine how political struggle might begin to take place in the face of external conquest, disadvantageous global economic relations and venal [*corrupt*] forms of postcolonial rule. Many have understood Africa's problems, both economic and political, as a result of a set of constraining *structures*, based on the factors noted above. In other words, African states have been integrated into global economic structures in ways that impoverish them, domestic class structures militate against democracy, class structures in African societies necessarily exploit the peasant majority, and ruling classes are structurally located to serve the needs of foreign capital. Much of this epistemology came from the rather patchy transposition of dependency theory from Latin America to Africa (Leys, 1996; Rodney, 1972).

This book finds this approach unsatisfactory, for the following reasons.

- This approach provides an excessively rigid evaluative framework for political action. Only clear progress towards delinking is seen as politically progressive and significant. The mode by which this is supposed to take place is not very clear (a problem for dependency theory in Latin America, at least in the Gunder Frank version). Amin (1987) speaks of a popular national alliance which includes parts of the ruling class; others have theorized forms of social revolution in the periphery. This then leaves any other forms of political action as either insignificant or under-theorized.

- It conceives of class politics in terms of economic structures rather than in terms of historical configurations based on economic, political and social interaction with other classes. There is a Althusserian flavour to this structuralism which relegates political forms and actions to the realm of superstructure, or a product of a more powerful economic 'base'. This book will approach struggle within a more integrated political-economy framework in which the base–superstructure approach is seen as a false dichotomy. Classes do not exist by virtue of their structural location; they are created through social struggle, interaction and forms of accumulation. As such, social struggle and interaction will constantly modify, or even transform, class relations.

- The main contradiction and conflict in this schema is between the West and the Third World. This leads to a quite stark set of political possibilities: either reformism which will not make any real difference to anything, or a break with the world system dominated by the West, what Amin calls delinking (Amin, 1990 – although some have tended to caricature Amin's argument). No serious attention is paid to other more modest forms of political action, whose effects might be complex and important but not 'structurally significant' in the terms of a core–periphery system. This framework also creates an epistemology too starkly based on internal and external, or nationalist and imperialist. It is not clear that national resistance to forms of external intervention are necessarily progressive; they might be part of a strategy to shore up domestic power in an authoritarian form. It is also excessively reductionist to identify all external intervention as necessarily damaging (although the historical record tends to confirm that this is most often the case). This book will try to capture the complexity of political interaction within states, recognizing that global interaction almost always plays a role in shaping these interactions. It is too easy – and politically vacuous – to blame everything on the West.

We can suggest an alternative analytical framework which will be loosely applied in this book. The main aim of the book is to investigate the nature of political struggle rather than develop a theoretical model, so I will not attempt a full theoretical excursion. Instead, the approach can be outlined in the following points, with some references to the chapters to follow.

- It would be fanciful to abandon the notion that in African politics forms of political struggle face severe constraints, imposed by and large by powerful actors outside the reach of ordinary people. In this sense, we can speak of structures. This will become especially apparent in Chapter 2, which details how forces with external origin have powerfully dominated and exploited peasant farmers, or in the latter parts of Chapter 4, where the 'good governance'/ democratization agenda is analysed.
- These structures are not entirely the product of an economic logic. Rather, they are *social*, that is the product of a variety of forces which have been rather falsely separated into sociology, political science and economics. For example, as noted earlier, imperialism was not just a process which obeyed an economic logic; it also involved political rivalries and aggrandizement; specific imperial histories also reveal significant cultural components to imperialism, based on ideologies of liberalism, christianity, 'civilizing' missions, *lusotropicalismo* in the Portuguese colonies, modernization and so on. There is limited use in trying to identify a 'determining' factor in what is only really understood as a historical and social process. Without this recognition, it would be necessary to condemn movements for multi-party democracy as ineffectual as they have made no difference to 'economic structures', but – as we shall see in Chapter 4 – these movements are still significant (albeit modest) historical developments. In Chapter 5, we will investigate the complexity of interaction between historical change, political movements based on identity, and political economy in a way that would be substantially outside the scope of a concern with structures as a purely economic phenomenon.
- An awareness of structures does not necessarily require that we treat some social relations as immutable. Structures are robust and resilient, but they are also reinforced and undermined by human agency. The long-running structure–agency debate in the social sciences has produced a thread of work in which the rigidity of structures does not endow them with permanence, and changes in social relations and the actions of agencies allow structures to change slowly, rapidly or collapse altogether. It is in this sense that Giddens

speaks of structuration (1995), and Gill argues that 'structures are transformed by agency' (1993: 23). The salience of this point derives from its repercussions for the way we understand struggle: there is no pre-emptive logic which prohibits us from entertaining the possibility that struggle *can* make a difference to structure.

- *Structures and struggle*. The recognition of the existence of structures, and their constant reproduction or reconfiguration in the context of social relations, leads us to recognize that there is *struggle* embedded in all structures. Structures can be dominating, but still contain an element of social contest and resistance. If they did not, the structures of capitalism would be dire indeed! Just as it would be facile to see postwar capitalism in Europe and the emergence of social democracy purely as structures of the bourgeoisie, rather than the outcome of union and labour/communist activity (as well as the threat of the Soviet Union), it would be equally mistaken to imagine that political structures in African societies do not contain within them a 'moment' of resistance. In Chapter 2, we will see that forms of peasant resistance can substantially define state structures in rural societies; in Chapter 3, the imposition of economic reform by outside agencies can only be understood by looking at forms of resistance and struggle between classes and social groups and their engagement with the politics of executing a structural adjustment programme. As Chapters 3 and 5 make clear, struggles do not have to be explicitly opposed to a structure to make a difference to its contours.

The underlying normative approach (or 'feel') of the book derives from these points: powerful forces have made Africa's political history one of oppression, marginality and poverty. But this is not the whole story, and to imagine that it is is actually to evacuate Africans – individually and collectively – of agency. In fact, all processes of domination contain within them, and provoke, acts of resistance, even if these acts do not necessarily directly challenge an oppressor. In a way, the power of structural forces in/on Africa (as defined above) serves to underline the significance of *any* political resistance, bearing in mind the severe context in which they are elaborated. The message that the book wishes to convey is that politics is not absolutely determined by structures in Africa, that eschatologies of inevitable decline are politically vacuous, and that the analysis of any political problem in Africa (as in any other part of the world) should not preclude the *possibility* (not the prescription) of resistance and resolution. We will return to these arguments in Chapter 7, but in sum, Marx's aphorism nicely sums up the approach taken here: 'men [and women] make their own history, but not in circumstances of their own choosing' (Marx, 1978: 595).

Africa and the politics of representation

> Africa is a unity, but it is not homogeneous.
>
> (Mamdani, 1995b: 17)

It is the normative charge to the notion of struggle that leads us to consider briefly some epistemological questions concerning our unit of study. Is Africa a valid 'field of study'? Over the last ten years or so, increasing attention has been paid to the way in which writers have constructed representations of Africa which can be quite diverse. This raises the question of the extent to which writers are actually analysing the reality of Africa, as a region of the world, rather than making their own images of Africa as a result of their cultural background or political predisposition. Undoubtedly, for some readers, these questions will have already come to mind in respect of *this* author when reading the first sections of this book. We will engage with these issues here, again to illuminate something of the methodology of struggle.

Africa and homogenization

'Africa' is indeed a dangerous word. Running courses on African politics in British universities, I find myself at the start of courses constantly policing the tendency of students to treat Africa as a country ('when France colonized Africa...'; 'she visited Africa in...'). This is reflected in public discourse: the broadsheet newspapers spoke of an 'arms to Iraq' scandal, but also of an 'arms to Africa' scandal, rather than an 'arms to Sierra Leone' scandal. The Band Aid lyrics to the song 'Feed the World', making an appeal for relief during the Ethiopian famine of 1984 state: 'There won't be snow in Africa this Christmas.' Throughout the late 1980s and 1990s, the outbreak of civil conflict in states such as Somalia, Liberia and Sierra Leone led journalists to make grand generalizations about an 'African malaise' or even a 'dark continent' in their opinion pieces (see *New African,* July/August 2000, for a review of this form of reportage). In this book, I have already used the word 'Africa' in ways that are very generalized. Can one make this generalization in a way that does not reduce the diversity of the continent's politics to a homogeneous entity? Can one employ the term

'Africa' without summoning up the ethnocentrisms that were eloquently detailed in Edward Said's (1995) concept of orientalism?

Let us first set out some clear boundaries. In this book, Africa will be used as shorthand for those countries south of the Sahara which are not currently subject to ongoing civil conflicts, and excluding South Africa. Other countries located geographically within the continent are referred to in the text, but where this is the case, explicit associations to the argument will be made to justify this. Conflict-riven societies will not be included partly because this would create too excessive a diversity to allow us to make meaningful generalizations. That is not to say that there is a small number of distinct factors which divide conflict-riven states from generally peaceful ones; but it is to say that civil conflict raises too many important and distinct issues to be incorporated within the general focus of this book. To integrate these states into the book would involve a consideration of struggles for peace, struggles over territory and resources, forms of secession, an analysis of 'complex emergencies' and so on. South Africa is left out because of its somewhat unique history, although researchers argue about whether South Africa is extreme or exceptional compared with the rest of the continent (Mamdani, 1996; Bernstein, 1996a). Thus, our focus is somewhat narrower than the geographical entity of Africa, but the term is used as a shorthand for sub-Saharan states not riven by civil conflict. One might use the term 'Europe' to connote the European Union to the exclusion of some eastern and central European states in the same fashion.

However, we can also identify some key common features of African politics derived substantially from the points made above concerning Africa's experience with capitalism.

- The origins of contemporary African states lie in the recent and brutal colonial project. For the three cases in Chapter 6, Mozambique, Nigeria and Burkina Faso were colonized by Portugal, Britain, and France respectively.
- African economies still engage with global markets principally as primary commodity exporters. In 1992, the 12 poorest African states relied on primary commodities for 89 per cent of their export revenue (World Bank, 1994: 190–1; see also Barratt-Brown, 1995; Sutcliffe, 1986). Again, for our three cases, Mozambique: prawns, cashew and cotton; Nigeria: oil; Burkina Faso: cotton.
- Postcolonial ruling elites were derived from a small collection of social groups close to the colonial state in the decade before

independence. In Mozambique, this social group was a progeny of the colonial state and concentrated in the south; in Nigeria a complicated situation was created by the way colonialism created a politically powerful northern bloc and more 'modern' and economically developed elites in the south through the missionary schools, cocoa production and trade. In Burkina Faso, an elite was created out of the colonial bureaucracy and Mossi ethnic power.

- African countries are substantially agrarian societies, to a greater extent than other regions of the world except South Asia. Seventy to eighty per cent of Mozambique and 80 per cent of Burkina Faso's population live in rural areas. In Nigeria, despite a more substantial industrialization and the growth of cities, the majority still reside in the countryside.

- All African states are undergoing (or have recently undergone) a programme of economic reform under the sponsorship of the World Bank and IMF. SAPs (Structural Adjustment Programmes) were signed in Mozambique, Nigeria and Burkina Faso in 1986, 1987 and 1991 respectively.

Not all of these criteria are exclusive to Africa, and there are some exceptions to some of the 'rules' set out above (for example, Liberia was never colonized by Europe) but their combination certainly does define a substantial regional politics which gives 'Africa' as an analytic unit meaning. One can see that Africa's common characteristics derive from a particular historical experience with global capitalism: 'the extreme dependence of the continent as a whole on external forces has conditioned developments within specific countries and also given Africa, *a certain uniformity*' (Goulbourne, 1987: 40, emphasis added). There are two other 'binding features' which are more complex in their origin and explanation.

- African states are *poor*. Mainly an effect of the points noted above, African states occupied the lowest 19 places in the United Nations Development Programme's Human Development Index in 1997, although some of this is accounted for by conflict-riven states. Sub-Saharan Africa contains 34 of the world's poorest nations (*Financial Times,* 27 April 1993). For 1997/1998, excluding South Africa, Africa's GNP per capita was US$ 316; its average life expectancy was 50 years.

- African countries have a binding social trait, based in *lineage*. However one formulates this statement, it will inevitably appear controversial, but some formulation of the statement lies implicitly within most social scientific research on Africa. The difficulty with the statement is that it might connote all kinds of chauvinisms, references to colonial and postcolonial racism and such feeble-minded ideas as Africa as a 'traditional' or 'savage' place (Harrison, 2002). But, as we shall see in Chapter 2, a diverse and fluid dynamic of lineage is central to African political life. In other words, for most African people, one's extended family, village/neighbourhood community, language group, family name or common ancestor have a great deal of salience in day-to-day social life and in the forms and features of African politics (Bayart, 1993; Mamdani, 1996; Berman, 1998; Allen, 1995). Lineage is not just a synonym for 'rural' because lineage associations and politics are produced in cities as well as villages; in fact lineage politics pervades the strategies of the modern ruling elites as a flexible structure to channel accumulation and patronage. Nor is lineage a synonym for 'ethnicity', although most ethnic identities make a claim to some form of common lineage structure and a myth of origin based on a founding patriarch or matriarch.

Taken together, these seven points constitute an acceptably robust social entity, defined as 'Africa'. The points do not make a perfect delineation, but then what concept or social entity does have absolute boundaries? In one sense, academics need to make an open and honest choice, between an explicit methodology which allows for meaningful generalization, or resorting to a postmodern epistemology in which not only does 'Africa' not exist, but neither does 'Kenya', 'peasant', nor 'Luo'; rather, there exist significations evoked by these words which produce discourses on 'Africa', 'Kenya' and so on.

Of course, defining a set of common features does not tell us anything about the extent and form of diversity, even within a fairly robust general unity. The existence of some broad similarities does not preclude very significant differences. To illustrate with one example: the Democratic Republic of Congo (DRC – formerly Zaire) was a Belgian colony, forged out of the fiefdom of King Leopold's Orange Free State, and bequeathed a sudden independence in 1960, only to face strong secessionist forces in Katanga, quashed with external intervention. From 1965 Zaire was ruled by one man, Joseph Mobutu, until Laurent Kabila took power in 1996. All of the DRC's neighbours are quite different in important respects: Angola was a Portuguese colony which gained independence in 1975; Uganda was a British colony which gained independence in 1962; and Congo was a French colony which gained independence in 1960. In order to remain cognizant of the diversity within unity, Chapter 6 presents three case studies, applying the points made in previous chapters to particular postcolonial histories.

Images of Africa and ethnocentrism

Another point concerning our focus in this book has less to do with levels of analysis and more to do with the images that the analysis produces. This was alluded to earlier with reference to Said's concept of Orientalism. Said argued that Western culture has historically – even before capitalism – defined itself vis à vis the Other, that is an 'eastern' or 'oriental' non-Western-ness. Said shows how these constructions of orientalism are based on exoticism and notions of savagery. In respect to Africa, Said's idea has a lot of resonance (see the various articles of the journal *Race and Class*). Africa has suffered from a whole range of cultural biases and prejudices generated by Western writers since the colonial invasions, producing tropes of savagery, primitivism, sensational accounts of 'ritual' (itself a word that has contested connotations), anarchy and what might be best summarized as infantilism (African societies and individuals as 'innocent' of modernity, Africa as an 'untouched' continent and so on).

Of course, no serious study of Africa would recall these tropes in the present day, despite the persistence of some of these in dampened form in the print and electronic media (a clear example being the reportage on the genocide in Rwanda – see Karnick, 1998). But is there a deeper epistemological continuity which underlies even the most clearly 'Africanist' writing within the West? Mudimbe (1998) defines a Western epistemology, based in European culture and the Enlightenment, which has imposed a system of knowledge on African societies and intellectuals who have subsequently integrated and reconciled this with other forms of knowledge. Amadiume (1997) argues that European concerns with visible and public power structures have rendered them blind to forms of matriarchy within many African societies. One response to this epistemological orientalism (to coin a cumbersome phrase) is to evoke counter-currents based on an assertive African identity, explicitly *not* Western. This is Amadiume's argument (although it is less than convincing). Much of the recent construction of an 'counter African-ness' has derived from Afro-Americans, making references back to some image of a 'homeland' (Lemelle and Kelley, 1994). Howe (1998) gives a brilliant account of how problematic these counter-currents can be, even if they are based on sentiments of challenging biases and prejudices against Africa. In fact, it seems just as problematic to challenge one set of dualisms with another, however progressive they purport to be (Appaiah, 1992). A more interesting and convincing approach is to understand Africa's experiences with ethnocentrism as an unequal encounter that has generated resistances, assimilations and innovations in identity (a leading text here is Gilroy, 1993).

Moving from issues of culture back to methodology, the point concerning a rejection of dualities is important here as well. For some, the crux of the politics of African–Western relations is the ideological force of liberalism. Young (1995) and Williams (1999) conceive of African–Western relations as, in essence, a liberal project being imposed on African non-liberal societies. Young and Williams provide sophisticated and insightful analyses, which are not as starkly dualized as some forms of dependency theory, but the key to their analysis is a supposed contradiction between an imperialist liberalism – forcing men to be free (Young 1993a) – and a set of cultures in which the self is embedded in forms of community. Therefore, there is an authoritarianism in liberalism's imposition – through Western-sponsored economic reform and political conditionality to promote multipartyism – and a violence in its effect, as culturally embedded selves are wrought into individuals as nuclearized citizens.

There are repercussions in this analysis for methodology. The analysis above argues that the force of liberal ideology produces a kind of epistemic authoritarianism, as Western academics impose liberal frames of analysis (neoclassical or marxist) on African realities. Perhaps notions of human rights, civil society, democracy and so on are so embedded in Western liberalism that they can only be culturally authoritarian (Hopgood, 2000). So, why are these terms used in this book in more or less conventional terms?

- African societies are not different from other societies in a fixed and stable manner. Differences between societies are complex, and can be recently constructed as well as historically embedded. The contours of difference change over time, and not just in response to overbearing external forces. It is therefore possible to employ universal concepts, as long as one is aware that they contain a 'health warning' concerning their culturally and historically specific origins.
- We have already seen that colonialism and capitalism have *imposed* similarities on Africa, in terms of class formation, modern states and

national economies. This is certainly not to say that all of these features have made Africa in the image of Europe – far from it. But, for all the differences in the historical construction of states and classes in Africa, they do still exist and deserve to be analysed as such with an awareness of a tension between homogenizing and differentiating forces.

- Again, following the previous point, it is true that one can employ the concepts of Western social science in ways that do not restrict all *flexibility* in their application. Concepts can be adapted and employed to make insights into specific forms of cultural politics. Some have used Weberian notions of a moral community or E. P. Thompson's moral economy (1980) to understand quite clearly non-liberal forms of political action. Others have used a fairly standard Western epistemological approach to 'de-exoticise' the politics of sorcery, magic and witchcraft with considerable success (Meyer and Geschiere, 1999a; Wilson, 1992). We will return to the flexibility of established political concepts, as well as recently established (but no less Western) poststructural concepts in Chapter 5.

Having made these points, I would not wish to refute the insights of Young and Williams *tout court*. Most importantly, it is certainly the case that the Western–African encounter has been one of cultural arrogance from the former, and a belief/conviction that what African countries need is to become modern, that is Western/liberal in their cultural forms. This book accepts this point, but understands the force of liberalism's 'imperialism' within a broader framework of imperialism based on the emergence of capitalism in Europe and the dynamics that it created. It is not clear that one can impute to liberalism as an ideology a primary historical agency, unless one follows Fukuyama's (1992) approach in which history is the contest of political ideologies. It is worth bearing in mind that liberal theory in its classical form is based on *two* founding ontologies: individual freedom and private property. Liberalism's effect is to conflate the two, and the persistence of this conflation is a result of the historical ascendance of capitalist societies.

One final point concerns the role of theory in a more fundamental sense. As mentioned earlier, there is no theory or methodology which does not contain a normative premise. The critique of liberalism connotes a normative position of *cultural relativism*, that is an assumption that the world contains fairly distinct and coherent cultural systems which work according to their own social and moral norms. Consequently, one cannot judge other cultures because one inevitably applies criteria from one's own culture. I am not convinced by this approach. Cultures are significant and diverse, but also fluid and porous: there are no hermetically sealed cultural boundaries, and to suppose that there are can generate alarming normative standpoints (Huntington, 1996). Does cultural relativism imply that the West should disengage with Africa entirely? Academic endeavour in the (liberal) social sciences has always been concerned to make abstractions, generalizations, associations based on some normative base that *humanity* exists, with certain similarities and, consequently, rights. This book is willing to entertain a degree of 'cultural imperialism' – historically rooted in the European and liberal origins of the University (Wallerstein, 1997) – for the sake of maintaining a normative standpoint that condemns hunger or torture as a violation of human rights, in whatever society they occur.

This brings us to our final methodological point: the normative contours of our concept of liberation.

An analysis of struggle implies an ideal of *liberation*. Notions of liberation can be explicitly expressed or abstracted from an analysis of political action, even if not held explicitly by the agents of political action. In this book we employ liberation in both senses. We do not employ liberation in a third sense: what people *should* do in order to produce political meaning. There is no overarching theory or prescription of liberation, based in the heroic narratives of revolution, delinking or an achievement of 'modernity'. To employ such a concept would be to dress an authoritarian methodology in progressive clothing which hides an excessive positivism (in order to achieve *a*, agent *b* must do *c* ...). As such, explicit references to liberation rarely appear in the book; rather, the concept is employed to calibrate our evaluations of political struggle. This 'background' liberation is based loosely on:

- a sympathy with mass action, or the political actions of the oppressed and marginalized;
- an awareness of the contradictions generated by the social relations of capitalism;
- a concern to locate agency, as struggle, at the centre of an analysis of structures that constrain, exploit or oppress;
- an awareness of the complexity of politics as action, in terms of organization and the repercussions of action. In other words, liberation does not prescribe a strict organizational or mobilizational pathway within the 'messy' terrain of struggle;

- it is noteworthy here to establish what *isn't* seen as liberation. Political actions of revenge and violence and actions based on an identity which denies other groups basic rights are not considered under the rubric of struggle and liberation. Rather, liberation here relates to ideals of equality, widening political participation and resistance to overbearing power.

The aim of this concept of liberation is modest. It is not to state that a definitive step along a pathway to liberation has taken place; nor is it to predict a definitive end-stage for struggle. Rather, it is used to employ a framework – if nothing else at least explicit and honest in its formulation – which can give analytical meaning to political struggle which, despite the powerful forces that render so many dire images, is an essential component to a full understanding of African politics. The aim of this book is to review structures of power and, through this, identify 'spaces' of struggle or resistance.

Further reading

One of the best general historical introductions to Africa is Freund (1988) and subsequent editions. Clapham (1996) and Schraeder (1996) provide good accounts of Africa's global relations, the former more theoretically, the latter empirically. On the much-disputed issue of class in Africa, see Berman and Leys (1994) and Kitching's (1980) seminal study of Kenya. A very stimulating book on how to conceptualize Africa is Appaiah (1992). Other books which deal with 'African-ness' from very different points of departure are Bayart (1993) and Howe (1998).

2
Peasants, Politics and the Struggle for Development

Moving beyond the prejudices

Sub-Saharan Africa contains a majority of peasant farmers. Broad demographic trends reveal that – along with South Asia – sub-Saharan Africa is the world's main agrarian region. Over one half of sub-Saharan Africa's aggregate economic output derives from rain-fed agriculture using basic production techniques (Gibbon, 1996a: 775). It is also the case that many of the identified 'problems' or challenges which Africans face derive from the ways in which rural societies have changed in reaction to external powerful forces: famine, civil conflict and environmental change, among others. For these reasons, any analysis of contemporary issues in African politics should start with the peasantry, the majority of the population of most states, and those faced with some of the most intractable difficulties in securing sustainable livelihoods, both politically and economically.

As the previous chapter established, much of the politics in any analysis of Africa's contemporary situation derives from the way problems are (re)presented in the first place. This applies not only to notions of struggle, but even to the essentials of categorization and definition. This issue is particularly germane to an analysis of the peasantry because debates concerning the actual definition of 'peasant farmer' already have a long lineage, dating back to the rise of capitalism, the Industrial Revolution and discussions concerning the role of the peasantry in socialist revolution (Harriss, 1982; Kitching, 1982; Cowen and Shenton, 1998).

So, let us begin by asking: what is a peasant? Within Western culture – so urbanized and so infused with pernicious values from the colonial period – 'peasant' immediately takes a derogative form, associated with images of primitiveness or childishness at its extremes, likened to isolation, simplicity and innocence in its more moderate guise. The idea of 'primitive peasant' certainly reflects the colonial legacy. The associations of peasant with isolation, simplicity and innocence have broader and deeper socio-historical origins in what Brass calls 'the agrarian myth' (Brass, 1997). The agrarian myth that Brass describes is a complex and constantly modified idea of *peasant-ness*, based around coordinates of difference and a peasant essence derived from working the land.

The arguments that peasant societies are primitive or 'simple' and that they are isolated or innocent of the powerful social relations of modernity have both come under sufficient criticism to render them defunct. More sympathetic (and diligent) writers have identified the varied and complex funds of peasant knowledge which direct decisions concerning production, migration and socio-cultural behaviour. For example, the frequent (colonial and postcolonial) concern with population pressure on land with a limited carrying capacity is often presented as a question of educating peasants to reduce family size. But in many cases, population growth is regulated within peasant societies through the distribution of livestock or the timing of ceremonies to mark the passage into adulthood which in turn manages the formation of new households. Others have argued that peasant knowledge about the environment and production is more sophisticated and appropriate to the challenges of production in arid and semi-arid zones (Leach and Mearns, 1996), or that Western technical advice constitutes at best benign blunder and at worst unmitigated disaster. One famous example of the latter is the groundnut scheme in Tanzania which invested in Western technology-intensive groundnut farming and did not produce a single nut.

The encounter between various hues of Western 'expert' and peasant farmer provides a history of failed development projects and misunderstandings. This raises a very important point – key not only to an understanding of the agrarian myth, but also to the ongoing interventions of external agencies in peasant life: consultants, researchers, development workers and (as we shall see) also national bureaucrats, politicians and technicians rarely feel it incumbent upon themselves to make sufficient effort to understand the 'target' of their intervention. The seminal text here is Chambers' *Putting the Last First* (1983), in which he identifies a series of biases implicit in the normal process of research which provide the researcher with a partial and misleading view of what is actually happening in a peasant community. This is the ignorance of the 'outsider' (Chambers' phrase), not the peasant.

One might also consider here the work of some 'postcolonial' writers, who have argued that the 'subaltern' cannot fully express themselves vis-à-vis the powerful – at best they might achieve a dialogue, with each speaking a different language both only partially understood by the other (Spivak, 1988). The problem with this idea of peasant 'other-ness' is that, once again we stray into the realm of peasant essentialism. As we shall see, things are more complicated than this dualism would allow – not least because what has been central to the politics of the peasantry is a dynamic of interaction with other classes and agencies.

Especially from the 1960s, anthropologists and others have identified the ways in which peasant societies interact with other social groups and institutions, at first through the notion of acculturation (a modernist concern with the decay of cultural facets in the face of other imperialistic or overpowering cultural forces), and subsequently through the development of ideas related to the articulation of modes of production (about which more later). Previously, the ethnographic orthodoxy of the colonial period was to study each culture as a self-contained social unit, functioning according to its own laws, and reproducing itself accordingly more or less in a way that maintains a social equilibrium (from a very large literature, see Crehan, 1997; Ranger, 1980, 1985). This was certainly not the case, as we shall go on to see. It is actually very questionable whether peasant societies were *ever* self-contained and stable (Neimeijer, 1996). Coquery-Vidrovitch (1976: 91) makes the same point with a rhetorical question:

> How far back do we go to find the stability alleged to be characteristic of the pre-colonial period: before the Portuguese conquest, before the Islamic invasion, before the Bantu expansion? ... [T]he static concept of 'traditional' society cannot withstand the historian's analysis.

So far, we have carried out a basic 'ground-clearing' exercise: we have established that peasant society is not primitive in any essential sense: the notion of primitiveness has been generated by the biases of the observer, often confirmed through poor methods of research. We have also recognized that peasants are not isolated or backward, removed from the intrinsic dynamism of modernity. But this is merely to make a start. If we have some idea of what peasants are *not*, we need to ask what peasants are.

Conceptualizing the peasantry

Let us begin with an important caveat – one that recalls another general lesson from the previous chapter: peasant societies are extremely diverse. Diversity works along many axes: matri- or patri-lineal; arid or semi-arid; highland or lowland; settlement pattern; mono- or polytheism; decentralized or centralized polities; relations to trade networks; the forms of artisanal skill; language or family of languages; relations with neighbouring societies; the use of livestock or not; forms of age-setting or gender relations; techniques of house construction, grain storage, to mention the most obvious. The matrilineal peasant of northern Mozambique speaks a different language, cultivates different crops, has a different experience of colonialism, and dresses herself in a very different way to the patrilineal male elder in the cocoa-growing areas of Western Nigeria. So why call both of these individuals peasants?

The principal unifying characteristic which has allowed writers to generalize across Africa's diverse rural social tapestry is the prevalence of family or lineage-owned and run smallholdings. A proportion of the produce on the farm is destined for consumption within the family/productive unit. Production techniques are labour-intensive – typically involving a hoe and other tools, perhaps involving livestock and a plough, and occasionally a tractor. But once we move beyond these basic characteristics, we need to employ more analytically useful and less descriptive terms. We will look more closely at analytical issues, and in doing so identify some key points concerning the ways in which peasant farmers have interacted with broader processes of socio-economic change or development. This will allow us to put forward some key points about peasants as agents of political action and struggle.

Peasants and class

In the first place, the peasantry is defined as a class. Classes are intrinsically *relational* concepts – one class cannot exist unless in relation (often opposition) to others. Much of the study of African peasantries has attempted to look at the insights that class analysis brings to issues of agrarian change, the latter of which is often known as 'the agrarian question' (see Box 2.1).

Box 2.1: The agrarian question

How do peasant societies change as a result of deepening and expanding forces of capital accumulation and commoditization?

Main issues:
- Integration of peasant production into national/global markets.
- Commoditization of peasant production, that is the increasing presence of money within circuits of peasant production and consumption.
- The undermining or modification of peasant production as a result of the expansion of capitalism.

Main questions:
- Do peasantries dissolve as capitalism expands?
- Will peasantries differentiate into rich aspiring capitalist farmers and landless farm workers?
- Can peasants resist the forces of commoditization? *Should* they resist these forces?

Peasantization

Let us begin with the process of peasantization itself. Within analyses which put questions of class at centre stage, there is no such thing as a 'natural' or timeless traditional social group. In fact, class-based approaches to the peasantry did a great deal to debunk the *Gesellschaft* images mentioned in the previous section. For those who analysed peasants as a class, peasants were created through a historical process related to the expansion of capitalism.

One of the best-known works on this process is Colin Bundy's *The Rise and Fall of the South African Peasantry* (1979) which makes conceptual points of relevance to the rest of the continent. In this book, Bundy shows how the black farmers of South Africa maintained a sufficient degree of autonomy from the forces of English and Dutch power and business. They did this by maintaining control over their land and by engaging with markets only at their discretion, in other words when they thought it appropriate to do so. So effective was this autonomy that indigenous farmers often successfully out-competed settler farmers: by exploiting their own family labour, they could put crops on the market at a lower price than those offered by the settlers. This was the process of peasantization: an integration into capitalist networks of trade and production and – like West African farmers after the First World War – peasant farmers often showed themselves to be quite capable of taking advantage of spreading colonial markets where they had the chance. From 1913 the South African state introduced marketing institutions which offered settler farmers higher selling prices for their crops. Settler farmers also enjoyed access to extension services and credit. And – of massive historical significance for South Africa – the state began to evict African farmers from their land until, by the 1970s, black Africans, who constituted 83 per cent of the population occupied just 13 per cent of the land. This constituted the 'fall' of the peasantry.

As mentioned in Chapter 1, there is a debate concerning the extent to which South Africa was extreme or exceptional vis-à-vis the rest of Africa; but the process of peasantization was one which worked beyond the boundaries of South Africa. In fact, peasantization constituted one aspect of all colonial states' policies, and it reminds us again of the importance of colonialism in creating a component of commonality between African societies. In the rest of southern Africa, where most countries had a significant settler presence, peasants had to deal with states that created institutions with dualized price systems in favour of settler farms (Thompson, 1991; Mackintosh, 1987). For example, the Maize Control Act 1931 established a two-tier price system in Rhodesia, setting the buying price of maize for settler farmers above that offered to the peasantry. There is a particularly rich literature on forms of peasantization in Kenya from the 1930s onwards (Cowen, 1981; Heyer, 1981; Orvis, 1993; Kitching, 1980). In West Africa, where there was a negligible settler presence, peasants did not suffer evictions as they did in southern Africa, but nevertheless, they were integrated into politically structured agrarian markets on terms that subordinated their previous (relative) autonomy. Talking about the peasantry in Ibadan, Nigeria, Beer and Williams give the following account:

> Prior to the First World War, the price paid to the cocoa producer was higher in real terms than it has been ever since. But the commitment of resources to cocoa... has forced the farmer to bear the brunt of subsequent collapses in the world price and of the exactions of the intermediaries on whom the farmers are dependent for marketing their crops. The colonial administration subjected them to the power of the State and to manipulation by the possessors of a

literate culture. In short, *cocoa farmers were incorporated into the colonial political economy as a peasantry.*

(1975: 235–36, emphasis added)

What both the accounts from Nigeria and South Africa have in common is the identification of a politically guided process of peasant subordination to markets. The pivotal policy within this process was the imposition of a tax regime which compelled all peasant households (with some exceptions for the infirm) to engage with the money economy on whatever terms were available in order to pay tax, usually organized as a poll tax (known as a 'hut tax'), that is a tax on households. Failure to pay one's taxes meant one or all of the following: imprisonment, a beating and a period of forced labour. A similar fate met the many peasants subject to compulsory cash crop production, especially in respect to cotton (Isaacman and Roberts, 1995; Isaacman, 1996; Vail and White, 1978). The encounter between state and peasantry was profoundly affected by the question of tax-raising: taxation bequeathed a difficult legacy for postcolonial states as we shall see later on.

It is the integration of African farmers into broader political economies by states that constitutes the key to the process of peasantization. Having established that the peasant class was created out of the political and economic forces of colonialism, we now turn to consider how relations between peasants, states and economic forces have developed over time.

Perspectives on agrarian change: modes of production

Consider the social location of peasant farmers during late colonialism (1960s onwards) or during independence: locked into a broader set of political–economic relations over which they have minimal control and which work in the interests of external and powerful forces, perhaps as far away as the main players on the coffee and cotton markets in Europe and America. Does this spell the beginning of a process of historical decline in peasant farming? The historical persistence of peasant societies (Bryceson, Kay and Mooij, 2000) requires us to look at ways in which researchers have theorized the social relations of the peasantry and their interactions with other social forces.

One set of writings, mainly from French radical anthropologists, suggested that peasant farming would not decline as a result of the ongoing development of capitalism. In fact quite the reverse: systems of capitalist production *actively maintained* peasant farming systems in order to extract surplus from them. In other words, because of the resources that states and capitalists could extract from peasant farmers, policies and economic relations developed which, in one sense, under-mined peasant production (by extracting surplus) and in another sense reproduced peasant production as part of a broader social formation. So significant was the idea of the persistence of peasant farming to these writers that they located peasant farming entirely outside of capitalism, as a separate mode of production – the peasant mode of production.

The notion of a peasant mode of production (MOP) has significant connotations, because it raises the question: what exactly is the rela-tionship between peasant and capitalist systems? The answer to this question is based on the idea of an *articulation* of modes of production: both modes of production encounter each other, modify themselves during the encounter but reproduce themselves with their own discrete 'logics'. Needless to say, the encounter between capital and peasant was not one of equals. Rather, the encounter is described as one in which capitalism establishes a relationship of domination over the peasant MOP. The analysis of modes of production can become rather abstract and complex, and its details will not detain us here (see Foster-Carter, 1978; Wolpe, 1972, 1980; Meillassoux, 1981; Seddon, 1978). But it is worth outlining the principal mechanisms of articulation as they impacted on peasant livelihoods.

The principal means through which articulation was effected was migration (see also Chapter 5). Particularly in southern Africa, peasant societies were integrated into a migrant wage labour system, oriented around the plantations and mines of South Africa, but also in Rhodesia (now Zimbabwe). These systems of labour migration were enforced and regulated by colonial states, albeit with varying degrees of success. This was not a process of *proletarianization* in which peasants left the land for the factory or mine. Rather, wage labour was arranged around a system of short-term contracts managed by state agencies, most impor-tantly WENELA in South Africa. Peasants only had the 'right' to work at a particular mine for a period of six or nine months, before being 'exported' back into the countryside (Munslow, 1981; Cohen, 1980; Van Onselen, 1980; Harries, 1994).

It was thus that a system of *rural reserves* emerged – sustained through agriculture and wage remittances. This system of reserves and migrant labour was the key to the social geography of southern Africa (Cliffe et al., 1988). But how did it work to the advantage of capital?

What interests did the mine owner have in the migrant labour system and the peasant wage labourers it yielded? The system of wage labour meant that employers never had to pay a wage that encapsulated the costs of maintaining a household with a family near the place of work. The costs of childcare, house maintenance, food production and part of the worker's own recuperation and sustenance were borne in the farming areas or reserves, and they were borne principally by the wife. Her labour subsidized the labour of her husband at the mine to the profit of the employer. Writers who identified this relation called it *superexploitation:* the peasantry was being reproduced by capital through the migrant wage system in order to allow the costs of labour to be borne outside the domain of the employer (Marcus, 1980). There is no doubt that there is a significant truth to this argument. Its significance is only augmented if one considers that hundreds of thousands of migrant labourers were pulled into the system (and then spat out again) every year, and that South Africa's industrialization was centrally premissed on the mining sector (Fine and Rustomjee, 1996).

So, the concept of an articulation of modes of production has given us some insights into the fortunes of peasant societies in the face of the forces of capitalism, modernization and social change. But it does raise some further critical questions.

- If there is a peasant *mode of production*, can we still conceive of the peasantry as a *class*? After all, modes of production contain within themselves class relations.
- Is there a danger of understanding too many aspects of peasant society as a function of the reproduction of capital? In other words, does the MOP approach suffer from a *functionalism* in which everything works in order to maximise profits?
- Following on from the above, does the MOP approach allow space of flexibility, contradiction and individual agency without which notions of political struggle cannot exist? There exist forms of worker resistance within the migration system (Van Onselen, 1980; Cohen, 1980) which disrupt the smooth workings of the migration machine. There are also important issues of culture which influence the ways in which worker-peasants have acted both 'at home' (in the villages) and 'at work' (in the mines) (see especially Harries, 1994). Research on southern Mozambique (the major source of migrant labour for South Africa) in the 1970s identified processes of social differentiation in which some migrants served perhaps ten stints in the mines as part of a strategy to build up a base of wealth

in their rural area of origin (First, 1977; van den Berg, 1987). These people – tailors, tractor owners and so on – do not fit the model of impoverished migrant labour working under the compulsion of the dominance of one MOP over another.

Perspectives on agrarian change: peasants as petty commodity producers

Another perspective on the peasantry attempts to reconcile some of the difficulties of the MOP perspective. One might call this approach the petty commodity producer approach. Here, peasants do not have their own mode of production; rather, they constitute part of the class structure of a capitalist society. Because they own their own property (land), but do not employ other labourers (as a capitalist would), they work as petty commodity producers. This means that they exploit not workers but themselves in order to put goods on the market and thus earn money.

This model has been most clearly developed by Henry Bernstein, although his own approach has changed over the years. Bernstein argues that capitalism has gone to the core of peasant production. That is to say, capital has not reproduced peasant production 'at a distance' across modes of production, but has profoundly changed the logic of production itself. Peasant households are *compelled* to involve themselves in capitalist markets not necessarily as a result of state compulsion and migration, but as a result of the fact that production has become so profoundly commoditized that it is impossible not to. Bernstein, employing Marx's concept, argues that peasants' simple reproduction requires engagement with capitalist markets. Simple reproduction is, to all intents and purposes, the ability to subsist, or to get adequate food and shelter to survive. This involves engagement with the market because all peasants need to buy some food during lean periods or to purchase basic tools for farming (1977: 62–3).

Again, as with MOP, Bernstein identifies the state as a vital institution in defining and enforcing the 'vertical integration' of peasants into broader circuits of exchange (1981: 174). But what exactly does Bernstein mean when he speaks of capitalism extending into peasant production systems (Bernstein, 1977: 64)? The state and markets regulate the peasant production process, influencing the amount of land and labour given over to certain crops, affecting labour relations, especially between men and women within the household (Bernstein, 1990: 73–4), and intervening with various rural 'development' projects, the end result of which is a deepening of commodity relations within peasant agriculture. Bernstein takes the example of Tanzania to illustrate these processes, and to emphasize the importance of state actions within peasant society. The state rearranges peasant production, technically and spatially; it uses its party offices as 'mobilizers' of labour; and it uses its marketing/extension apparatus as regulators of the interrelations between peasants and capital (1981; see also Raikes, 1982; Coulson, 1981, 1982; Havnevik, 1993).

Central to the state's ability to transform peasant production and to extract surplus is its control of the *terms of trade*. Because prices have been determined by state marketing agencies (partly in response to world commodity prices), they can be set in ways that involve a hidden transfer of value from peasant vendors to the state. The ratio of peasant selling prices for crops against the prices of the goods peasants wish to buy are called the terms of trade, and these terms are almost always stacked against the peasant sellers. States have frequently bought peasant crops at a fraction of global prices and resold them at a massive mark-up. Remaining with the example of Tanzania, Ellis estimates that 'the share of producers in the final sales prices of their [export] output declined from 70 per cent to 42 per cent between 1970 and 1980' (Ellis, 1982: 221). This has led some writers to identify the state marketing boards as the main obstruction to agrarian development, and with good reason. Nigeria is another well-treated example (Helleiner, 1966; Williams, 1985). We will return to the nature of state involvement in peasant society in more detail below.

The notion of peasants as petty commodity producers provides a more integrated and flexible understanding of peasants' interrelations with other classes and economic structures. Like MOP, this perspective has little to say about culture, although it does allow space for peasant politics and resistance, and is thus less functionalist (Bernstein, 2001). Perhaps the main problem with the concept of petty commodity production is that, unlike the family shop or shoe repairers, peasants produce not just for sale but also for self-consumption, and some peasants sell cash crops grown in specific fields allocated for that purpose, while others sell in a more occasional fashion, sowing food crops in the hope that an adequate surplus will be generated to make enough money at the market to buy a new shirt or machete. The second kind of peasant farmer may find him or herself working for the first kind for a period of the year, perhaps creating households of both land and labour scarcity. Orvis outlines the importance of these distinctions for an understanding of the agrarian question in Kenya (1993). Can the petty commodity model encompass these kinds of social relations and the differentiations that they produce?

Bernstein argues that, despite the profound social transformations which accompany the deepening of commodity relations within agriculture, peasant differentiation does not necessarily spell the oft-ordained historical decline of the peasantry (see also Bryceson, 1999, 2000). There is no *necessary* process of class formation within the peasantry, that is a process of differentiation in which some employ labourers and others lose their land. One feature of accumulation within the peasantry which is apposite here is the tendency of wealthier peasants to diversify out of agricultural production: rather than expanding and capitalizing a farm, rich peasants often set themselves up in trade, transport, retail and so on (for a Nigerian example, see Berry, 1983, 1985). However one interprets differentiation, it is certainly the case that, in the face of inauspicious external forces, peasants have proved to be remarkably resilient. This is a result of peasants' flexibility and capacity to exploit their own labour, that is to intensify work and undergo increasing hardship.

This resilience of peasants during processes of 'modernization' is something which both MOP and petty commodity producer models try to understand. The conventional understanding – based on social histories written about Europe (Barrington-Moore, 1966) and theories of capitalist development – is that peasants are exiting the historical stage as a result of the development of capitalism, which supposedly tends towards scientific technology and large-scale production. But such linear understandings have been found wanting on a number of counts (Neimeijer, 1996), and there have been recent processes of peasantization, de-peasantization and even *re*-peasantization, although not in sub-Saharan Africa (McMichael, 1997; Bernstein, 2001). The lesson here is an important one: that it is not possible to identify linear and immanent futures for peasant society in sub-Saharan Africa – there is a necessary process neither of de-peasantization, nor of ongoing peasant 'relative autonomy' in the face of social disturbance. This leaves our analytical terrain open for a range of possibilities for peasants as agents of political struggle.

Peasants and culture

Considerations of culture are not absent from class-based analyses (Bundy, 1979; Murray, 1992; Kitching, 1980). But what all class-based approaches have in common is an attention to the powerful economic forces impacting on peasant production. These render cultural politics *contextual*, that is contemporaneous manifestations of social contradiction and change. They privilege the nature of peasant production and relations of exchange over lineage and communal land ownership.

Part of the reason for the downplaying of culture as an important explanatory factor in the understanding of change in peasant societies was the desire to reject the legacy of colonial research, in which peasant production worked according to a kind of cultural logic. The reintroduction of culture to centre-stage came with Goran Hyden's work on peasants and modernization (1980, 1983). Hyden argues that peasants have successfully avoided the turbulent forces of modernization altogether: they have not become part of a capitalist system. The phrase Hyden uses is that peasants are an *uncaptured* class: they have escaped the predations of both state and capital and have successfully maintained their independence. In this sense, peasants maintain an essential non-modernity. This non-modernity is identified through what Hyden calls an 'economy of affection' (1980), and it is this notion that allows Hyden to put culture at the centre of his analysis. Modern economies are defined by instrumentalism and individualism; economies of affection are defined by ethnicity and communalism, or in Hyden's words 'blood, kin, community or other affinities, for example, religion' (1983: 8). Peasants retain their culture and it is this that explains the fact that peasants do not produce for profit or engage in markets unless forced to. They would rather produce to distribute gifts to kith and kin than accumulate and expand; they would rather satisfy than maximize. Their obligations are not to themselves but to their community and their chief. Hyden paints a picture of a kind of historically obstinate class, infused with lineage-based mores which keep them at one remove from the commoditized and technically advanced interventions of state and capital.

Unsurprisingly, Hyden's arguments created strong reactions from researchers who understood peasants as part of contemporary capitalist political economies. The main reaction of these writers was to argue – convincingly – that it was misleading to understand peasants as 'uncaptured' when such a wealth of historical evidence revealed their (often, but not always, coerced) integration into wider circuits of exchange and production (Kasfir, 1986; Cliffe, 1987; Bernstein, 1990: 73; Williams, 1987). So profound are these interconnections that peasants' 'exit option' from official markets does not produce a refuge in self-sufficiency, but an engagement with other markets and forms of production, as Nabuguzi (1993) shows in the example of Uganda during state collapse. But another aspect of the uncaptured peasant debate relates to Hyden's arguments about the notion of progress. Hyden argued that the future lay in the destruction of the peasantry. Their inimicability to modernity required their eradication by state or capital (Hyden put more faith in the state). This is not to say that peasants themselves should be destroyed of course, but their autonomy, their culture, and their livelihoods must be undermined in order to allow progress in the countryside. The main problem that Hyden identifies is that states are too weak and peasants too independent for this historical encounter and its subsequent progress to take place. Peasants can ignore, undermine or escape state schemes and policies, or, as Hyden phrases it, they can exercise their *exit option*.

Williams strongly rejects this argument, saying that peasants are quite capable of 'modernizing' or taking advantage of social change. Rather, the problem is that states are always trying to prescribe what is best for the peasantry rather than allowing them to decide for themselves, based on their own judgements about the nature of markets. This constitutes part of Williams' argument for 'taking the part of peasants', and in an earlier argument he identifies the central problem that peasants face:

> Modernization and development represent the achievements of advanced, industrial societies and define the objectives of backward, nonindustrial societies... 'peasant' denotes cultural and technological backwardness. Peasants are assumed to lack initiative and innovation. *They are unable to develop. They must be developed* [...] Modernization and development have been achieved only on the backs and over the dead bodies of peasants or by the liquidation of peasants as a class. The recalcitrance of peasants to outsiders' conceptions of progress and the peasants' place in it defines the peasants as backward and delineates the peasant problem.
>
> (1976: 131–2, emphasis added)

Williams puts more emphasis on politics, particularly the politics of the encounter between states, international institutions (Williams, 1981) and peasants. He rejects Hyden's dualism of a state and an uncaptured peasantry by emphasizing the dynamics of the interaction between the two, and more than most writers from a class-based approach, he integrates a political dynamic which is not necessarily wedded to the analysis of a specific economic process. He has been criticized by others for placing too much emphasis on the kind of analysis which flows from the quotation given above, as it leads to an image of 'virtuous peasants and vicious states' (Bernstein, 1990), but Williams does place the state–peasant encounter on its own terrain and he is willing to entertain that a less economistic process of 'development', 'modernization' or simply state consolidation is a vital component in the analysis of the peasantry. He also provides space for peasant agency and struggle based not on resistance to 'modernization' per se (Hyden's approach), but the terms under which change is prosecuted. We will come back to this in the next section, but we need to review one final way in which peasant society has been analysed.

Exit the peasant and enter the smallholder?

Even Hyden, for all his opposition to other radical writers, claims for himself some affinity (affection?) for marxist methods. The final part of this section outlines an analytical framework which is in many ways quite removed from all notions of class. For this reason, the term 'peasantry' is often replaced by 'smallholder' (or 'family farmer'). What distinguishes a smallholder from a peasant? The answer to this question derives from the context in which the smallholder is placed. Smallholders are small property owners. The property that they own is a form of capital which the family (and possibly others) work on in order to make profits. In this way, smallholders resemble small businesses: able to flourish in a market society, not be exploited by it. In the words of the World Bank's influential 'Berg Report': 'all the evidence points to the fact that smallholders are outstanding managers of their own resources [and]... can be counted on to respond to changes in the profitability of different crops and of other farming activities' (1981: 4).

There are repercussions of this recasting of peasants, which distinguish this perspective from the previous ones. Where there was once a class, engaged in contradictory relations with other classes and institutions, there is now a class of property owners, who potentially can flourish as capitalism develops (more on this later). Where there was once a peasantry which organized life according to the logic of 'affection', there is now a rational-thinking maximizing group of individuals or households, balancing considerations of profit and risk (Lipton, 1982b). The context in which smallholders are placed provides the nub of the agrarian question for these writers. It is the state, and especially its marketing boards, that stymie the efforts of smallholders to flourish in rural markets. States distort market forces; they exploit smallholders through setting the terms of trade (a phenomenon noted by many other writers); they introduce inefficiency to the supply of services which progressive smallholders require (Bates, 1987).

The reason for these Leviathan-like interventions by the state into rural areas is the state's urban bias (Lipton, 1982a). States have an immediate constituency in urban areas – vocal middle classes, militant working classes and unruly informal sectors. All of these groups are spatially concentrated, and near to the centres of power. Peasants are dispersed and remote; they express their demands in less direct ways, often without engaging in the lingua franca of the state itself, and for these reasons, they are vulnerable to the predations of an urban-biased state, desirous to keep its urban citizens at least minimally content. If it wasn't for the state's intervention, agrarian development along free-market lines would do the trick: '[rural development] is not a case of efficiency versus equity, but both versus power' (Lipton, 1982a: 67).

Again, this approach has produced responses from others (Byres, 1982; Corbridge, 1982), and one powerful criticism is worth brief mention here. Byres argues that the urban bias argument fetishizes space at the expense of class: there are extremely poor people in the cities, and there are dominant groups within the countryside. In fact, Lipton does allow space for a rural elite, but only in so far as it is in alliance with the ruling urban bloc. The model presented is rather like a miniature version of dependency theory's core and periphery, and thus it suffers from similar shortcomings: is the periphery (rural area) really an undifferentiated mass of poverty? Are divisions between space and social inequality really so clear-cut? Does this model reveal any possible solutions to rural poverty? Lipton has a set of possible answers to this. Each of the possibilities he suggests is subsequently written off because the existing balance of forces pushes against it, in other words Lipton reproduces the tautologies of dependency theory. Lipton's preferred solution – tautologies notwithstanding – is the development of a rural bloc, uniting landlords and the most impoverished smallholders, together to support a rural agenda of fairer prices and better social services in the villages.

Urban bias revolves around one particular mechanism which deserves separate mention. This is the *rent-seeking* tendency of the state, that is its inclination to employ political fiat or force to generate for itself monopoly rents or profits. Moving away from the neoclassical economics that provides the theory for rent-seeking, we can translate this into one particular issue, already mentioned above: the state marketing board. Marketing boards were most often a product of the late

[margin annotation: Marketing boards]

colonial period, but they often passed into African management after independence. These boards became the sole buyers of principal cash and/or food crops, and they might have been the only licensed retailers of commodities in rural areas. Official prices thus become the only prices in rural markets. States set these prices at levels which allow them to extract value from the peasants by buying low and selling high. Bates has contributed most to analysing the political economy of marketing in rural Africa, but the issue has also arisen centrally in writings from outside the smallholder schema.

Which way forward?

Table 2.1 provides a résumé of the contending representations of the peasantry and the relations between how we perceive the peasantry and how we understand peasant agency. The previous narrative has

Table 2.1 A schema of theorizations of the peasantry in sub-Saharan Africa

Peasants as ...	Class	Culture	Smallholder
'Logic' of peasant production/ development	Exploited by capital; petty commodity production.	Production to fulfil subsistence and then demands of family/lineage/chief.	Rational-thinking and maximizing small property ownership.
Relations with the state	Controlled by the state which deepens commoditization.	'Uncaptured' by the state; can avoid state interventions and maintain its economy of affection.	Subject to rent-seeking by the state; encumbered by state-induced inefficiency.
Answers to the agrarian question..?	Peasants: struggle against capitalism; are destroyed by capitalism; or differentiate into rural capitalists and workers.	No shortcuts to progress: before development must come the destruction of the economy of affection.	The creation of a 'rural bloc', lobbying in the collective interests of the rural population and countering urban bias.
Agency/struggle	Struggle as effect of class relations, tendency towards economism.	Peasants act against modernization; 'traditional' peasant.	Peasants as entrepreneurs, marginalized by 'urban bias'.

identified the shortcomings of some and strengths of others. Class-based analyses have been keenest in identifying the historical sub-ordination of peasant producers to powerful social forces deriving either from capital or the state. Dangers emerge with excessive economic functionalism, but it does seem that – in the absence of a powerful new paradigm – the best way forward is to work flexibly within this tradition. The alternatives seem to suffer from flaws which cut right to the core of the agrarian question: peasants are neither historical exceptions defined by an archaic culture, nor are they societies of petty entrepreneurs. The most rewarding pathway in analysing peasant politics is to concentrate on the ongoing dynamics of interaction *between* peasants and other social groups, and to pay attention to the ongoing battles *within* peasant society concerning the control of wealth, capital and power. These questions will be investigated in the next section, which looks at relations between states and peasantries.

Peasant–state relations

We have already established that there are some important contradictions in the relationship between state and peasantry. Let us bring those points together and explore them a little more deeply.

- *Peasants are subject to exploitation by the state.* Here the marketing board and its ability to control the terms of trade is the main culprit. This exploitation reflects and contributes to the deepening of commodity relations in the countryside.
- *States are not accountable to the peasantry.* Recall the notion of urban bias: although flawed, it is certainly the case that the diffuse and remote nature of peasant politics renders the notion of accountability problematic.
- *States' designs for rural development are hostile towards the peasantry.* Recall Williams's 'taking the part of the peasants'. He argues that states do not afford peasants their own agency: they must be acted on by more technically literate and progressive actors. The old dualisms of peasant tradition and backwardness have proved to be very enduring with many postcolonial governing elites.

These three points focus our attention on questions of power and ideology as much as economics and class. Although it is dangerous to de-link each of these areas of study from one another, it is certainly the case that politics has been brought back into the study of state–peasant relations in the last ten years. In fact, the politics of the agrarian question has itself yielded a series of important issues.

States, peasantries and top-down development

Let us begin at the apex of the structures of power: the central institutions of the state. Most research into postcolonial politics – especially in the decade after independence – has remarked on the continuity in forms and practices of power from the colonial period. This led some to speak disparagingly of 'flag independence': a kind of formal change in the ownership of essentially untransformed power (see First, 1970; Rodney, 1972; Davidson, 1992; Winchester, 1995).

What were the repercussions of this flag independence for newly 'independent' peasantries? A variety of writers have identified key continuities in the oppressive or contradictory practices of postcolonial states: for example, marketing boards (such a key institution in colonial agrarian policy) were not abolished (Williams, 1985; Bates, 1987; Helleiner, 1966). These institutional continuities relate to a broader continuity of institutional duality, studied by Mahmood Mamdani (1996). He identifies a key distinction between the urban citizen and the rural subject, produced through institutions of law, labour migration and taxation, which remained intact after independence. Peasants are maintained as rural subjects through the *ethnicized* forms of state power in the villages: most notably state-approved chiefs constitute a 'clenched fist' of power in rural societies, conflating executive, judicial and administrative power in one institution and often one person (1987, 1996). The continuities of this state of affairs with Indirect Rule during colonialism are patent (Berman, 1998).

But why should postcolonial states reproduce much of the political logic of colonialism? The answer lies partly in the nature of the decolonization moment (Young, 1988) in which previous careful reform and the ongoing presence of Westminster/Paris constitutions and personnel tried to moderate the scope of political change after independence. But postcolonial elites themselves actively reproduced some aspects of colonial power in ways that cannot be explained solely through the notion of European influence. The reason for this was that the social characteristics of these elites were themselves a historical product of the late colonial period. These elites were schooled in missionary schools or perhaps Western universities and armies; they worked within parties with a limited presence in colonial assemblies; they often had a European language as their first language; they keenly read and involved themselves in the internationally spread ideas of development, modernization, socialism and national planning. All of these latter ideas might not have been colonial strictly speaking, but they were certainly *Western*.

The social experiences of these elites left them with a difficult relationship to peasant society. While claiming to represent 'the masses', at the eve of independence political leaders often had to fight for a place at the negotiating table over lineage chiefs from the countryside; and after independence, elites understood government in Western terms, consequently concerning themselves with plans, institution building and the consolidation of formal political power.

But postcolonial states provided weak bases from which to act, and elites had to act within – and react to – particular sets of circumstances. Let us highlight two with particular repercussions for state–peasant relations. Firstly, one immediate challenge facing elites was the consolidation of a nation – both in terms of infrastructure (administrative, economic, military ...) and in terms of culture (citizenship, imagined community, language ...). This led most elites to act in a hostile manner to the diverse cultural politics of rural society. In fact, states had to deal not with rural society but *societies*: different peasantries, with different economies, ethnic identities, patterns of migration and so on. For an elite intent on establishing a social homogeneity through which to construct a national identity, much of this plurality could only be seen as a problem – the more so for its 'primordial' or 'tribal' features. Hence the (in)famous dictums of some African presidents: 'for the nation to live, the tribe must die' (Samora Machel of Mozambique – see Cahen, 1990); 'our aim is to remove all that tribal business to be citizens of a single nation' (Julius Nyerere of Tanzania – see Feierman, 1990; Coulson, 1982: 140). A Ugandan minister explained the centralization and consolidation of state control over agricultural cooperatives as part of the 'essence of nation-building and the new political culture' (in Bunker, 1984: 67)

Secondly, postcolonial elites faced what Davidson calls a 'crisis of rising expectations' (1978). Nkrumah famously said 'seek ye first the political kingdom and all else will be added unto ye', meaning that once Africans had control of the political apparatus, steady progress would be made towards wealth, equality and progress. It followed that in order to maintain legitimacy, elites had to at least *appear* to be making *progress*. Certainly, in the early years after independence, many African states increased investment in the countryside, notably in social provision – a fact often lost now in historical hindsight and the inauspicious denouement of most rural development plans. Progress came in packages of technical planning, modernization, and large-scale investments, often within some form of national plan over three or five years, supported by international donors (Raikes, 2000). In this, African elites could rely on the 'expertise' and funds of international institutions such as the World Bank (Lele, 1975; Williams, 1982). The result was a constant stream of plans to villagize peasants, to organize them into producer or consumer cooperatives, to force them to grow certain crops, to set regulations on cultivation techniques (sowing times, arranging single crops in lines, using certain amounts of chemical fertilizers and so on), to resettle them as part of an irrigation or conservation scheme, and to require from them 'voluntary' labour for public/conservation works.

Together, these two challenges produced a key feature of agrarian policy in postcolonial states, irrespective of their ideological colours: the national development programme. These programmes took too little account of local variations in ecology, social relations and ethnicity; they were imposed 'top-down' by technicians and administrators on the supposedly passive peasant subjects; and they involved a strong dynamic of the expansion of control by the state – replacing local influences with state-sanctioned power (chiefs for party cadres) (Cruise O'Brien, 1971).

States, peasants and the limits of top-down development

The picture so far is strongly dualized: on the one hand we have a peasantry remote from the centres of power; on the other hand we have a state with a social base which leads it to implement its designs and desires on agrarian societies with little account of the subjects upon which projects are being imposed. This account is useful in framing a general contradiction between states and peasantries, but it is not sufficient. As it stands, our account resembles the more dualized narratives of 'urban bias', and in fact reality is considerably more complex.

In the first place, we should acknowledge that – for all their pretensions to the contrary – postcolonial states have proved to be very *weak* (or 'soft'), both institutionally and socially. The repercussions of the state's fragility are that it cannot realize its own designs for peasant society. The repeated encounter between state and peasant community is one of *partial successes*: states might assert their presence as an important actor in a village or region, but they rarely establish a hegemony which affords them a consent to rule in peasant society and they rarely have the resources and institutional capacity to ensure that plans and projects are fully realized. Sara Berry's astute and encyclopaedic review of the agrarian question in sub-Saharan Africa makes this point to refute the dualisms within the arguments of Hyden and Bates. She speaks of an *inconclusive encounter* between peasants and states, 'in which the objectives of a project or program are neither achieved nor resisted in a consistent fashion, and its effects on rural economic performance are often contradictory or unclear' (1993: 45). She goes on to illustrate this with reference to failed cooperativization, the proliferation of institutions which are inadequately funded and the devices through which peasants succeed in avoiding aspects of state fiat.

State power and the grassroots

But Berry's nuanced analysis does not take us on the entire journey. She leaves us on the edge of a social relation between state and peasant, with an understanding of the limits to state power. She provides a useful antidote to the high-minded plans of states and development agencies to transform the countryside through the implementation of a programme designed in offices by technicians and other 'experts'. But how does the state actually reproduce itself within peasant society? How successfully can it establish its authority and how well can it gain localized agrarian roots?

There is no single answer to this question because the state's fortunes depend on the dynamics of a particular society or region – perhaps varying from village to village. But some examples do reveal some key processes through which state power works, 'at the grassroots'. In aLuund areas, in the southwest of the Democratic Republic of Congo (DRC), local government politicians evoked a mixture of images – some from local notions of chieftaincy and others from the iconography of the power of the nation-state (at the time almost one and the same as Joseph Mobutu). This mixture produced political-official ceremonies which contained within them a distinct flavour of local 'tradition' (De Boeck, 1996). In his studies on northern Mozambique, Harrison looked at the interaction between lineage and state power. In some villages state power reproduced itself along lineage lines, making use of the authority of influential families (Harrison, 2000; see also Geffray, 1991). The important point to note here is that the ruling elites' ideals of national modernization and state omnipotence can be compromised when the state is actually forced to negotiate its presence in a local situation in which it has no established hegemony.

Examples such as these have led some to argue that, at the local level, the state is built from the bottom up – not imposed from the top down. Bayart (1993) makes this argument in a very general sense (mainly taking examples from Francophone Africa) by talking of a *rhizome state* – produced almost in subterranean fashion and growing upwards into specific nodes of power. Feierman makes a related point compellingly in his study of Tanzania. He identifies a rural cadre of peasant intellectuals, educated in rural missions, who articulated a discourse which subsequently became central to the ruling TANU party's thinking (1990: 227). Staying with the example of Tanzania, Kelsall (2000) has recently argued that decentralization in rural areas has increased the salience of localized contours of power for the construction of state authority.

There are other aspects to the hybridity of local state power. The most important of these is the fact that state institutions which organize production and sale can be bypassed. In states with a particularly weak 'hold' on their territory – for example Zaire in its last decade of existence – or in states where extremely ambitious and totalized projects of rural development were attempted – for example in Tanzania where villagization was enforced in the early 1970s – peasants took recourse to illicit forms of economic activity (Maliyamkono and Bagachwa, 1990; Swantz and Tripp, 1996). Government-organized cooperative fields would be left unkempt and surpluses would be sold illegally across national borders (MacGaffey, 1991). Peasants exercised a relative autonomy (not the absolute autonomy of Hyden) to minimize the damaging economic intrusions of the state. The same 'multiple channels' strategy also occurred within the political realm: in Mecúfi, Mozambique, peasants would go to state authorities for adjudication or ratification in some cases but not others (Harrison, 1999b; see also Berry, 1993).

So, once we begin to look at local instances of state power in rural society, we find that peasants are not passive in the face of top-down homogenizing and modernizing programmes ill-fitted to local circumstances. State power often has to work compromises through networks of local power and it reproduces itself in a context of partial authority, in which people might decide to visit a chief or elder as much as a party cadre. This brings us to those more visible examples of peasant agency: forms of rural resistance.

Peasants and resistance

Let us begin by recalling the broad structural tensions between postcolonial states and the peasantry. States, and their modernizing imperatives, have been all too keen to impose centrally designed plans of agrarian change upon peasants, neglectful of peasants' own know-ledge, culture and ecological conditions; they have also been con-cerned to extract resources from the peasantry – partly to enrich the governing elites, and partly to expand and deepen market relations into peasant production. Although, as we have seen, these struc-tural contradictions are 'negotiated' as weak states have to pro-duce a contested authority in the day-to-day situations of vil-lage life, there remain cases where peasants actively resist state policy.

Since colonial times, states have been imposing development pro-jects on peasants which have upset peasants' conditions of life and rarely presented a clear and secure improvement in the standard of living. The most notorious example of this is villagization (Tanzania, Ethiopia, Mozambique and, to a lesser extent, other countries such as Zambia); but there are other examples of resettlement (as part of an irrigation project), forms of ecological conservation (often labour-intensive and of marginal benefit) and orders to cultivate certain crops. Peasants have resisted development projects not by lobbying gov-ernments to change policies, and rarely by rebelling against the state in direct confrontation. Rather, the strategy has been one of *sabotage and subterfuge*: the aim is to render a project defunct without the state officials realizing that failure is a result of purposive peasant action. That way, peasants do not attract the force of punishment or more intense interventions from the state. In another context, Scott calls these actions 'the weapons of the weak' (1985).

Colonial and postcolonial forced crop cultivation has led to peasants boiling seeds, planting them upside down, or infecting stands of the crop (Beinart and Bundy, 1987; Feierman, 1990: 41; Isaacman, 1990; Rimmer 1988: 42; Jewsiewicki, 1980; Crummey, 1986). In one part of postcolonial Mozambique, peasants maintained 'toy' communal vil-lages which they would occupy only when officials were visiting to maintain the image of villagization as a success, before moving back and working in dispersed hamlets (Geffray, 1991). One might also recall peasant culture and resistance during the process of labour migration, mentioned in the discussion of MOP above. Peasants have also occasionally made more drastic gestures of resistance against the state's interventions. Beer and Williams describe a series of rebellions which involved peasants arming themselves and pushing state officials out of areas of Ibadan, Nigeria as cocoa bushes were cut, taxes were imposed and cocoa prices set extremely low (1975). When marketing prices have become extremely low, peasants have 'struck' by retaining their crop, leaving the marketing board with no produce.

Virtuous peasants and vicious states?

There is one final aspect of state–peasant relations that we need to account for. We have spent quite a lot of space identifying conflict between the state and the peasantry and, even if we allow for the fact than in local circumstances states can at best attain inconclusive encounters with peasant societies rather that absolute hegemony, this is only to *qualify* the established relationship of vicious state and virtuous peasant which Bernstein sees as part of the prevailing wisdom (1990). Although we can use this broad structural contradiction to guide our understanding of state–peasant relations, it is also the case that there are counter-tendencies.

If we recall the notion of 'multiple channels' from the section on grassroots power and think through the implications of this strategy, we find a different tendency. In these circumstances, peasants can use the state rather than vice versa. There are many examples of richer peasants 'capturing' government cooperatives for their own ends (Harris, 1980; Cruise O'Brien, 1971; Bowen, 2000). In Kenya, peasant self-help (*harambee*) groups have effectively pressured local politicians and the central state for more resources (Holmquist, 1984). Peasants might take recourse to the state only when it is to their advantage to do so; otherwise they might undermine or ignore it. Some wealthier and more influential peasants might lend weak states their authority on the grounds that they will receive some form of return through their closeness to official power. It is important not to fall back into the 'romantic peasant' frame which we reviewed in the first section of this chapter: peasants, like all groups of people, are devious as well as honest, acquisitive as well as community-minded.

There are also examples of public action which has improved the circumstances of the peasantry. Robert Bates, whose seminal contribution (1981) set the scene for a powerful anti-state invective, has subsequently integrated considerations of progressive state action within peasant societies. Where peasants have produced important cash crops and gained a certain amount of wealth and power, states have related to them far more positively, for example in the cocoa growing areas of Côte d'Ivoire (Crook, 1988, 1997). In states where peasants contributed centrally to a liberation movement, states have made real efforts to 'give something back': in Mozambique, the Frelimo government carried out vaccination campaigns which made a significant and rapid improvement to health in rural areas (Walt and Melamed, 1983). In Zimbabwe during the first ten years of independence, the provision of credit, marketing infrastructure and extension services saw a marked improvement in peasant production (Stoneman, 1988). Other smaller examples of success exist (Coquery-Vidrovitch, 1988; Mengisteab, 1995: 171–3; Ferraz and Munslow, 1999).

Concluding remarks

In this chapter we have looked at the ways in which we can conceptualize the peasantry, and we have traced the main features of peasants' relations with the state. These two tasks have yielded a complex picture, but we can highlight a number of key points.

- Peasants are neither passive nor traditional, but are part of modern social systems, acting and reacting from a position of relative weakness.
- Peasant society is internally differentiated but has not followed any linear path towards the formation of a landed and landless class.
- Peasant society is defined by its resilience and flexibility in the face of external forces.
- A key feature of postcolonial agricultural 'development' has been the extraction of resources from the peasantry by state institutions.
- State elites have been antagonistic towards the plurality and 'tradition' of their peasant societies.
- Any policy or programme from a state or international agency must negotiate a set of local circumstances.
- Peasants have elaborated a series of responses and strategies to these externally contrived circumstances including: avoiding and bypassing the state, subverting the effects and purpose of state action, 'capturing' the state at the local level, and selectively engaging with it where it is advantageous to do so.

This chapter serves to re-engage considerations of agency and struggle for the majority of Africa's people. In the chapters that follow, we will be prepared to consider how peasants have reacted in the face of two important contemporary processes, namely economic reform and democratization.

Further reading

A readable and theoretically engaged overview of peasantries in Africa (and elsewhere) is Bryceson, Kay and Mooij (2000). Brass (1997) provides a subtle engagement with perceptions of peasants and broader intellectual trends, which makes interesting reading in conjunction with Chambers (1983) who also analyses the engagement between peasants and intellectuals from a more pragmatic standpoint. There are a number of excellent historiographies of peasant societies, including Bundy (1979), Murray (1992) and Kitching (1980). The best introduction to peasants' relations with capitalism is Meillassoux (1981) or the various works of Bernstein. Hyden (1980) raises key issues concerning peasant–state relations; an impressive broader engagement with this issue is Berry (1993). On local peasant politics, see Harrison (2000) . On peasant resistance, see Isaacman (1990).

3
The Politics of Debt and Social Struggle

Introduction

'The debt crisis' has entered general vocabulary alongside terms such as 'the Cold War' or 'New World Order'. Most people can say something about what the debt crisis is but there is a great deal of discussion and debate concerning its actual nature and dynamics, and their interpretation. Also, one can fit a wide variety of themes under the rubric of the debt crisis: analyses of the World Bank (Caufield, 1998; George and Sabelli, 1994; Kapur, Lewis and Webb, 1997), economic reviews of solutions to the debt crisis (World Bank, 1981, 1989, 1994a; Mosley, Subasat and Weeks, 1995), or research into the social and environmental impact of debt (Gibbon, 1992). The debt crisis has become a central reference to all those interested in understanding contemporary development issues in Africa. This chapter will concentrate on one aspect of the debt crisis: its interactions with African politics. More specifically, this means identifying how debt relates to concentrations of power – especially the state – and how it has influenced political movements and organizations with different approaches to the 'debt question'.

There is no orthodoxy in this area which can easily be recapitulated as a basis for our discussion. It is important, then, to be explicit about how we will approach the issue of debt, politics and struggle. It is fruitless analytically to isolate debt and its repercussions from the rest of Africa's postcolonial political economy. What point is there in analysing the impact of the debt crisis in an analytical vacuum when its real impact derives from the way it relates to ongoing crises and balances of power? In this sense, we will follow Ihonvbere's approach in his discussion of the politics of debt in Nigeria: the debt crisis emerged 'on a sea of corruption, poverty, instability, unproductive disposition of the dominant classes, foreign domination of the economy, rural decay and urban dislocation' (1993: 141). Counterfactual arguments (how would things have been if the debt crisis hadn't happened?) enjoy a central place in many debates about the debt crisis, especially regarding structural adjustment, an issue to which we will return presently. The point here is that the debt crisis is neither an 'original sin' imposed on a previously sound state of affairs, nor is it excused from its damaging effects on the grounds that 'things were already pretty bad'. This is particularly important for our interest in the politics of debt because it is the *real* effects of debt and the real (re)actions of collectivities to these effects which constitute our field of study in this book.

In order to begin a consideration of the politics of debt, it is necessary to begin with a brief introduction to the nature of the debt crisis. Especially important here is *structural adjustment*. Subsequently, we will look at the way in which structural adjustment has affected the scope and nature of state and market action. We will do this with particular attention to the way in which the debt crisis has affected different social groups. These changes in state action should suggest to us some 'natural constituencies' for support or resistance to structural adjustment, and this will be the subject of the subsequent section. We will see that political reactions to structural adjustment are more complex than a methodology of 'political accounting', generating 'winners' and 'losers' (Wieland, 1998; cf. Nelson, 1990) would suggest. Instead, we will highlight the interplay between a legacy of state power, changes in markets (especially processes of differentiation) and the dynamics involved in the construction of political movements.

The creation of a permanent crisis

Setting and springing the debt trap

In most accounts, the debt crisis began in 1981 when Mexico announced a moratorium on debt repayments to its creditors. It was followed by Brazil, another big debtor, leaving Latin America's creditors – mainly private banks – with a crisis of liquidity. At the same time, across the Atlantic, debt burdens in Africa were growing rapidly, generating unsustainable debts, but in economies which were small enough not to attract the same amount of attention as Brazil or Mexico. In fact, the debt crisis was a 'trap' which was set over the decades before: a culmination of both longer historic factors and sharper conjunctural changes. Let us briefly identify the main factors which created the debt trap.

- The generalized faith in debt-led development from the 1960s. Students of development economics, Third World governments and international organizations, especially the World Bank, believed that the main problem for the Third World was capital shortage, and that the solution rested mainly in lending. The World Bank especially developed a culture of lending, and even argued that a highly indebted country meant a healthy economy. Thus, from independence, African states ran up large international debts in congruence with the prevailing consensus about development. This constituted a key international dynamic in the 'top-down' modernizing proclivities of the postcolonial elites mentioned in the previous chapter.

- More than other regions of the world, African economies were integrated into global markets in a difficult position – mainly as the exporters of primary commodities, that is unprocessed crops and minerals. Although primary commodity prices have risen for some periods, they have been in decline from the 1980s onwards, and show a long-term decline. This means that African economies, which are dependent on primary exports for their export revenue, have had to export more to earn the same amount of dollars. This is expressed as *national terms of trade* (not *peasant* terms of trade, dealt with in Chapter 2: this is the same economic ratio, but between two different economic entities), that is the ratio between the price of a country's main exports compared with the prices of the main (manufactured) imports. If one conceives of Africa's role as primary commodity exporter as a position in an *international division of labour*, it is important to bear in mind that primary commodity production involves little value added, which is generated as a result of processing and involves more lucrative productive technologies.

- African governments have frequently run up debts in pursuit of goals which yield low returns on loans and generate renewed desires for loans. The various processes of corruption in postcolonial African politics have meant that loans have been salted away into personal bank accounts through various devices. The venality of particular regimes (Joseph Mobutu's Zaire is usually held up as an extreme example) should be accompanied by considerations of the nature of accumulation in many postcolonial societies. As we have already seen in the previous chapter, after a short period following independence, governments rarely made effective efforts to support the majority of crop producers within their national territories. Also, the industrialization that did take place was often inefficient and relied heavily on imports from overseas (part of the general import substitution industrialization strategy pursued by most states). In essence, a whole series of inefficiencies were introduced (or consolidated) in African economies because they allowed ruling cliques to enrich themselves with little concern for the masses. The fact that loans were not being used productively was not a concern for those in many governments, and lenders such as the World Bank made few efforts to ensure that project lending was spent properly. Often, the solution to various forms of 'project failure' was actually more loans.

Taking the postcolonial period as a whole, then, we can identify a 'conspiracy' of structures which consolidated themselves through the years: an international system happy to allow high levels of indebtedness in the name of 'development'; a global division of labour which put Africa 'at the bottom of the pile'; and a postcolonial politics which developed a greed for loans to create networks of clientelist support or merely for enrichment. This structural balance of forces was exacerbated by certain conjunctural events.

- *Oil price hikes.* The price of oil rose from $3.22 per barrel in 1973 to $34 per barrel in 1982. As most African states were oil importers, this created a drain on their external accounts: from 1973 to 1982, Africa's external balance of trade moved from a small surplus (selling more than buying on the world market) to a $6 bn deficit (Singh, 1986: 104). The oil price hike exacerbated Africa's long-term vulnerabilities, noted earlier: for example, in 1960 one ton of sugar would purchase 6.3 tons of oil; in 1982 the same ton of sugar would purchase 0.7 tons of oil.
- *The rise of the petrodollar market.* The oil price rise also created a flooding of European capital markets with 'petrodollars', that is the increased revenues from oil sales. European banks needed to lend this money out very quickly in order for it to make an income. Thus banks lent enthusiastically to Third World states – especially as it was believed that sovereign debtors could not go bankrupt: after all, how could a state go into receivership? Debts to private banks increased as a result of the on-lending of petrodollars.

- *The results of neoliberalism.* From 1979, a virile form of neoliberalism took hold in the powerful Western states, associated with Reagan and Thatcher. The monetarist policies that these regimes imposed had two deleterious effects on debt (Szeftel, 1987).
  - The recession created in Western economies led to a fall in demand for the main exports of African states, and thus a fall in African states' terms of trade. This meant that it became harder to earn the dollars to pay off debt interest.
  - The raising of interest rates in the UK and the USA created a global increase in rates of interest. Between 1979 and 1981, real interest rates rose between 10 and 15 times (Engberg-Pedersen et al. 1996a: 3). This meant that loans became more expensive. Merely keeping up interest payments became impossible for many African states during the 1980s. The aspiration actually to pay off the debt became a progressively more remote possibility.

These events – the rise of the petrodollar market in Europe, the decline in terms of trade and the global rise in rates of interest – constituted the 'trap' which turned high levels of indebtedness – previously the signs of a healthy growth trajectory – into a *crisis*. Debt became unsustainable as countries struggled merely to maintain interest payments and were taking out new loans merely to pay off interest. This trap ushered in a period of permanent crisis, defined not only by indebtedness but by Structural Adjustment Programmes (SAPs).

Structural adjustment

Since the early 1980s, African governments have renegotiated their debt repayments with their main creditors. Most African states owe most of their debt to individual governments and the international finance institutions (IFIs), that is the World Bank and International Monetary Fund (IMF).

The role of the World Bank and IMF in renegotiation has been key for two reasons.

1. The international finance institutions play an important role in the monitoring and evaluation of indebted economies. Commonly, bilateral creditors only entertain the possibility of renegotiation if a debtor country is given a fairly clean bill of health by the World Bank and IMF. The IFIs have dedicated considerable resources to the monitoring of economic change in its member states: in some countries this has involved an overhaul of

statistical agencies with World Bank support. The World Bank and IMF use this information to produce a large number of research papers and documents, and also to make decisions as to whether to continue providing loans to a debtor state, making them the 'preeminent source of the continent's economic data and studies' (Schatz, 1996: 240). An IMF or World Bank decision not to provide loans (within an existing agreement or in considering new lending packages) will result in most other lenders following the IFIs' lead, because of their domination of intelligence and monitoring functions, for example in Nigeria (Olukoshi, 1995: 167, 169).

2. It is World Bank and IMF finance, lent as part of a structural adjustment programme, that has kept almost all African states away from the brink of national bankruptcy. Where other creditors have acted, they have acted within the overarching structures of the structural adjustment programme. This is most evident in the Consultative Group meetings of bilateral creditors and donors, which are chaired by the World Bank, and in which the content of the meeting is basically oriented around a consideration by bilateral creditors of the extent to which a debtor country is adhering to an adjustment programme (Martin, 1994). A strong example of bilateral donor support for the IFIs is Tanzania which had a particularly rocky relationship with the IMF during the 1980s: during that decade 'Tanzania... depended on an agreement with the IMF: no donor was willing to guarantee bank credits prior to an IMF agreement' (Bierman and Campbell, 1989: 75). In sum:

> The influence of the IMF and the World Bank in the formulation of the economic policies of African states has become all-pervasive. Because of the relatively high dependence of African economies on external financing and because of the severity and length of economic crisis in sub-Saharan Africa, this part of the world is particularly vulnerable to the terms of conditionality imposed from outside.
>
> (Campbell, 1989: 23)

The World Bank and IMF's power has allowed them to condition further loans on a series of neoliberal policies, collectively known as structural adjustment programmes. However, there are some complexities here.

• SAPs are not all identical; the circumstances of 'adjusting' states even less so (Simon et al., 1995).

WB = developmental

- Donors have not always lined up with the IFIs: for example, Scandinavian governments did not always act within the SAP logic in the 1980s, although they have reconciled themselves to it in the 1990s (Bierman and Wagao, 1986: 143).
- The World Bank and IMF have different forms of lending, the former being associated with economic restructuring and the latter with financial stabilization. The World Bank disburses Structural Adjustment Loans and the IMF (Enhanced) Structural Adjustment Facilities, and most recently a Poverty Eradication and Growth Facility. The distinction within the division of labour between the IMF and World Bank has progressively become less clear, to the extent that Mosley, Subasat and Weeks suggest that the two IFIs have become akin to 'identical twins' (1995: 1459; Feinberg, 1988). The usual procedure is that a debtor country reaches agreement with the IMF (characterized as more technicist and hard-headed) before negotiating an SAL with the World Bank (characterized as more 'developmental'). And there have been occasions of disagreement between the two IFIs (Tarp, 1993) as well as within each institution.
- A final complexity which is noteworthy here is the issue of policy 'slippage', or the extent to which an adjusting country fails to implement the policies set out in a loan agreement. 'Slippage' can be substantial, especially towards the end of an SAP term (Mosley et al., 1995; Engberg-Pedersen et al., 1996a: 19–21). The concern with the extent to which paper agreements were being implemented is one reason for the methodology in one of the World Bank's major reports on SAPs in Africa: *Results, Reforms and the Road Ahead* (1994a), which categorizes countries as 'good' or 'bad' adjusters in terms of policy slippage.

These complexities are important to bear in mind, but they should not detract from the bigger picture of the ascendance of the IFIs as a result of the debt crisis, and the common direction within the broad sway of adjustment policy. Not all SAPs are identical, a good example of this being the absence of devaluation criteria in the SAPs of the African franc zone up until 1994. But it is certainly the case that they contain many common policy measures, and are driven by the same neoliberal ideals (Williams, 1999). It is also the case that during the 1980s the vast majority of African states negotiated SAPs with the World Bank and IMF: already by 1989, 89 structural adjustment loans had been agreed between the World Bank and sub-Sahara African states (Geest, 1994: 189; see also Riddell, 1992: 56). It is therefore not unreasonable to work from the premise that the debt crisis has provided an opportunity for the IFIs to increase their power vis-à-vis African states and to use this power to impose neoliberal reform.

Structural adjustment programmes have been introduced to Africa through *conditionality*: in order to qualify for further credit and debt rescheduling, governments must implement economic reforms which collectively constitute an SAP. Without an SAP, it is unlikely that an indebted country will receive any finance or debt rescheduling in order to prevent it failing to make debt repayments. Failure to make repayments and the absence of an SAP would lead to virtual isolation from the world economy.

There is a clear set of common objectives within SAPs, based on the economic theories of monetarism and neoliberalism. The key components of SAPs are:

- *Rolling back the state*. Removing the state from many areas of the economy, for example: the dissolution of state marketing boards, the privatization of state-owned enterprises and measures to reduce budget deficits.
- *Liberalizing the economy*. Allowing prices to be determined more closely by supply and demand, for example: removal of subsidies on consumer goods, the introduction of user charges for medical and education services.
- *Opening the national economy to the world*. Encouraging a closer integration into the world economy through the removal of barriers and the provision of incentives, for example: removal of controls over foreign currency market, incentives to encourage foreign investment and the rewriting of investment codes in a more capital-friendly direction.

In order to implement these broad policy directions, a series of more specific policies are implemented, for example 'second windows' of foreign exchange auction, the creation of new 'one-stop' investment agencies, the removal of political control over the central bank and programmes of retrenchment within the public services. Each SAP contains different emphases on different components (Mosley and Weeks, 1993: 1589; Engberg-Pedersen et al., 1996b) and with different approaches to the sequencing of different policies. Rather than looking at the issues raised by this in more detail, we will take the broad neoliberal thrust of SAP and consider its political repercussions, paying particular attention to the politics of struggle and liberation.

The social repercussions of structural adjustment

In order to examine the politics of structural adjustment, we need to be explicit about our methodology – not least because much of the controversy over assessments of SAP has come down to differences in this respect (cf. World Bank 1994a; Economic Commission for Africa, 1989; Parfitt, 1990; Mosley and Weeks, 1993). In order to clarify our approach, the following points are important:

- Structural adjustment did not constitute a 'clean break' from the previous regime. Therefore notions of 'before and after' can only reveal a partial picture of the impact of SAP, confusing or obscuring continuities in place of an interest in change. Before and after analyses evoke shaky counterfactuals which derive from the unanswerable question: what would have happened if a country had *not* adjusted (Brett, 1997)? The important point is to analyse SAP as a new set of social processes which can undermine or build on previous relations of power and economics.
- SAP is not an omnipotent force. Economic growth rates depend crucially on climate, global economic change, war, and other factors largely external to structural adjustment. In Mozambique, SAP was implemented during a civil war (see Chapter 6), and Zimbabwe's SAP was implemented the year before a severe drought. But, despite the importance of war and drought, one can reasonably ask how structural adjustment affected the impact of these factors (Wuyts, 1991; Stoneman, 1992). Furthermore, as mentioned above, the *declaration* of structural adjustment is a very different thing to the *implementation* of individual policies.
- Politics is not a direct reflection of economics: socio-economic change which has been promoted by SAP does not allow one to 'read off' political constituencies of support and resistance to SAP, or 'winners and losers' to use the public choice vocabulary. Having said that, the socio-economic impact of SAP is certainly pivotal in understanding the political effects of adjustment; it is just that we must carefully think through the linkages between the economy and polity. We will use categories of social group and consider the impact of SAP on these categories, not in order to identify a direct line towards a prescriptive political reaction, but in order to identify the context and motive within which a certain form of political action has emerged.

The social impact of structural adjustment

Debates about research methodology and the politics of adjustment have been no more keen than in terms of their impact on levels of social provision and well-being – mainly in health and education (see, for example, Sahn, Dorosh and Younger, 1999). The basic argument that emerged in the early 1980s was that the demands for fiscal austerity from the World Bank and IMF led governments to cut back on social provision. Thus structural adjustment made the poor and vulnerable more so (Adepoju, 1993; Onimode, 1989). Here the issue of 'before and after' became central to the debate: it was clear that levels of social spending had been declining before SAP in many cases (Mengisteab and Logan, 1995). It is also the case that the new funds provided after a structural adjustment programme has been agreed can lead to an *increase* in social expenditure in some cases, for example in Ghana. The World Bank has highlighted the issue of *how* money is spent as well as *how much* is spent, criticizing governments for their preference for tertiary education and curative (not preventive) health care. Nevertheless, the IFIs did not shake off the strong concerns articulated about the neglect of social well-being within an essentially neoliberal reform package, especially when these concerns came from UN organizations that were broadly supportive of the World Bank's efforts, and it is fair to say that – bearing in mind the levels of poverty in Africa – SAP has not come near to addressing the social components of development (Cornia et al., 1987).

Consequently, the World Bank has developed a series of social components to its structural adjustment programmes, or social dimensions of adjustment (SDA). The most well-known example of this is the Programme for the Amelioration of the Social Consequences of Adjustment (PAMSCAD) in Ghana (Hutchful, 1994; Zack-Williams, 2000). SDAs are usually funded by bilateral donors. Another component of Bank funding – project funding – has also counteracted the 'intuitive' desire to reduce public expenditure that one can identify with the broad sway of World Bank and IMF adjustment programmes. The World Bank has funded social provision projects aimed at primary health care and education.

Obviously, the actual social repercussions of structural adjustment are very important as a grounding to an understanding of the way social groups react to SAP. There is great debate concerning the question of whether SAP is good or bad for general well-being. When considering the extent to which social programmes have dealt with the social detriments of SAP, it is important not to get too involved with aggregated numbers: each country has its own experience of adjustment and (perhaps) SDA, obscured by continent-wide figures; there are also important issues concerning *what kind* of social provision is maintained, for example how social support is administered, or how much money goes into staff and how much into material costs. Also, political struggle does not develop in strict correlation with trends in GNP or percentage changes in spending on education (although clearly both of these indices will be crucial to a country's political dynamics). There are issues more apposite to political economy which will prove to be pivotal to SAPs medium-term political effects.

- The social components that the World Bank and bilateral sources fund are generally 'tacked on' to existing SAPs rather than integrated into the logic of adjustment (Gibbon, 1992). The expectation is that economic growth will relieve the need for loans and aid in the social sectors, but the fact is that economic recovery is not clearly evident in structurally adjusting Africa (Mosley, Subasat and Weeks, 1995; Schatz, 1994).
- Social provision programmes are based on the concept of providing a 'safety net' (Elson, 1994: 518) to reach particular 'target groups'. The minimal provision for the specific groups approach means that the generalized and extreme levels of poverty remain unaffected. For example, in Mozambique, the second structural adjustment programme, was launched with an added social component aimed at about 25 per cent of the population when about 66 per cent of the country's population subsisted below the poverty line (Herbold Green and Mavie, 1994).
- It is equally important to consider the way in which SAP changes different classes and social groups' opportunities to secure a livelihood or accumulate wealth. Social indices of a 'before SAP and after SAP' nature may identify important conjunctural patterns in poverty (and may make the point of the author who wishes to defend or condemn structural adjustment), but there are also important repercussions for structural poverty which derive from adjustment. The question then becomes: how is structural adjustment reconfiguring class relations in African societies? How does structural adjustment affect social groups' capacity to defend or promote their own well-being? In order to answer this question, we need to look with more detail at the way adjustment has had different impacts on different social groups, not just *directly* through short-term changes in prices but *indirectly* through changes in social

relations (Messkoub, 1996). In doing so, we will also look at the political *responses* that have been generated by SAP.

Wage workers' adjustment and austerity

One of the first concerns articulated by those studying SAP was the impact of removing the state from social provision. In 1981, the World Bank published the strongly worded and influential 'Berg Report'. This report argued that, because the state was the source of much of Africa's contemporary economic malaise, central attention should be paid to minimizing its scope of action. But did this central concern with efficiency and faith in the market create a new set of vulnerabilities?

The *removal of subsidies* on staple foods meant that the poorest groups (especially in urban areas) could buy less for their money. This led to the so-called 'IMF riots' in Zambia, a key moment in the decline of Kenneth Kaunda and his party UNIP, as well as in Sudan, the Côte d'Ivoire, Morocco and recurrently in Nigeria (Walton and Seddon, 1994). Rising staple goods prices created urban discontent in other countries which did not manifest itself as out-and-out rioting. Workers' purchasing power fell, and this hit the lowest wage earners disproportionately because it was these strata who spent most on basic staple foods – precisely the commodities hit by the removal of subsidies (Hutchful, 1996: 380; Lugalla, 1995b).

In Mozambique, where SAP was introduced in 1987, prices had previously been partially liberalized, but in 1988 subsidies were removed from basic staple foods. As a result, the price of rice per kilogram rose by 575 per cent, maize (kg) by 317 per cent, bread (250 g) by 50 per cent, and sugar (kg) by 428 per cent (Marshall, 1990: 31). This rendered a basic subsistence way out of reach of the average wage earner (Hermele, 1988a). In Tanzania, where SAP was introduced in 1986 (after a series of 'home-grown' attempts at adjustment), basic commodity prices followed a similar trend: from 1985 to 1988, the price of sugar (kg) rose by 266 per cent, soap by 396 per cent, and *kangas* (cloth for clothing) by 920 per cent (Messkoub, 1996). In Zimbabwe, during the first two years of Bank-sponsored adjustment, average earnings fell by 24 per cent in real terms (Gibbon, 1996b: 379). In Sierra Leone in 1986, after adjustment and devaluation, a bar of soap went from Leone 0.5 to Leone 2, a gallon of kerosene from Leone 9 to Leone 23 and a chicken from Leone 20 to Leone 80 (Riddell, 1992: 57).

Many SAPs also included policies of *retrenchment* in the public sector – the largest employer in most African countries. Consequently,

SAP has led to higher numbers of unemployed. In Uganda, a World Bank-supported retrenchment programme had cut the public employee list from 320 000 to 150 000 between 1990 and 1995 (Bigsten and Kayizzi-Mugerwa, 1999: 64–5). In Ghana, retrenchment as part of its SAP led to the retrenchment of 53 000 civil servants by 1989 (Rothchild, 1991: 9).

Thus, it appeared that SAP created or exacerbated poverty within the wage-earning sector of the cities. In fact, Elliot Berg, the author of the founding text of the World Bank's anti-statist innovations of the early 1980s, reflects on the course of SAP and notes that 'civil servants have suffered a wages loss of 30 per cent to 40 per cent in the past decade and it becomes clear that the civil servant class represents clear "losers" in adjustment reforms' (in Dieng, 1995: 113). How did this affect working-class politics during the adjustment period?

Wage workers and political responses to SAP

Labour unions have often challenged the economic austerity of SAP, but it is fair to say that labour resistance has not been as great as some predicted, bearing in mind the way in which SAP reduced their well-being. Most research on this question has been focused on Ghana, which implemented a determined adjustment programme from 1983, received strong external backing and has undertaken a series of living standards surveys. SAP has created many of the deleterious effects outlined above (Herbst, 1991: 176). But there has been no strong political backlash from organized labour in the public or private sector. Herbst explains the weakness of labour's reaction primarily as a result of the measures taken by the government to suppress independent labour politics. In the early years of revolutionary fervour in Ghana (1981–83), party cadres and militias dealt with 'anti-revolutionary' actions (suspected or real) with zeal and brutality (Herbst, 1991: 179 et seq.; Jeffries, 1991: 165; Oquaye, 2000: 69). Repression was also employed in 1986/87 over the trade unions (Hutchful 1995: 572; 1989). This recalls earlier general works on the politics of adjustment, which argued that SAP necessarily required authoritarian regimes with determination to impose the 'shock therapy' of adjustment on restive populations (Gibbon et al., 1992; Lall, 1983). Social opposition to SAP also produced authoritarian reactions in the Babangida regime in Nigeria (Ihonvbere, 1993: 144; Ibrahim, 1993). In Ghana, the PAMSCAD also concentrated of compensation for retrenched public sector workers who were seen as politically volatile (Hutchful, 1995: 575).

Despite the fact that it is states that implement structural adjustment, and the fact that most wage labour is employed by the state in sub-Saharan Africa, one should not overplay the antagonisms between unions and states. Although there are clear tensions between the two, it is also the case that organized labour often receives some access to government offices, recognition and funding from government. More generally, the corporatist relationship between unions and governments (on the particularly clear example of Tanzania, see Barengu, 1997: 66) in postcolonial Africa has allowed governments to 'rein in' union leaderships in the 'national' cause. It is also the case that the government managed to engage labour unions with strategies of 'divide and rule'. Union leaderships have been manipulated and co-opted (Herbst, 1991: 179). In Nigeria, the Babangida regime exacerbated divisions within the Nigerian Labour Congress (NLC) between 'progressives' and 'democrats' in order to frustrate anti-SAP labour politics (Beckman, 1995; Bangura and Beckman, 1993). In Zimbabwe, the Mugabe regime has only been partially successful in controlling the Zimbabwe Congress of Trade Unions (ZCTU) (Skalnes, 1993: 424–5), but the government has also encouraged splits within union organizations (Gibbon, 1996b: 357).

The World Bank itself has been very concerned with worker politics with respect to retrenchment in the public sector. This is because the link between adjustment policy and unemployment is direct and clear: political struggle against retrenchment would necessarily aim directly at SAP and its sponsors. But fears of mass unrest have not been accurate. Despite radical retrenchment, as mentioned earlier, Ghana has not experienced strong resistance to this policy. The World Bank explains this as a result of the fact that ex-public employees can move fairly easily into the informal sector or agriculture. It is also the case that public employment has long since been an unsustainable form of employment: wages contribute little to a family's subsistence, pay is often delayed and the functions of many jobs can be minimally held down in a fraction of the working time. Consequently, bureaucratic office has been as much a base for a series of other forms of work as a job in itself. There is no discrete movement from full-time employment to total unemployment, rather an imposed switching of strategies within what Mustapha calls 'multiple modes of livelihood' (1992).

So, one can identify a set of potential political responses to the social processes engendered by SAP: protest, 'coping' strategies, institutional co-option by the state and repression by the state. These responses are generated by the specific political economy and history of a country as much as by the effects of structural adjustment. Anti-SAP agendas have emerged in some cases: the ZCTU and NLC have provided alternative economic programmes or at least strong counter-arguments to SAP based on forms of national protectionism and stronger state social provision, as well as making arguments about the scope and nature of democracy (Beckman, 1995: 305; Sachikonye, 1993: 261 et. seq.). In Mozambique, May Day parades always carry placards denouncing structural adjustment (Harrison, 1994). These mobilizations have interacted with struggles for democratization which will be returned to in Chapter 4.

Adjustment, gender and women

Another social group which has suffered as a result of structural adjustment, and which certainly also suffered before structural adjustment, is women. Now, the concept of a homogeneous social group identified as 'women' obviously hides as much as it reveals, and feminists argue that women's experiences are extremely varied, leading some to argue that the founding feminist notion of a women's struggle is now defunct. But, as argued in Chapter 1, identifying complexity and variety does not necessarily require us to abandon the concept of liberation or political struggle – I recall a postcard I saw on a colleague's office wall: 'I'll be a post feminist in a post patriarchy.' Pearson puts the point clearly when she 'starts from the premise that all women share a common experience of oppression and subordination. It is possible to gain some notion of women's common interests, even though the forms of women's oppression and subordination vary widely' (1992: 292–3).

So, how did SAP affect women, and how did women respond to this environment? The central arguments which defined research into gender and adjustment were set out by Diane Elson (1991). She began by making clear distinctions between the social arenas in which women laboured: domestic and public. Women work within the household as mothers, carers, educators, cleaners and cooks; they also perform various roles as wage labourers, petty producers, farm workers and traders (the latter especially in the cities of West Africa). Elson then asks: how does SAP reconfigure the relation between private ('family') and public ('economy')? By reducing public expenditure in the name of fiscal austerity or balancing the budget, structural adjustment imposes higher burdens of work on women within the household as public provision contracts further. As wage rates fall, women have to budget with smaller amounts of cash: this has resulted in women buying cheaper food which requires more labour to cook. Women are also working as wage labourers to a greater extent in order to bring a higher level of income into the household and compensate for the general decline in real wages, for example in Tanzania (Messkoub, 1996). Women may spend more labour time producing petty commodities such as foodstuffs or beer to increase resources within the household (Musyoki and Orodho, 1993; Brand, Mupedziswa and Gumbo, 1993). In sum, 'the problem with SAPs is that ... they are ... grounded in a gender ideology which is deeply and fundamentally exploitative of women's time, work, and sexuality' (Antrobus, in Zack-Williams, 2000: 36).

These are the immediate effects of SAP which relate to price changes and the redistribution of labour between public and private. Economic planners relocate much of the burden of adjustment to the domestic sphere (in which women's labour is 'invisible') with little consideration as to the consequences (Elson, 1991; Sparr, 1994) The effect is to make women work (even) harder and increase their vulnerability. Malnutrition, overwork and childbirth have conspired to make women less healthy and more vulnerable to illness. Economic vulnerability has also led to sexual vulnerability as women have been compelled to undertake sex work in the context of increasing poverty (Lugalla, 1995a).

Falling levels of public provision also 'run' along the contours of existing gender inequalities, thereby exacerbating them. Obasi (1997) provides an illustrative example of this in respect to primary education in Nigeria. The implementation of Universal Primary Education led to an increase in female attendance at school; the introduction of fees as part of SAP has led to a return to the household for girls and young women as households calculate that male children are more suited to success at school.

Women's responses to SAP have been mainly associated with 'coping' strategies: that is, taking on new activities to maintain households. Indigenous NGOs have formed to express the collective concerns of groups of women, sometimes with the support of Western NGOs. NGOs have stressed the socially damaging impact of SAPs on families, women and children. But more assertive public political protest has been restricted by the longer political history of gender inequality in Africa (Hay and Stichter, 1984). Throughout the post-colonial period, women's actions as political agents have been repressed or co-opted into governmental structures such as a Ministry of Women's Affairs (which has low prestige), or the pet projects of the male elite's wives (for example the 31 December Women's Movement in Ghana).

Structural adjustment and the liberation of the peasant smallholder?

As mentioned earlier in the chapter, structural adjustment has its origins in the rise of the 'New Right' and neoliberal theory. Neoliberal theory is based on a fundamental faith in the market to allocate resources in the best way. This fits well with one of the perspectives on the peasantry covered in Chapter 2: peasants as petty entrepreneurs. Recall that this perspective was based on the notion that each small-holder production unit was akin to a small business which would flourish if only the intrusive rent-seeking state would allow markets to work their magic. By threading this smallholder perspective on the peasantry with structural adjustment, we have the main intellectual defence for SAP. Structural adjustment aims to redress the urban bias of postcolonial economic policy, it aims to liberate the peasantry from overbearing state control, and consequently it is a programme designed to assist the poorest who reside in the countryside.

The mechanism through which adjustment works in favour of the peasantry is the <u>roll-back of the</u> state. SAP often involves the dissolution of state marketing boards; where it does not it certainly demands the raising of producer prices for crops. Once prices more closely approximate world prices, peasant producers will have the incentive to produce more and to gain more revenue. They will become dynamized by the market.

It is certainly the case that the roll-back of the rent-seeking state is to be welcomed. It is also true that higher producer prices have been welcomed by peasants and that in many cases they have responded positively, for example in respect to cocoa production in Ghana (Mikell, 1991). But there are a number of problems with this model of rural development.

- Peasant recovery is based on *export production* (or tradeables). Devaluation (another key component of all SAPs) makes exports more competitive and complements the raising of export crop prices. But world prices for many crop exports are very volatile, or have been falling for a long period of time. There is some controversy concerning the falling prices of export crops, but Tiffen and Barratt-Brown put the matter clearly and with reference to the World Bank's own figures:

Prices in world markets for African products have been falling sharply since 1950, with only the occasional blip for oil and most minerals in the 1970s. The downward trend is particularly pronounced when falling prices for Africa's exports – mainly primary commodities – are compared with rising prices for Africa's imports – mainly manufactures.

(1992: 3)

As mentioned earlier, the downward trend in crop primary commodity prices (the bulk of primary commodities) is very clear for the period from 1980 onwards – exactly the period in which SAP became the continental orthodoxy (see also Sahn et al., 1999: 16). Tiffen and Barratt-Brown also question the long-term prospects for export crops in the face of new technologies, substitution effects and declining markets in the West (1992: 28–40; see also Raikes and Gibbon, 2000: 60).

- Freeing the market in agriculture takes no account of the processes of *differentiation* at work in rural areas (Bryceson, 2000). Following on from the previous point, price changes can provide advantages for larger peasant farms which are oriented towards exports, but provide little respite for smaller peasant households which produce mainly food crops which are either consumed by the household or sold in local markets (Mikell, 1991: 90 et seq.; Campbell and Clapp, 1995: 440). Indeed, there is evidence that export promotion might undermine food crop production (Bassett, 1988). SAP also impoverishes those in rural areas with very slight resource bases (Zack-Williams, 2000: 61). The fact is that different peasant households have different capacities to respond to market liberalization, and although responses are complex and often involve activity in non-agrarian sectors (see Chapter 2), it is probable that in the absence of countervailing pressures, liberalization will benefit the wealthy and powerful more than the poor and politically weak. The World Bank's penchant for land privatization would almost certainly accentuate rural differentiation.

- As mentioned at the end of Chapter 2, the poor record of *state action* does not entirely preclude the possibility of positive state action when looking at the prospects for rural development. And it is yet to be proven that the market is any better than the state at providing vital components of any agricultural regeneration. Freeing the market does not, through some ethereal dynamic, produce the infrastructure of trade and commerce. Remote rural areas require roads, trading posts, credit and grain storage facilities if peasants are to respond positively to price signals. Private commerce does not automatically provide these things: in fact where it has tended to do so, it has been in response to incentives or directions from the state. Markets are as much constructed by state action as they are the invisible hand (Ponte, 1998). Furthermore, in remote areas, a public monopsony (many sellers, one state marketing board purchaser) can be replaced by a private monopsony (many sellers, one private trader), leaving peasants vulnerable to the trader where once they were vulnerable to the marketing board.

- *Devaluation* can offset crop price rises, reducing peasant terms of trade (see Chapter 2) or even making them negative (Campbell and Clapp, 1995: 441–2). Devaluation makes exports more competitive, but it also makes imports more expensive. Because African economies are often highly import dependent, rises in the prices of imports can have strong inflationary effects which make basic consumer and producer goods increasingly expensive. The net result is that, although peasants might gain more revenue from the crop sales, they find that they have to spend more to purchase the same basket of goods. In Mozambique, this has led to peasants' terms of trade falling under structural adjustment (Harrison, 1998).

In sum, we can see that the intuitive neoliberal logic is actually quite difficult to sustain once we abandon the premise that markets by their very nature have progressive social effects. It is difficult to give much detail on peasants' political responses to structural adjustment because peasant politics is very much defined by local political relations which have endured over a longer period than just the 1980s and 1990s (but see Harrison, 2000; Berry, 1997; Boone, 1998). Peasants encounter SAP as local changes in the nature of state action and market forces, which can display as much continuity as change even in the context of quite radical structural adjustment (Galli, 1990). Removed from the more intense circuits of written information and political organizations in the urban areas, it is difficult for peasants to understand SAP as a series of social processes sponsored by international finance institutions often underlain with an element of coercion produced by indebtedness. Peasants may condemn the declining levels of health or education (Rudebeck, 1990, 1997), but much of the politics of this discontent will be embedded in more complex and problematic state–peasant relations in a particular context. Processes of differentiation during the era of SAP have created an increase in the politics of witchcraft, in which the enrichment of some is represented as a magical process most often associated with 'sucking the blood' of others, or morally dubious and Faustian activities (see Chapter 5).

Structural adjustment's 'natural constituency'? Business and liberalization

SAP is based on a faith in the market and entrepreneurship. Markets will allow business to flourish as a result of the rigours of competition, so the argument in its essentials goes. The economic relations created by SAP in respect to business are complex, and depend on the kind of business activity as much as the effects of SAP itself. Devaluation (which as we mentioned earlier makes imports more expensive) can be very damaging to import-dependent manufacturing; rising interest rates have made credit more expensive; the removal of quotas and reduction in tariffs has reduced the protection afforded to national industries; the privatization of parastatals can provide 'rich pickings' for politically connected entrepreneurs; rapid price changes can provide opportunities for speculation; open economies can increase competition from foreign firms.

In addition to these complexities, the political responses of business have been strongly conditioned by their relations with states. As mentioned in Chapter 1, bourgeoisies have often been substantially the creation of political power as much as economic power in postcolonial Africa. If structural adjustment threatens the umbilical cord between political and economic power, then some sectors of business might well articulate a nationalist and anti-SAP posture, especially when structural adjustment involves the opening up of domestic markets to foreign firms:

> Local investors, in the face of deregulation of the economy [*sic*], trade liberalization and heavy devaluation of the currency, simply find it difficult to remain afloat in the face of foreign competition. This is why the Manufacturers Association of Nigeria has been on the forefront of those opposed to the way the [structural adjustment] programme has been implemented.
>
> (Ihonvbere, 1993: 144)

In Zimbabwe, the Confederation of Zimbabwean Industries, the Chambers of Commerce and Mining and large-scale commercial farmers all supported structural adjustment as a way gradually to remove the high tax burden and regulations imposed by the government (Skalnes, 1993). But the CZI has not uncritically accepted SAP in

Zimbabwe (Sachikonye, 1993: 246). Zimbabwe has a history of a strong and fairly independent bourgeoisie, generated during colonialism and especially during the import substitution period of the Unilateral Declaration of Independence, which provides it with a critical independence from the state and other agencies. The Nigerian example fits more clearly with Gibbon's argument that manufacturing industries which have relied on state support suffer under structural adjustment (1996a, see also Hutchful, 1995: 57). In fact, Gibbon argues that while businesses with strong state connections have stagnated or declined during SAP, other forms of business based on import–export commerce and involving illicit activities have flourished.

Where SAP has had a recessionary impact, businesses have been critical of adjustment, even if they support its general direction. This was the case in Zimbabwe, where the pace of reform became a bone of contention between business and the World Bank (Skalnes, 1993). It was also the case in Ghana, where the Ghana Employers Association criticized the impact of SAP which generated 'severe liquidity problems, rapidly rising interest rates, sluggish sales… just to mention a few such matters' (in Kraus, 1991). Similar concerns were expressed in the Manufacturing Association of Nigeria's critique of SAP (Olukoshi, 1993a). For the World Bank and IMF, the desire to control inflation through a 'cooling down' of the economy was calculated to have a deleterious impact on national business which would then allow the most dynamic or efficient firms to emerge all the more strong, a kind of 'Darwinian process of natural selection amongst enterprises' (Gibbon, 1996a: 775).

Thus, as with peasant farmers, SAP induces processes of differentiation, growth *and* stagnation which render any unified political response unlikely for the time being. It is also the case that the politics of structural adjustment for the capitalist class is strongly conditioned by ongoing relations with the state. Let us now turn to the state itself to examine how it has responded to structural adjustment.

The state and adjustment

So far, we have identified two social groups (wage labour and women) which have suffered significant deleterious effects from structural adjustment, producing some resistance to SAP. We have also seen how the two main social groups which should benefit from SAP (peasants and businesses) have in fact experienced a process of differentiated change under adjustment, consequently producing equivocal political responses. All of these social groups have produced forms of political response which are in significant ways generated by ongoing state–class relations. This provides the complex terrain of the politics and struggle under structural adjustment: class responses to liberalization refracted through the contours of the state. But, in a way, we have so far omitted the most political aspect of structural adjustment: its implementation by the elite which directly detains state power.

There is a central paradox in the World Bank and IMF's structural adjustment programmes (Williams, 1994): the latter are based on an economic model in which the state is conceived as a tendentially overbearing rent-seeking institution. It is responsible for 'red tape', directly unproductive activities, 'bloated' and ineffective administration, and so on. Consequently, SAP involves the rolling back of the state – the removal of the state from the economy, the scaling-down of the administrative apparatus, and so on. But SAP must be *negotiated with states*, and agreements must be implemented by the same. In other words, adjustment requires state elites to author and implement their own disempowerment and exit from the economic stage.

The politics of state–donor relations are only partially understood and are very complex. Until recently, both states and the IFIs tended to be very secretive about the way in which adjustment programmes are agreed, and the details of SAPs were not made public, much less the mechanics of their design, although this has changed to some extent since 1995 or so. The World Bank began its interventions with very little regard to the politics of the states implementing them, but soon had to address itself to questions of agency and political support. Much of this thinking was condensed into the notion of governance, which emerged in the 1990s. *Good governance* (see Chapter 4) was required to ensure structural adjustment a smooth implementation. This involved attempts to create an open and transparent bureaucracy, some degree of institutional capacity building (not just less state but better state action), and some form of accountability (with the most powerful bilateral funders of the World Bank and IMF supporting multi-party democracy). Through the notion of governance, the Bank managed to argue the case for a *complementarity* between state elites – properly motivated – and adjustment. On the tails of good governance arrived a new vocabulary more closely focused on the power relationship between state and donor: partnership, participation, principal–agent issues, incentives, decentralization and so on (Harrison, 2000a).

But the politics of states during structural adjustment have not only developed within the negotiation process; they have constituted part of the process of social change itself. Most importantly in this respect, state elites have employed a series of 'straddling' techniques in order to maintain or enhance their political and economic power during adjustment (Bayart, 1993; Bayart, Ellis and Hibou, 2000). That is, they have used political power, knowledge and connections to consolidate positions for themselves within the economy. In fact, the initial implementation of SAP has often created such sudden and rapid price changes – in imports, exports and currencies – that speculative activity by the politically powerful has consolidated the socio-economic position of a state class. Mamdani identifies this in the *mafutamingi* class in Uganda, as does Galli for the *ponteiro* class in Guinea-Bissau (Mamdani, 1990; Galli, 1990; see also Loxley, 1990). Williams (1994) identifies the inability of the World Bank to address the dominance of this class – and the latter's ability to work within the SAP to maintain its privileges – as the reason why structural adjustment is necessary and why it doesn't work. This argument is supported by the case of Niger, for example (Gervais, 1995).

Despite the apparent conflict between the IFIs with their faith in the 'free' market and state elites who have relied on political power to create markets that work only for them, there is also a *mutual reliance* between the two. States require loans and aid from the IFIs and bilateral donors – and the more 'fungible' (that is the more one can put these funds to discretionary use) these funds the better – to elaborate strategies of class empowerment or at least defence. The World Bank and IMF require states to be compliant with the schedules of liberalization that SAP produces. Ghana has received relatively large amounts of funding because it has implemented adjustment fairly faithfully, and (even better) has yielded positive economic indices. Where regimes have started to 'slip' in their policy implementation, the IFIs have sometimes indulged these failings on the grounds that the political costs of cutting off a further tranche of lending would disrupt the image of SAP or its possibilities of maintaining influence with the state elite afterwards (Harrison, 2001b).

One of the conceptual points around which significant resistance to SAP emerges is *sovereignty*. Clearly, it is difficult to maintain conventional notions of sovereignty when the Ministry of Finance has World Bank or IMF staff in senior positions, or when negotiations in Washington or Paris become more important than negotiations with domestic constituencies (Mkandawire, 1992). A good example of how significant sovereignty can become can be found in the case of Tanzania where the sticky issue of devaluation revolved around who had the right to set the Tanzanian shilling's external value (Loxley,

1989; Singh, 1986; Malima, 1986; Raikes and Gibbon, 1996). The eventual capitulation to the World Bank and later IMF was only achieved after the first president, Julius Nyerere (who had been a close ally with Peter McNamara, a World Bank president from the pre-adjustment era) stepped down. Since the implementation of an IFI-approved SAP (1986 to the present), some have argued that adjustment has undermined the entire edifice of nationalism in Tanzania, so closely was it associated with state-based social provision and planning in the name of national self-reliance (Kaiser, 1996).

The notion of sovereignty can itself be employed for a variety of purposes which again add complexity to the IFI–state relationship. The Mozambican government has presented SAP very much as an externally imposed project (Saul, 1990), which in many ways it is (Plank, 1993). But reference to an external and politically untouchable agency also allows the government to *depoliticize* its own policy decisions: for example, the privatization and liberalization of the cashew nut industry was a conditionality over which the World Bank was intransigent, but the government failed to take up the World Bank offer to provide compensation for the economic damage wrought by privatization. In substance, the imposition of SAP constitutes one more innovation within a longer authoritarian relationship between state and society, in which socialist or capitalist top-down planning and state action has been the order of the day since the 1950s. One of the reasons why there has not been a stronger reaction to the externally imposed austerity of SAP is that it does not violate any pre-existing substantial participation or egalitarianism within indebted societies. Thus, with some parallels to the Mozambican case, the Zimbabwean government has presented ESAP (Zimbabwe's structural adjustment programme from 1990) 'as a fact of economic life, perhaps similar to drought', and has not been keen to encourage debate over its logic or its impact (Gibbon, 1996: 357). There are echoes of this in the way that the Babangida regime presented SAP in Nigeria: whatever one thinks of SAP, 'there is no alternative', as the President stated (in Beckman, 1995: 304).

So, the politics of the state–IFI relationship is more complex than a simple principal–agency model (African states executing Bank-funded SAPs) allows. These complexities are rooted in two vital relationships: first the unity of political and economic power within most postcolonial political economies, and secondly the mutual antagonism *and* mutual reliance that exist within the mechanism of conditionality: policies will threaten the incumbent elite, but it is only the latter that can effectively implement them, and if they do, it is likely that they will receive more aid and an 'indulgence' of policy slippage.

Understanding politics and resistance in the age of structural adjustment

In the previous section we looked at the political economy of adjustment and investigated the ways in which this political economy affected political responses to SAP. If there is one fundamental point which one can take from the complexity of 'the politics of adjustment' investigated above, it is that SAP – for all its external origins and coercive dynamics – has necessarily worked within the relief of existing country-specific political economies. The mutual antagonism and/or mutual dependence between social groups and the state significantly define the actual form of implementation and resistance to SAP. Both organized labour and business have equivocal relations with the state, and each class can become divided as structural adjustment demands a reconsideration of links with the state. For some social groups – peasants and women – relations with the state have always been so poor that any damaging effects deriving from SAP appear as 'more of the same' rather than a serious challenge to previously attained or desired rights. More generally, the ascendance of the free market has created processes of differentiation – perhaps a struggle of all against all – which can work against organized political resistance.

It is also the case that the changes in class relations which SAP creates are the 'raw material' for a series of other political responses within civil society which cannot be directly related to a particular class constituency. Church organizations have been at the forefront of resistance to structural adjustment, for example, in Zimbabwe and Mozambique because of their declared interest in protecting the vulnerable from the socially regressive aspects of austerity (Gibbon, 1996b). In Nigeria and other West African countries, students have been central in anti-SAP politics partly because of intellectual convictions, but also because grants and resources to tertiary education are very often cut during structural adjustment.

Are there alternatives?

As suggested earlier, it is a lot easier to find critiques of structural adjustment than it is to find alternatives. But if we agree with Bond and Mayekiso that the logic of TINA (There Is No Alternative) be replaced by THEMBA (There Must Be an Alternative – also the Zulu word for 'hope') (Bond and Mayekiso 1996), it is important to consider these alternatives and the political struggles upon which they are based.

It should be noted at the outset that very few would argue that there was not something 'broken' which needed to be fixed in the early 1980s. The 'Berg Report' did indeed contain trenchant criticism of the rent-seeking state, and it seems fairly pointless to defend the state and thus portray it as victim of a crisis which was not of its own making. We have seen in the previous section how important the ongoing contradictions of postcolonial politics gave form to the experience of SAP in specific societies. So, is it possible to conceive of ways in which debt and economic crisis be addressed without recourse to SAP? We will review some of the main lines of thinking in this area.

A strong set of arguments against SAP and towards an alternative model have emerged from various groups within the African intelligentsia. The best known is the United Nations Economic Commission for Africa's Alternative Economic Framework (Economic Commission for Africa, 1989; Tarp, 1993: 143 et seq.). This Programme is based on the ideas of selective state planning and regional economic integration. Unfortunately, the alternative framework fails fully to consider the issue of *agency*, beyond references to 'popular' desires for an end to SAP. This shortcoming presents itself as a paradox. Let us take one particular work – a very well-argued and recent text – in order to illustrate the problem. Mkandawire and Soludo argue for an alternative to SAP based on the reclaiming of 'Our Future' (2000). They begin with a critique of SAP which includes references to the elite and authoritarian nature of postcolonial states. But once they begin a consideration of an alternative model, the state is ushered in again, as a 'developmental' institution, crucial to Africa's future. At no point is the question asked: why should the state act any more progressively outside a structural adjustment regime? The assumption that states will act according to the new agenda allows Mkandawire and Soludo to become rather lazy with their alternative model (see also Carmody, 1998). Where agencies are important, the authors can assert that 'The state must ...' (117) or 'African countries must learn ...' (111).

One useful way to understand the realities and possibilities for an alternative to SAP is not so much to chart out a specific socio-economic model but to understand how a variety of different political actions and struggles can affect the SAP regime. Responses to SAP which do not directly deal with neoliberal reform can still make a difference if they contribute to the modification of the terrain upon which structural adjustment acts. This is the case to some extent in respect to movements for democratization, as we shall see in Chapter 4. In the South African context, John Saul has employed the concept of structural reform after this fashion (1991). He uses it to get around the polarized perspectives on the 'New South Africa' – that democratic elections constitute the endpoint of a political struggle or that without a deeper revolution there can be only social decline and poverty. Structural reform allows space for a less determined set of political activities which might not revolutionize social relations but could change the conditions within which revolution or liberation (however defined) might become possible. In respect to structural adjustment, demands from labour organizations for a more 'nationalist' aspect to economic planning (as articulated by the Nigerian Labour Congress periodically for example) does not necessarily challenge structural adjustment in its fundamentals, nor does it chart out a flawless alternative model; but it does subject the state to countervailing pressures, making it less difficult to argue a case against rapid wholesale privatization of state property most often to foreign companies with concomitant retrenchment.

As previous sections have shown, much of the impact of structural adjustment is filtered through a national state. This means that one crucial axis of any consideration of structural reform vis à vis SAP will involve struggles against and within the state – both to assert rights to act politically (hold meetings, lobby governments, create working relationships with other political bodies and so on) and to subject the state to countervailing pressures to those emanating from the IFIs.

To get down to brass tacks, it would be inaccurate to imagine a strong, clearly directed popular resistance to structural adjustment. But because of the pervasive nature of structural adjustment – subject to an ongoing 'policy creep' from macroeconomics to administrative reform, relations with civil society, governance, and so on – many forms of political activity (current and future) will affect the future prospects of adjustment *and* the terrain upon which the struggles against adjustment *do* take place. For those who think that ending this chapter on this note is a little too biased in favour of the 'optimism of the will' over the 'pessimism of the intellect' (to recall Gramsci's phrase), the question is: is it more naive to remain open to possibilities of structural reform towards an end to structural adjustment or to preclude them in spite of contradictions generated by the adjustment regime? Remaining with the former approach, the next chapter looks at the context of political struggle from the late 1980s: the process of democratization.

Further reading

There is a massive literature on debt and structural adjustment. Good introductions include: (Mosley et al., 1995a; Simon et al., 1995; Tarp, 1993; Mohan et al., 2000). A detailed set of case studies is presented in Engberg-Pedersen et al., 1996b). On the social impact of structural adjustment, see Adepojou (1993) and, in contrast Sahn et al. (1999). More empirically detailed political-economy approaches are Gibbon et al. (1993) and Mkandawire and Olukoshi (1995). Walton and Seddon (1994) investigate anti-IMF protests in various regions of the Third World – the chapter by Parfitt and Riley is well worth reading. Elson (1991) is the definitive text on gender and adjustment. The impact of structural adjustment on the state has been intensively covered in the *Review of African Political Economy* from issue number 47.

4
Contesting Democratization

Introduction

Any book on contemporary African politics needs to deal with the marked political change during the 1990s during which most African states have 'opened up' politically in one way or another. By and large, this *abertura* (Joseph, 1998) has taken the form of the introduction of multi-party constitutions: from 1990 to 1996, 37 out of 48 African states held multi-party elections after a long period of single-party politics. In analysing this *abertura*, most academics have taken multi-party politics as their point of departure. This has led to a fairly strong literature on political transitions (Osaghae, 1995b) which has a general concern with institutions and elites (Diamond et al., 1988). Our concern is necessarily distinct: we must start with the processes of popular politics which might be characterized as part of a democratization process; and we must ask the question, partly paradox: has democratization been implemented in *undemocratic* fashion through concentrations of power?

As with the rest of the book, then, our concern is with struggle and its interactions with thematic political changes. This is in fact a very sound starting point in a broader academic and theoretical fashion. The best studies of democratization with a broad historiographical sweep have located social struggle at centre stage (Rueschmeyer et al., 1992; Wood, 1995; Barrington-Moore, 1966; Therborn, 1977). With a little bit of licence, one might say that democracy is only as good as people's capacity to struggle for and defend democratic rights.

A critical approach: democratization?

This shift in focus requires a few notes on its repercussions for the way we critically evaluate democratization. In this first place, we cannot *assume* democracy, nor even democratization, merely by the fact that institutions or leaderships have changed. Instead, this chapter will be less ostentatious in its claims to political change, identifying popular empowerment or struggle where it exists and considering its import in light of an array of distinctly undemocratic forces which hold sway over ordinary people (about which more later). In evaluating democratic change, which is the focus of the first section, a series of issues emerge which are quite cynical of much of the 'high politics' of multipartyism, new constitutions, watchdog agencies and elites who claim to have undergone some form of moral repentance for their previously undemocratic ways. The final section will contextualize democratic change within an analysis of the involvement of external agencies. This is necessary because of the important influence of external agencies, and the warning signal that this raises: does the pervasive intervention of external forces significantly attenuate the extent to which democratization can be based in popular participation and struggle?

Democratization or popular struggle?

If it is legitimate to assume that democratization is a *partial* process, whose success is a result of struggles ongoing, it is equally apposite to note that democratization does not necessarily begin in the 1990s, when the Berlin Wall fell followed by many a 'big man' African dictator, and when national conferences and referenda ushered in constitutional change. In fact, one could realistically narrate a history of democratization as a history of struggle within and against the nation-state, imposed through the violence of colonialism and the bankruptcy of postcolonial rule. This is in a sense the argument that Basil Davidson sketches out (1978, 1992). This history would include the labour struggles of the 1930s, the politics of popular nationalism in the 1950s, the liberation struggles in the Lusophone and settler states of the 1960s and 1970s, and the ongoing flowering of small political organizations based on popular empowerment that have more often than not been crushed or co-opted by postcolonial states. It would also include the postcolonial struggles of peasant societies (Chapter 2) and labour unions (Chapter 3).

There are many more books on authoritarianism or the supposedly democratic content of 'socialist' states in Africa than there are studies of struggle against the state. One useful collection of studies is Anyang' Nyong'o (1987), which portrays postcolonial Africa in the throes of a battle for a 'second liberation', this time not against the colonial oppressors, but against the presidents and their cronies who inherited the state and wielded it against their own citizenry. There are three obvious reasons for this paucity in the literature. One is the fact that there has rarely been a strong political movement of popular demo-cratic empowerment in any African state during the postcolonial decades. Consequently, our conclusions in this chapter must be necess-arily cautious concerning the significance of the recent 'winds of change'. Secondly, academics have been little inclined to consider this topic, either because of their alignment with a conservative worldview, or because of their solidarity with African governments out of an affinity for socialism in Africa or a dislike for the powerful imperialist forces that batter postcolonial states. Thirdly, the lack of democracy, accountability and participation in postcolonial states does not necess-arily provoke organized opposition to a form of power and its prac-tices. It is just as likely to lead to various kinds of *political distancing*: a subversion of state politics or a desire to establish a realm outside of the state. This is why probably the most influential study to con-sider responses to authoritarian states in Africa before the 1990s detailed a dynamic of 'political exit' through the construction of civil societies which put distance between people and the state (Rothchild and Chazan, 1988). So, this historical frame cautions against too keen a search for political novelty, and it requires us to be quite modest about the scope and prospects for democratization in present-day Africa.

A political economy of democratization

Much of the academic attention to democracy from the 1990s has led to a strong emphasis on institutions, leaders, parties and political behaviour. Even if some space is given to social and economic processes (Bratton and van de Walle, 1997), it is understood that it is in the formal political realm that the action takes place. Hyden goes further in his notion of governance, closely associated with democrat-ization: 'we can adequately grasp the current political changes ... only by treating politics as an independent variable' (1992: 4). In this book, it is argued that political change, and particularly its impact on the general population, is best understood as an integral part of a broader political economy. As we have already seen, the politics of the peasantry and of structural adjustment are about markets, eco-nomic regulation and income levels as well as political organiza-tions, policies and accountability. In this chapter, we cannot separate democratization from the changes taking place in African econ-omies. This means, *inter alia*, revisiting the dynamics of structural adjustment, this time with a closer focus on its repercussions for democracy.

In summary, our analysis of democratization has three guiding coordinates:

- to understand current processes of democratization as modest developments on a longer political trajectory;
- to relate domestic and international forces promoting or restricting democratization;
- to ensure that democratization is studied as political economy;
- to evaluate democratization principally in terms of collective political action

Evaluating change

Three criteria

Our concern with struggle does not allow us solely to rely on formal indices of democratic progress. We cannot declare a country democratic by virtue of the fact that it has successfully held two peaceful elections which have ushered in a change of government (Huntington, 1991: 226 et seq.; Lawson, 1999: 2), because this does not necessarily connote any great popular participation in the polity or empowerment of the masses. Nor can we rely on the calculations of the Freedom Index by Freedom House International, as these rankings take very little account of political economy. Instead, we propose a triad of analytical criteria, not amenable to rankings or the definitive statement regarding how far a country has democratized. The three criteria elaborated here focus our analytical eye on issues that illuminate the popular nature of democratic change.

1. Is democratization shallow or deep?

A shallow democracy would be one which has not made much of a difference to ordinary people. There might be quite radical changes to a constitution, and an expansion in party activity, but this might well be accompanied by a sense of *plus ça change* among ordinary people, especially those living in rural areas:

> Having candidates who come to the village before election day to fish for votes, but who return to the capital once they have been elected, this makes as little sense as keeping a spare wheel for a car 110 kilometres distance away from the car.
>
> (In Baker, 2000: 186)

The picture painted by this 'African elector' is probably not dissimilar to the nature of formal politics in many African countries before 1990.

The image is one of the party official from the city arriving in his four-by-four once a year to make grand promises and elicit support before disappearing and doing nothing. Lonsdale's opposition is instructive here. Rather than opposing shallow and deep politics, he poses a duality between high and deep politics (1986: 135). The point Lonsdale makes is relevant here because shallow politics is also high politics – largely divorced from the struggles, organizations, and life chances of the masses.

A deeper democracy requires more than merely a theatre of participation and accountability. It requires that we identify actual processes of popular influence on the state which subsequently make a difference to the way the state acts. In other words, democratic deepening is not the holding of two or three peaceful election events, but is a *process* of political organization and engagement with the state. As a social process, democratization is likely to be a complex and incremental affair.

2. If democratization is a process, is it a process of popular participation?

Democracy, as we have already mentioned is as good as people's capacity to construct and defend it. Democratization is a process of struggle to participate in the affairs of state, and this is a process which does not start and stop according to the caprice of academics' periodizations. Rather, it has a history as long as the state itself, and has been part of Africa's postcolonial politics generally (Aké, 1995: 77). When evaluating developments in the period from 1990, we must ask: how much has change involved a growing practice of popular organization and participation? This is different from the previous question because the issue is not how much difference a political development has made, but how much people have participated in the dynamics of the development itself. In other words, the concern is with the means as much as the ends, or – to use another metaphor – the question is not so much the destination as the nature of the journey itself. This is an important point which raises some difficult issues. Which is more significant for democratization: a popular movement for democratization which creates new and fairly accountable organizations but is crushed by the state, or the decision by a president to legalize political parties and create two political parties, one 'a little to the left' and the other 'a little to the right'? Both of these processes have been part of the Nigerian democratization process since 1986.

3. Does democracy make a difference?

This simple question has profound repercussions as well. In the words of Joaquim Chissano, Mozambique's president, 'you can't eat democracy'. The general tenor of this book is that one cannot separate political and economic rights, therefore it makes no sense to celebrate a process of political opening which makes no difference to the material well-being of the masses. People have a right to a minimum intake of calories, as well as a right to basic health care and education provision. Rights do not stop at the ballot box, but extend into the market and the workplace. This is not just a question of understanding democratization as 'bread and butter' issues; it is also a question of keeping a keen eye focused on the *scope* of democratization, that is the boundaries of state action and popular influence over the latter. In this age of 'globalization' and quangos, this is hardly a question peculiar to sub-Saharan Africa.

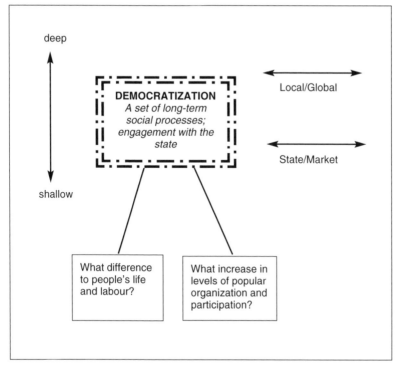

Figure 4.1   Analysing democracy

Figure 4.1 sets out a conceptual map of our approach to democratization, summarizing the points made so far. Let us now go on and look at some democratic developments that took place in the 1990s.

Democratization and political activity

The media

A key part of the constitutional changes that have taken place as a result of the introduction of multi-partyism has been the removal of restrictions, formal and informal, on the media. This has involved the legalization of independent publishers and the loosening of governmental control over the publicly owned media.

In a number of countries, the print media have been pivotal in constructing a new critical discourse in urban literate politics. In Mozambique, a group of journalists previously working within the state established a number of independent publications which have identified corrupt or incompetent practice in the higher echelons of the state, argued against the undemocratic involvement of international finance institutions in Mozambique's polity, and generally put politicians and officials under an intense critical spotlight (a taster of the reportage in Mozambique can be found at http://www.sadirectory.co.za/mediacoop). At the time of writing, one of the most prominent investigative journalists in Mozambique and editor of the excellent *Metical* news-sheet, Carlos Cardoso, was assassinated as he investigated a large-scale bank fraud. In Tanzania, a moderate oppositional voice has emerged since the cautious political liberalization there (Sandbrook, 1996a: 83) and in Benin, 40 new newspapers and magazines emerged after 1989 (Karikari, 1993: 55). In Uganda, *The Monitor* (http://www.monitor.co.ug/) provides a critical alternative to the government-owned *New Vision*. *The Monitor* suffers from a problem which affects all print media: a lack of funds. The urban market is both small and generally low-income. One could add examples from many other countries. In Nigeria and Ghana, strong independent publishers have been fighting to maintain a presence throughout the postcolonial period. In Zimbabwe, a strong independent press is increasingly having to defend its right to free expression. In each of these cases, newspapers have been the focus for a critique of the government, sometimes directly aligned with an opposition party, sometimes just as critical of opposition parties as of the ruling party.

But it is also the case that this discourse is itself extremely limited in scope. Few people can read the print language of the newspapers. Forty-two per cent of sub-Saharan Africa's adult population (over 15 years old) was illiterate in 1997 (World Bank, 2000: 329). Furthermore, newspaper circulation is mainly restricted to urban areas (Karikari, 1993). It may be that provincial towns receive a small selection of newspapers every week or so, but nothing more. There are, by and large, no newspapers in the villages. More likely, people tune in to the official radio station (government owned), or the shortwave international stations such as Voice of America and the BBC World Service.

It is also important to note that the legalization of the independent media does not necessarily mean increasing political activity and an improvement in the political awareness of the reading citizenry. Firstly, states still find ways to restrict freedom of expression, perhaps through an enthusiastic use of the courts and accusations of libel, perhaps just by detaining editors on trumped-up charges. Baker reports that arbitrary seizures, censorship and detention of the media took place in 24 African countries between 1995 and 1998 (2000: 204). Nongovernmental journalists are also often informally kept out of the information loops of government (Burnell, 1995: 683; interviews, Kampala, 2000).

Secondly, freedom of the press does not necessarily lead to heroic struggles to establish freedom of information. In both radio and print media new enterprises have emerged to sell sensation and tacky commercialism. Thus in Mozambique *Fim de Semana* (The Weekend) reports fictional stories of sex and death not dissimilar to Britain's *Sport* or the American *Enquirer*. Ugandan independent radio DJs emulate the delivery of a flow of banalities common in commercial radio the world over. Mahmood Mamdani, speaking of democratization in Uganda, laments this kind of liberalization and the culture it produces, which celebrates the market at the expense of democracy.

> The global village is more like a selective, highly-priced hotel. Its global inhabitants are like a thin layer of cream, socially cosmopolitan and culturally increasingly homogeneous. Steeped in vulgar consumerism, they have a fragile national identity. If you want to identify this group in today's Uganda, just look for those who consume CNN television uncritically, and those on its fringes who devour the new FM Radio stations. Their global integration goes alongside an increased distance from the mass of working people.
>
> (1995a: 232)

So, liberalization can be about an expanding critical public discourse and citizen awareness, and it can mean more cola adverts. Even worse, the independent media can publicize incendiary messages which will likely undermine democracy, as some papers did in Côte d'Ivoire in the run-up to the 1995 elections (Crook, 1997: 234).

Thirdly, even well-researched media reports do not necessarily mean that states or citizens change the nature of their actions. In Mozambique, the media have been central to changes in government action, for example in political leaders declaring their assets before entering office, or in dismissing an extremely unpopular Minister for the Interior (Harrison, 1999a). In Benin and Togo, the independent media were central to the push for the holding of National Conferences to usher in a new multi-party constitution (Nwajiaku, 1994: 434). In Cameroon, the oppositional *Le Messager* became central to the politics of opposition after 1991 (Krieger, 1994: 610). But, in many other cases, the presentation of a political issue in print does not result in a political response. It might be that, once the 'shock' of a new investigative journalism subsides, governments just ignore the accusations. This has repercussions for citizen action and attitude as well. In Uganda, as the press has become more critical and as parts of the Ugandan state have taken the struggle against corruption more seriously, a paradoxical effect has been created, in which citizens perceive that corruption is on the increase (because more cases are exposed), although both exposure and increased publicity by anti-corruption agencies is part of the process of reducing corruption. Unless this representation can be changed, people will become increasingly apathetic and less likely to entertain the possibility that something can be done about corruption (interview, Inspector General, Uganda).

Labour unions

Throughout the postcolonial period, organized labour constituted part of the corporatist bloc of power centred around the state. However, as we have seen in Chapter 3, the strength of governmental control over labour organizations was weakened as a result of the impact of structural adjustment, which restricted the ability of the state to provide unionized workers with certain (relative) privileges. As a result, a complex set of interactions have been created in many African states. These interactions are the result of the interplay of three principal forces: the desire of the state to control organized labour, the increasing restiveness of workers faced with economic austerity, and the desire of labour unions to assert their autonomy and involve themselves in pro-democratic politics. All of this is rendered more complex by the internal divisions and rivalries that often pervade union organizations, especially union congresses which bring a wide variety of specific industry unions together.

In Nigeria, the transition back to a civilian regime via elections was brought to a halt in 1993. As a result a wide range of pro-democracy movements emerged, demanding that the military recognize the results of the 1993 elections. The Nigeria Labour Congress (NLC) was a key part of the democratic struggle (Agbu, 1998: 250; Osaghae, 1998b: 297–9). The NLC, particularly the oil unions, Nupeng and Pengassan, supported the broader Campaign for Democracy, protesting the annulment of the presidential elections (Lewis, 1999: 147). The strikes held by the oil unions cost the oil industry, and the Abacha regime which took power after Babangida's exit, 25 per cent of its daily oil revenues for every day that the government refused to accept the outcome of the elections (*Financial Times*, UK, 25 September 1994). It was therefore no coincidence that the state's response in brutally quelling democratic protest involved demobilizing the NLC, Pengassan and Nupeng (*The Independent*, UK, 19 August 1994). Another aspect of the state's response was to sow divisions within the structures of the NLC, a strategy in which it was already well practised (Beckman, 1995). Mass strikes significantly boosted other pro-democracy demonstrations (Bratton and van de Walle 1997: 148). In Cameroon, strikes helped force a National Conference and subsequent elections (Krieger, 1994: 611).

Unions played a part in many other countries' struggles for political change. In Tanzania, where the corporatist binds were particularly strong, 'under pressure from within … especially from students and trade unions … the ruling party has slowly liberalised and begun to dismantle its monopoly of power over the state' (Ohlson and Stedman, 1994: 207). After 1987, Mugabe began to moot the possibility of constitutionalizing a one-party state. This plan eventually failed, partly because of splits within the ruling party, but also because of resistance to the idea within Zimbabwean civil society. The Zimbabwe Congress of Trade Unions (ZCTU) was 'the major civil institution which opposed the concept of the one party state' (Sachikonye, 1993: 262; Alexander, 2000). In Zambia, the success of the Movement for Multiparty Democracy (MMD) in ousting Kaunda and UNIP can only be explained by the role of the Zambian Congress of Trade Unions which provided organizational and logistic support, as well as providing the party with its leader. Note Chiluba's words in 1990: 'the Zambian Congress of Trade Unions believes that the one-party system is open to abuse; it is not the people in power who should direct political change, but the ordinary masses' (in Bratton and van de Walle, 1992: 425; see also Sichone, 1996: 120; Ihonvbere, 1995: 16). More recently, the Movement for Democratic Change (MDC) in Zimbabwe repeated this pattern: the ZCTU provided the support base and the leader (Morgan Tsvangirai) for the first significant opposition party in Zimbabwe since 1987 (Bond, 1999: 14). Strikes promoted democratization in Malawi (Ihonvbere, 1997: 225–9), Benin (Decalo, 1997: 51), and Côte d'Ivoire (Rapley, 1994: 51; Mundt, 1997: 189).

Political parties

The rise of new political parties has sometimes involved a struggle against state oppression and the mobilization of previously under-represented constituencies (Sandbrook, 1996). Examples include FORD in Kenya before it split, and some of the parties that emerged in Mali after 1991 (Vengroff and Kone, 1995: 49–64).

The rise of an opposition party can provide an unprecedented level of opposition to a single party which has consolidated its power throughout a state. A good example of this is the Movement for Democratic Change in Zimbabwe (MDC). In Zimbabwe, a de jure multi-party constitution has developed into a de facto single-party state since the unification of Mugabe's Zimbabwe African National Union (ZANU) and Joshua Nkomo's Zimbabwe African People's Union (ZAPU) in 1987. Since then, President Mugabe has effectively ruled a single-party state. The MDC's emergence out of the Zimbabwe Congress of Trade Unions has provided a real opposition to Mugabe, having taken 46 per cent of the seats in parliament (Krieger, 2000: 448), despite elections that were perhaps free on the days of voting but grossly unfair as a result of the widespread intimidation that preceded them. During the pre-election violence, MDC members were killed, injured or threatened by militias most likely acting through the party; 32 people were killed in electoral violence overall. The MDC's success derived from its ability to broaden its support base from the labour movement to a rather complex aggregation of social groups, including large-scale commercial farmers and urban residents generally (Alexander, 2000).

Like most new opposition parties, the MDC's opposition was based strongly on an anti-corruption theme and the mobilization of a desire for change. But the MDC also articulated an alternative economic agenda, reflecting its support base. Most importantly, the MDC defended the country's property relations against the state's increasing tendency to purchase compulsorily large-scale commercial farms from the white population. So, substantial issues of general policy were at stake in the party elections in Zimbabwe in 2000. As we will see later on, this was an exception in multi-party elections, not the rule.

In much of Francophone Africa, new parties emerged within the context of the *Conférence National*, or National Conference. National Conferences were established in a number of Francophone states (Benin, Cameroon and Niger), in opposition to enduring single-party governments. The conferences brought together a wide variety of political organizations, including opposition parties, principally to create an alternative forum of decision-making to that of the party-state. Enfeebled ruling parties were then forced to accept and/or recognize the Conferences or risk the repercussions of bringing out the police in numbers to destroy the Conferences. This did not happen, and in the case of Benin (the first country to usher in a multi-party system), the Conference gained a sovereignty that allowed it to make decisions about the scope and pace of political change (Allen, 1992). In Togo, the state managed to maintain a stronger control over the *Conférence National*.

Formal and informal civil society

Other organizations outside of the party structure also promoted democratization. In Kenya, Zambia and Malawi, the churches provided a focus for demands for democratization (Kanyinga, 1998: 56; Venter, 1995; Bartlett, 2000: 432; Throup, 1993: 389; Cammack, 1999; Bratton and van de Walle, 1992: 424 et seq.). Churches were resisting the moral vacuousness of increasingly authoritarian regimes in these two countries as well as articulating a human rights point of view. In other examples, students were key protesters in starting off a popular movement towards democracy, for example in Zimbabwe and Mali (Nkiwane, 1998). Students were mobilized by a mixture of ideology and corporate interest, as incumbent regimes found it increasingly difficult to pay student grants or to provide employment for graduates. (We will return to student protest in Chapter 5.)

There also exist complex and diverse networks of informal organizations within African societies, which have grown to resist state power, provide an alternative to public authority and at times to exert pressure on the state. This is not civil society in the conventional sense (civil society will be dealt with later), but a more evasive and less formally institutionalized set of organizations. Mari Tripp has outlined the contours of these organizations in Tanzania and Uganda (Swantz and Mari Tripp, 1996; Mari Tripp, 1998). In respect to Tanzania, she argues that the emergence of these 'local organizations' provided an important part of the dynamic which made the ruling Chama cha Mapinduzi (CCM) liberalize its political system, leading to multi-party elections in 1995 and 2000.

What can we glean from the examples given above? It is clear that a vibrant and diverse set of political forces have emerged during the democratization period which express popular sentiments and aim to influence the state. Referring back to the second criterion listed earlier, we can identify processes of popular participation and mobilization outside the strictures of the state. However, consideration of the first and third criteria strongly attenuate the significance of this emerging set of struggles. Conclusions about the scope and meaning of democratization within the multi-party schema must necessarily be quite modest. One can say that some groups have taken advantage of limited political liberalization to create the *possibility* of a wider democratization process. Any more radical a statement about the scope of democratization would be to depart from the evidence, and to ignore the very real social features which undermine democratization, at least in the sense in which it is understood in this book. We will now go on to look at some of these 'restricting' features.

Recognizing the limits

Elections and 'eating'

There is a need to make a distinction between form and content in respect to elections. That is, elections might take place and, in respect to the process of voting, appear to be free and fair. But the political dynamics of the elections might not be characterized by meaningful popular choice between parties.

Analyses of authoritarianism in sub-Saharan Africa frequently paid attention to the phenomenon of clientelism. Clientelism involved the use of political power to distribute or accumulate resources in order to shore up the power of a ruling elite. The reference to 'eating' in the heading to this section derives from a West African saying: 'a goat eats where it is tethered'. In this sense, eating connotes the consumption of public resources by those in positions of political power, that is, the goats. Although the saying applies to the petty official as much as to the president's palace, the use of political power privately to accumulate resources is inextricably interrelated with a clientelist system. Clientelism involves the strategic division of the spoils of 'eating' to groups inside and outside of the state in order to shore up power (Allen, 1995). These systems vary in their structure – extremely centralized in Sierra Leone (Riley and Parfitt, 1987, Zack-Williams, 1990), decentralized in Nigeria (Joseph, 1987) – but they remain an important common feature of most postcolonial authoritarian systems, with a direct lineage back into the colonial period (Berman, 1998).

The reason for this reference to the 'pre-democratic' years of the 1980s and before is that, in fact, the political dynamics of clientelism and the distribution of political largesse remain today, shaping the meaning and content of elections in a multi-party context. When elections took place in 'pre-democratic' Africa, they were elections fought and won through strategies of patronage:

> Political party leaders at the national level look around for local leaders who command appreciable support within their own areas. They offer the local leader ... a place in the party, perhaps as a candidate in his home constituency. The local leader gets out the vote, essentially through his contacts and authority, and delivers it to the national party. The national party in turn – assuming that it wins power – delivers benefits to the local representative, in the form of either economic allocations... such as a road or a water supply, or a purely personal pay-off.
>
> (Clapham, 1993: 64)

In Zambia, during the second multi-party elections in 1997:

> The MMD [Movement for Multiparty Democracy] took advantage of its control over government resources to bolster its electoral prospects. While the MMD was not the only party to hand out T-shirts, beer, and money to attract supporters, other parties lacked the resources that were available to the MMD by virtue of its position as the ruling party.
>
> (Bratton and Posner 1999: 396–7)

In some countries the electoral process imposes such pressure on the state purse to distribute largesse to voters and local elites alike that Finance Ministries abandon their imperatives to control inflation and reduce public debt. This was the case in Kenya, Nigeria and Côte d'Ivoire's multi-party elections (Mundt, 1997: 195; Falola, 1999: 219), and in Tanzania, 'the ... Government... borrowed 33 billion Tanzanian shillings in the run up to the flawed 1995 elections' (Young, 1999: 34). In Ghana's 1996 elections, increased public expenditure to sweeten the elections generated inflation that knocked Ghana's structural adjustment off course (Jeffries, 1998: 205–6). The substantive content of clientelism involves not just the distribution of resources but also the distribution of political postings: in Benin

> Although the CN [*conférence national*] had accomplished its ultimate task by creating the necessary conditions which would enable any future President to be peacefully replaced by another, his 'pay back' job-postings for those who had supported his candidature means that it is not at all clear whether continued clientelistic practices will allow the recently introduced 'democratic' procedures and institutions to function.
>
> (Nwajiaku, 1994: 444)

Returning to Ghana, it is worth mentioning a longer-term form of clientelism: development conditionality. This is the tendency of newly elected governments to condition public investment on a region returning a positive vote during the elections. This means that democratic governments tend to plough resources into regions that returned a solid vote for the incumbent (Oquaye, 2000: 58; Jeffries, 1998: 200; Kanyinga, 1998: 58).

So, the substance of elections has not changed as drastically as one might imagine: Clapham's quotation might be applied not only to the 'bad old days' but also to the contemporary democratic period in many cases. It follows that elections – even if free and fair by international observer standards – are not necessarily events of free choice by ordinary citizens: local chiefs and notables might still try to use their clout to 'bring the voters out' for a party through which he or she is receiving largesse, and people's choices might be influenced as much by the 'glamour' and free T-shirts as they are by questions of policy. Certainly this is what Frelimo believed in Mozambique's first multi-party elections in 1994: the ruling party invested considerable resources in a series of *showmícios* – a word that joins the Portuguese word for political rallies and the English word 'shows' to describe the spectacular rallies held by Frelimo which involved bands, free beer, and T-shirts and hats.

Elite transitions

The point here is made clearly by Schraeder:

> The contest over political ascendancy in Africa still largely takes place among the same group of contestants: a very small elite (whether civilian or military) that generally favours political self-preservation over policies and political structures truly designed to benefit the disempowered majorities of most independent African countries.
>
> (1995: 63)

The chapter by Schraeder comes from an edited book which argues that multi-party elections are a form of 'low intensity democracy', in that they are principally a means through which a small elite circulates in and out of ruling party and state positions. One can see this in sub-Saharan Africa through three main features. In the first place, there is a clear tendency for politicians to 'cross the floor' from one party to another for no obvious reason other than to realign with the ruling clique or to oppose a ruling faction that has ousted someone from a position of power. Burnell analyses democratization in Zambia and identifies a strong popular perception that democratization is mainly the politics of self-enrichment by elites. He concludes that the 'general tendency of self-seeking helps us to make sense of the flourishing practice whereby political figures migrate between parties, sometimes even retracing their steps by rejoining a party they had formerly left' (1995: 682; Baylies and Szeftel, 1997: 115).

Secondly, opposition parties have often emerged, split and collapsed as a result of the personality rivalries and instrumentalism generated by what Claude Aké calls counter-elites (1995: 83–4) and their strategies charting a road to the presidential palace. This is most clearly the case in Kenya, where the split of the Forum for the Restoration for Democracy (FORD) into two factions, and the generalized factionalism and bickering of the opposition, allowed Moi to stay in power with a minority of the electorate's support (Kanyinga, 1998: 57; Ajulu, 1992, 1993). In Zaire, Mobutu successfully encouraged divisions and factionalism within the already unstable opposition parties to the extent that he was able to shore up his own power and install a multi-party system under his own rule, known as *multi-Mobutisme*.

Thirdly, elections have not always sounded a death-knell for dictators. In the first place, there has been a notable rebirth of former dictators as new democrats, sometimes taking power again in second elections, for example in Benin. More generally, Baker (1998) finds that between 1990 and 1997, more than half of Africa's transitions have resulted in a former dictator remaining in office, mainly by surviving the ballot box. Much of the explanation for this can be found in the fact that incumbency allows those in power a considerably higher ability to distribute patronage, to manipulate the rules of the elections and to employ the security forces to intimidate and split the opposition. Looking at second elections in sub-Saharan Africa, Bratton and Posner argue convincingly that incumbent elites are learning how to 'play' the electoral game in ways that ensure their incumbency (1999: 381).

These tendencies collectively highlight that democratization, counter- intuitively, can be an *elite process* in which the notions of representation or franchise are actually quite removed from the real business (literally) of electoral politics. Democratic politics can be powered by a rivalry of personalities or factions rather than a rivalry of ideology (Hawthorn, 1993: 340). Democratic regimes can coexist with a variety of forms of 'informal repression', as Kirschke clearly shows (2000); political liberalization can be simultaneous with new forms of oppression (Bratton and van de Walle, 1992: 427).

So far, we have identified a cautious process of popular empowerment being built within political processes with significant counter-democratic trends: enduring forms of clientelism in which the electorate are at best seen as a means to an end and at worst are bullied by local patrons, and a form of political competition characterized by rivalries within tiny elites. This situation suggests as many *continuities* as *changes* during democratization – continuities which necessarily attenuate our optimism about popular empowerment and struggle. These continuities lead us to consider some of the broader structural relations within which political change takes place, taking us back to the third criterion.

Structure and struggle

As mentioned in Chapter 1, our approach to the dilemma of structure and agency is to understand structures in dialectical relation to struggle. As such, we can acknowledge the importance of structure without abandoning agency and contingency to the realms of effect or function. There are two important structures which we need to account for in respect to the restricted nature of democratization.

Rural democratization?

Once again, we return to the politics of the countryside. Democratic change has impacted mainly on urban politics, and its reach outside urban areas is by no means obvious. Although some recognize the geographical restrictions of democratization (Burnell, 1995: 682, 685; Baker, 2000: 186), few have considered the extent to which democracy has an impact in rural areas. This is partly because political parties, and civil society more generally, are conceptually as well as physically located within the urban real (Kasfir, 1998a).

In many countries, elections are the only time that peasant communities see or hear from their 'elected representatives'. The image here is one of the suited politician arriving in his Pajero, making his promises to an audience corralled by the local party structures (perhaps through a translator), before leaving again to the business of politics in the city (recall the quotation from Baker at the start of the chapter). In Benin, rural 'people commonly complained that candidates arrived in the village making promises about new roads, health facilities, schools, and electricity, but they would never be seen again' (Magnusson, 1999: 231). This certainly fits well with the general arguments of Chapter 2, and resonates with this author's interviews in the villages of northern Mozambique. But what of multi-partyism specifically?

Concrete case studies or theorizations about the impact of multi-party democracy on rural societies are thin on the ground. Owusu (1992) argues that village communities have their own forms of democracy, and makes some favourable comments about the PNDC's attempts to involve Ghana's villages in the political process. Guyer's (1992) informative and thought-provoking study of democratization in Nigeria is more focused on the politics of taxation than on multi-partyism. Harrison (2000) has provided some details from a district in northern Mozambique. Here, the politics of multi-partyism has been appropriated into more localized and embedded social tensions. For example, the opposition party, Renamo, took up a strong liberal stand on the right of people to live where they wanted, and this provided Renamo with support because the people of Mecúfi district had been ordered into villages by the ruling party and their subsequent experience of Frelimo villages was far from happy. Other evidence from Mozambique also stresses local factors, such as the popularity of a particular lineage chief in a village, and the party colours they had decided to wear.

However, it is also important to note that agrarian societies do contain a wide variety of socio-political organizations. These may be village-level credit societies, cooperatives, social groups which also mobilize members to undertake collective work, local groups of political advocacy and so on. A diverse account of these associations is given for rural and peri-urban Nigeria by Adedeji and Otite (1997). The fact that these organizations are 'informal' and work according to gender, age or kinship ties rather than 'interests' in the liberal sense has left academic researchers generally poorly equipped to make sense of the interactions of this 'rural civil society' and the state. Dia (1996) refers to this sphere of interaction as the 'missing middle', that is the key to reconciling the modern institutions of state and international organization with the vaguely defined 'community' which often constitutes the target of policy (see also Landell-Mills, 1992).

But one cannot say all that is local or 'grassroots' is good. The popularity of a local 'Big Man' is also related to the extent to which people consider him (or her?) able to bring resources into the area (Crook, 1997: 218). The importance of patronage and the local geography of clientelism is very powerful during the build-up to an election.

Class and state

As mentioned earlier, political power and accumulation have been unified in a single social process in most of sub-Saharan Africa. Democratization has not destroyed this relation; in fact clientelist politics have continued in new guises, for example in Zambia (Szeftel, 2000) and Mozambique (Harrison, 1999a, 1999c). As we have seen in Chapter 3, ruling classes can also survive – or even thrive within – structural adjustment. There are serious repercussions in this structural continuity for the prospects of democracy.

The struggle for political power is still infused by a 'sharpness' not experienced in other parts of the world because the possession of political power is so central to accumulation and the maintenance of patronage networks. As such, elections have more of a 'life or death' feature to them: incumbents who lose elections can find their private avenues to wealth cut off; worse still, they may be brought in front of a judge to explain their ill-gotten gains.

The centrality of the state to private economic activity leaves the institutions of civil society very weak, as they must either struggle merely to survive as institutions, or as they resort to requesting support from the state itself. The other alternative is to elicit funds from external sources. We will be looking at the question of donors and democracy below. But it remains a fairly sturdy generalization to say that civic organizations in sub-Saharan Africa are few and far between, have fragile resource and support bases, and are quite elitist in terms of their urban and middle-class social base.

In sum, democratization has produced an increase in popular mobilization, struggling against reactionary forces within a set of powerful structural continuities.

Western involvement in democratization

The context of donor involvement

Since 1989, Western governments and multilateral agencies have promoted good governance in sub-Saharan Africa. Good governance has been defined in various ways (Landell-Mills, 1992; Hyden, 1992; Jeffries, 1993; Doornbos, 1995). The core of the notion of good governance adopted by Western institutions can be gleaned from the World Bank's *Governance: the World Bank Experience* (1994b):

- public sector reform;
- accountability;
- stronger rule of law;
- transparency;
- participation in decision-making by non-state actors;
- reduced military expenditure.

These key components of the governance agenda clearly derive from liberal democratic ideals historically based in Western development (Blunt, 1995; Young, 1995; Williams, 1999). The Bank cannot explicitly propound multi-partyism, as it is bound by its Articles of Agreement not to intervene in the sovereign affairs of a member state's political system – even if this seems a rather flexible restriction (Mosley et al., 1995: 102; Caufield, 1998: 51, 57). However, bilateral donors have tied the notion of good governance and democracy together in their interventions (Baylies, 1995; Hook, 1998; Lawson, 1999). Western commitment to democracy should be questioned when other economic or geopolitical concerns arise, however (Olsen, 1998). Another facet of the governance/democracy agenda is the tendency to include NGOs in project implementation and negotiation, as part of the concern to encourage the development of civil society (Danaher, 1994; Howell, 2000). Again, there are questions concerning the scope and nature of participation in externally funded projects (Mayoux, 1995; Cleaver, 1999).

One can see then that democratization or political liberalization in sub-Saharan Africa have been promoted by a wide range of external agencies under the broad rubric of democracy and good governance. Strategies of intervention have included both negative sanctions – for example, the freezing of development aid in Kenya and Malawi in 1992 (Ihonvbere 1997) – and positive encouragement – for example the funding of comprehensive administrative reform programmes in Tanzania and Uganda (Harrison, 2001b). Thus governance and democracy have become components of the broader conditionality relation between African states and Western agencies. This relates back to the 'permanent crisis' of indebtedness, outlined in the first sections of Chapter 3, because it is indebtedness which allows donors such sway over the state, whether in terms of macroeconomics or governance. In promoting the 'governance agenda', external agencies have put positive or negative pressure on indebted states to undertake certain kinds of reform based on the governance components outlined above or the implementation of multi-party constitutions. They have also funded the emergence of civil society organizations. The question is, how has this external agenda affected struggles for democracy within African states?

External agendas and democratic struggles

Chapter 3 discussed the ways in which structural adjustment constituted an external imposition, or at the very least a project with profound external origins implemented in a far from democratic fashion. In the same chapter, it became clear that the social effects of SAP were clearly deleterious for a considerable swathe of the population. It does not seem unreasonable, then, to state that the general logic of structural adjustment goes against the grain of democratization, producing a paradox: an external policy agenda (with unpopular effects) implemented principally through the mechanism of *conditionality* onto the state, and a growing tendency for states to adopt democratic constitutions and aspire to be accountable to their citizens, again with external support. This contradiction has occasionally been thrown into bold relief during so-called IMF riots (Chapter 3), but even where an overt protest against the effects of SAP has not taken place, it remains true that states face a difficult reconciliation between external agendas (democratic or otherwise) and internal demands (democratic or otherwise).

It is in this sense that some have argued that the key feature of liberal democracy, a sovereign state, is absent in debt-riven sub-

Saharan Africa where conditionality and SAP enforce two constituencies – internal and external – on the state. One might say that
governing elites have to account to their national parliament *and* to
Washington.

We can explore this further. We need in the first place to recognize
the power of external agencies in the democratic period. Funding can
be increased or cut off, depending on the democratic performance of a
country and external observers giving the 'OK' to a country's first elections. (Foreign elections monitoring and the declaration of 'free and
fair' or at least 'reflecting the will of the people' is seen as the seal of
approval for a democratic transition, despite quite serious problems
with the whole observation process. See, for example, Geisler, 1993;
Anglin, 1988.) So powerful is this external pressure, and so vulnerable
are indebted states, that some argue that the democratization is essentially a donor-driven process (Young, 1993b; Bayart, 2000). The repercussions of this argument are profound: that political struggles within
states are not really related to the force of democratization. Rather,
they are contingent upon an externally driven dynamic. This would
reduce the import of our cautious evaluation of democratic struggle
even further. Others (Bratton and van de Walle, 1997; Wiseman, 1995)
have stressed the centrality of domestic political movements, even if
Bratton and van de Walle often mention the power of external agents
throughout their comprehensive and detailed text.

How are we to reconcile these oppositions? Theoretically, we must
recognize that the internal–external opposition which has been
employed in some studies of African politics is a false dichotomy.
Sovereignty has always been a *relative* concept (Halliday, 1997), and the
sovereign states that emerged in northern Europe (the birthplace of the
modern democratic model) were a result of the 'external' imperative of
war and (consequently) tax. An alternative to limited either/or formulations is to understand sovereignty in degrees, a product of the forces
that impinge on state power. This is hardly innovative in African
studies, where the notion of quasi sovereignty has already been around
for a decade (Chapter 1). The repercussion of this perspective here is
that indigenous political dynamics can be innovative and significant,
and they can reinforce external agendas or they can resist them either
through the vehicle of *claims* to sovereignty or against them. These
nuances should not allow us to lose sight of the considerable power of
Western intervention, and it certainly remains true that much of the
drive for democratization has derived from external actors, however we
perceive the interactions of these interventions with a particular state's

own social dynamics. The issue is, how does this powerful inter-national involvement affect the democratic possibilities of political change?

Donors and elites

Democratization in the era of structural adjustment means that the key macroeconomic policies which a state undertakes are not open for democratic discussion within a country. The fundamentals of neo-liberal reform are 'locked in' through the process of negotiation with the World Bank, IMF and Consultative Groups of donors who follow in the international finance institutions' trail. And, until recently, donor–state negotiations have taken place in conditions of secrecy, akin to elite pacting in smoke-filled rooms. An extreme example is Tanzania, where even ministers outside the Ministry of Finance or members of the Central Committee of the ruling CCM didn't know about the negotiations with the IMF (Campbell and Stein, 1992: 15).

A narrowed agenda

This state of affairs has meant that most debates between incumbent and opposition parties generate very little political capital out of sub-stantive policy differences. Where new parties come into power, however radical they might be in various respects, they still need to maintain negotiations with creditors and donors within the over-arching context of structural adjustment. In Zambia the MMD, which gained substantial support as Kaunda tried unsuccessfully to imple-ment IMF-sponsored adjustment measures, soon implemented the same neoliberal medicine with an even greater dependence on external funding and debt rescheduling. In sum:

> New democratic governments have very little freedom of action to organise ... economies in ways which may maximise their political support. They can only sit in the roller-coaster and hope that the policies provided by Western donors and creditors bring the necessary rewards before some jolt sends them flying.
>
> (Clapham, 1993: 437)

Much of this state of affairs fits within Mkandawire's analysis of 'choiceless democracies' in sub-Saharan Africa (1999). He also picks up on a broader shift in the discourse of politics, away from questions of political choice and towards issues of technocratic efficiency, which again restricts the scope of what is considered part of the political agenda. Thus external intervention reinforces those tendencies in opposition parties towards the politics of personality which is a characteristic of the elite rivalries and factionalism mentioned earlier in this chapter. In addition to the projection of personal images of leaders or counter-leaders, another central part of democratic discourse is the appeal for 'change', that is a specific change from the existing government, to an unspecified alternative – a product of elite rivalries and the narrowed possibilities under SAP. In Niger, the change ushered in after the National Conference and the 1995 elections was so poor that 'people soon coined the street-level expression *changer le changement!*' (Ibrahim and Souley, 1998: 163). Optimism about the potentials of regime has also been tempered in Zambia and Benin.

Corruption

The other component of general democratic discourse in Africa has been the desire to tackle corruption. Corruption is identified with extended incumbency in office and elite complacency. As has already been argued, the structures of clientelism have proved too durable to be amenable to an electoral 'quick fix'. But there are also linkages to donor intervention here as well. Donors have held up external funding in countries which have suffered high-profile corruption scandals (although the transformation from corruption to scandal is certainly politically contrived). One thinks of the IMF and others' freezing of funds after the Goldenberg scandal in Kenya (*Africa Confidential*, 20, March 1998). More generally, donors have funded administrative reform programmes, watchdog institutions and anti-corruption workshops throughout the continent (Hope and Chikulo, 2000; Harrison and Riley, 1999).

Donor efforts to reduce corruption produce complex effects: support for administrative reform and anti-corruption watchdogs of one sort or another are certainly welcome, at least in their motivations. But it remains to be seen if these efforts will have any tangible effects. Equivocations can also be generated when tackling corruption might seriously undermine the regime in power – especially if that regime enjoys good relations with donors. Uganda and Mozambique are suggestive in this respect.

Civil society

One aspect of the donor response to corruption is an interest in supporting the organizational growth of civil society and non-governmental organizations (NGOs). In the donors' vision, civil society provides a check on the state's power and plays the role of invigilator, not only in respect to corruption, but also in terms of human rights and gender policy. External support for these organizations has involved partnerships, most notably between country 'chapters' of Transparency International, an anti-corruption NGO, and the 'parent' organization in Berlin. It has also involved grants, either to help an organization establish itself, or to subsidize its running costs. This assistance has facilitated the growth of civil society in the urban areas of African societies, and inasmuch as these organizations influence the state or express the voices of the disempowered, one can say that donor-supported civil society initiatives have had a positive effect on democratization. However, there are three critical points that also need to be made concerning donor support for civil society.

In the specific area of external funding for development, increasing external preference to fund development via NGOs (a key part of civil society) rather than the state raises serious questions. States – however venal and cumbersome they might be – constitute the only infrastructure that can facilitate widespread social improvement. After twenty years of 'NGO optimism' concerning the potential of 'democratized development' (Clark, 1991), it is now increasingly recognized that NGOs are not necessarily capable of promoting widespread development, nor are they necessarily accountable for their actions (Fowler, 1992; Charlton and May, 1995; Sogge, 1996). NGOs' individual projects might create a poorly coordinated general effect, as some areas are ignored and resources are used inefficiently (Hanlon, 1991). They might also be co-opted into a governmental political agenda, thus giving the lie to their supposed independence or concern only with the grassroots (Gary, 1996; O'Keefe and Kirkby, 1997).

Returning to civil society more generally, it is necessary to note that external funding goes mainly to urban-based organizations which reflect the agendas of the funders (Howell, 2000: 13 et seq.; Kasfir, 1998b). The consequences of this are various: in the first place, externally funded civil society reinforces the neglect of rural areas; secondly, many civic organizations articulate ideologies which seem more concerned with activating the right responses from Western audiences than with reflecting the language or perceptions of the poor and powerless in their domestic society. I once attended a conference on development in southern Africa, and listened to a speech by a director of an NGO which claimed to be empowering women. The speech contained a dense set of references to empowerment, community, participation and so on, but no specific references to people's experiences, projects or problems. One was left wondering in whose interests the director was talking. Howell's excellent article makes the general point well:

> By setting up local branches, northern NGOs reproduce organizations in their own image, creating virtual clones, whose priorities, interests and structures are externally shaped. As donors command the resources, they also consciously or unwittingly shape the priorities, promote certain values and cultivate particular institutional forms ...
>
> (Howell, 2000: 17)

Thirdly, if civil society organizations do spend too much energy articulating a donor-friendly discourse rather than working as the 'organic intellectuals' of the poor and powerless, then this is partly a reflection of the dependence of many organizations on external funds. In Mozambique between 80 per cent and 90 per cent of Mozambican NGOs' finance comes from overseas (Harrison, 1999d). Although Mozambique is an especially impoverished and donor-dependent country, levels of dependence which are even half of this clearly question the sustainability of civil society organizations without donor support.

External intervention in democracy clearly involves a complex set of processes and a variety of organizations. But there are three themes which reveal contradictions in external involvement with democracy. First, there is the problematic interplay between democratization and structural adjustment; secondly there is the contradiction between a possibility of increasing democratic influence on the state simultaneous with the contraction in the latter's ability to act on behalf of its supposed citizenry; thirdly, there is the general urban-based and liberal preferences which get translated through local organizations, but often do not relate to those whose interests are supposedly served by the organization. These points lead us to understand external intervention at one remove from the issues of popular organization and mobilization covered in the previous section.

Conclusion

We can now add some detail to the schema set out in Figure 4.1. We have seen a real but cautious emergence of popularly embedded democratic activity. The difference that this has made to people's lives is at present outweighed by the continuities in the structures and processes of power, based as they still are in a tiny elite group, employing strategies of clientelism to further their aims. The state's scope for action (at least formal action) has been cut back by structural adjustment and economic recovery has been shaky or non-existent with some exceptions, the clearest of which is Uganda. Even in the cases where recovery 'on paper' has taken place, one must seriously question the extent to which this has 'made a difference' to the impoverished and mainly rural masses – the clearest example of this is Mozambique, the world's fastest growing economy in 1999, but still a society with widespread malnutrition and illiteracy. In terms of local–global interactions, we have seen that the fundamentally undemocratic disposition of the world system has contradictory effects on the processes of democratization within particular indebted states. In sum, if a democratic transition is taking place, it has only just taken its first step on a long road.

Further reading

A readable and robust overview of Africa's democratization is Bratton and van de Walle (1997). Other good texts are Wiseman (1995) who argues that democratization was driven by Africans, and Anyang' Nyong'o (1987) who agrees but from a more radical position. On democratization and popular movements, see Bratton and van de Walle (1992), Sachikonye (1993) and Agbu (1998). A lot of work has critically evaluated democratization by highlighting its limits, for example Clapham (1993) and Joseph (1998). Baker (1998) provides a useful overview of democratic transitions, showing how elections do not necessarily usher in change. Rural democratization is more patchily covered. See Kelsall's original work on Tanzania (2000) and my own on Mozambique (Harrison, 2000). On external constraints to democratization, it is worth noting the high incidence of rhetoric and polemic. Mkandawire (1999) provides a forceful but well-argued viewpoint. Howell (2000) and Kasfir (1998b) provide good analyses of donors and civil society.

5
New African Identities, New Forms of Struggle?

Introducing political identity

Previous chapters have analysed the ways in which political power and economic change have generated forms of political resistance and struggle. As mentioned in Chapter 1, resistance and struggle are terms associated with notions of liberation. This book chooses to couch its understanding of liberation within a consideration of the complex development of capitalism, and consequently we have identified forms of political action which can be located within classes: peasants, workers and capitalists. We have also been alert to the complexity of the political dynamics of these categorizations, especially in our considerations of state action, and we have also identified some of the gender dimensions of struggle. We have also acknowledged that the political dynamics of a society are not easily 'read off' from a class register: civil society contains within it a diversity of organizations and forms of power which have their own particular 'stories'.

So far, we remain within a fairly coherent and self-contained terrain: a political economy of struggle and resistance informed centrally by a left-leaning understanding of capitalism. But is this sufficient to allow us a comprehensive account of contemporary popular political activity in sub-Saharan Africa? In the last decade or so, researchers have identified forms of political movement or activity which do not apparently fit our schema. These can be collectively defined as *political identities*: ethnic, generational, religious, racial and gendered.

These are hardly new political categorizations, but their recent prominence rests on a broader epistemological basis. As we shall see, much of the research in the area of political identity has made a broader academic argument: that notions of class and capitalism are excessively 'structuralist' (or worse – authoritarian) and that new forms of political identity and action prove that African politics would benefit from a move towards a more poststructuralist realm.

Consequently, the tone of this chapter is a little different from its predecessors, but resembles Chapter 1 a little more: the narrative here must *engage* with writing on political identities in order to argue the case and maintain its theoretical standpoint. It will also take on board the benefits of a growing literature on political identity which has provided us with many insights. We shall begin by considering the broader innovations of poststructuralist research into political identities in Africa before considering two components of identity politics: worker and youth politics. We will also consider another form of identity more briefly, namely ethnicity.

Political identity and postcolonial studies

The concept of identity's main claim to distinction is its resonance with the 'personal' or the Self: it is affective and as flexible and multifaceted as the human personality itself. Identity is generated through culture – especially language – and it can invest politics with various meanings: ethnic, religious, age-based and so on. Thus, the operationalization of the notion of *political* identity has yielded a body of research in which collective political action is not guided by an understanding of the political economy of capitalism, but is instead informed by a desire to account for the psychological dynamics or historical evolution of an identity, bounded by such phenomena as language, religion (Brenner, 1993) and memory.

In African studies generally, there has been a recent shift in emphasis towards ideas such as identity, contingency, indeterminacy, performance, and complexity (for example: Werbner, 1996; Worby, 1998; Mbembe, 1991, 1992). All of these concepts fit into the poststructuralist approach to politics in which concepts such as class, nation and state are subject to deconstruction, and discourses are generated through language, collective memory and symbolism (Norval, 1996) producing multiple or fractured identities (Bloom, 1998). Often, studies which fit into this broad approach employ the word 'postcolonial' or 'postcolony'; revealing an underlying affinity with the poststructural and perhaps more starkly postmodern. The prefix 'post' affirms a cynicism with the Enlightenment and notions of progress, rational instrumentalism, a faith in science and technology, and – significantly for this book – the certainties of struggle and liberation. We will return to the rejection of the latter below, but first some illustrations of poststructural writing on political identity are in order.

Two of the most important contributions are an edited volume, *Postcolonial Identities in Africa* (Werbner and Ranger, 1996) and a special issue of the influential *Journal of Contemporary African Studies*, entitled 'The Politics of Identity' (Sharp, 1997). Both of these texts are concerned with case studies of societies within nation-states. This reflects the methodology of political identity in the post-structural mould: a rejection of grand social categorization, a preference for the complexity of localized situations and a desire to capture insights to which the liberal, Western-educated researcher is blind. The writers are more centrally concerned with anthropological and cultural politics. In these texts we find accounts of local ethnic groups which innovate their own symbolisms and memories in order to construct collective identities, and to identify forms of external identity ('otherness') to shore up the boundaries of their own collective. Myths of origin, discourses containing a normative or moral universe which determines individual agency, symbols and rituals and so on are elaborated and reinvented to produce political identities that are complex and fluid. At the same time, the epistemology of these studies is to highlight the porosity of socially constructed boundaries and the complexity of interaction between different groups or a community and the state. One can recall something of a similar approach in Chapter 2 in the section entitled 'State power and the grassroots' in that attention is paid in this work to the ways in which social power is *constructed* rather than *structured*. Here, African states are seen as decentralized forms of authority which permeate local social relations, producing an almost subterranean power which is not invested in formal state institutions as much as constructed by local elites and chieftaincies. Bayart (1993) explicitly opposes his account of African politics to those who have employed the 'old' structuralist language of imperialism, class, state and so on. He calls this latter approach 'paradigm of the yoke', in which Africans are all victims of external and immutable forces.

Let us take a brief look at two of the better chapters from Ranger and Werbner to get a flavour of the postcolonial approach to political identity. De Boeck details the ongoing elaboration of a kind of 'frontier identity' in southwestern Zaire amongst the aLuund ethnic group. In societies remote from the visible and coercive apparatus of the central state, local idioms are integrated into discourses of official power. But also, local idioms and cultural identities appropriate symbols of the central state: for example, the aLuund paramount chief took to wearing a leopardskin bonnet and glasses in the manner of Mobutu when trying to gain political and cultural ascendancy within the region through affiliation with the state (1996: 84). Popular identities are also constructed within the context of the frontier. For the area de Boeck is interested in, this is a frontier where the state is weak, where the diamond trade has had a massive influence, and where hopes for capitalist modernity guided by the state have been abandoned. In this context, forms of identity which stress self-sufficiency have emerged (95). Looking more closely at identity and globalization in the same part of Zaire, De Boeck (1999) analyses how diamond mining in Angola and identities of male adulthood and social responsibility have been intimately intertwined, creating a veritable flourishing of new patterns of dress and social action which have collapsed dualities between tradition and modernity, city and village.

Fisiy and Geschiere (1996) investigate witchcraft in Cameroon and its relationship to violence and identity. The authors introduce three short cases to illustrate how witchcraft constitutes a modern cultural politics, bound up with tensions between community and individual accumulation (1996: 195 et.seq.). In the case studies one finds that the adoption of modern identities – mobility, accumulation, individualism, or the building of a house with a tin roof – could raise accusations of witchcraft and allegations of occult and nocturnal activities. But, as with De Boeck, 'modern' and traditional' (spiritual) are not hermetically sealed from one another. Some *ngangas* (healers) employed both spiritual authority and a recourse to the procedures of the modern state (200–2). Both of these chapters provide insightful accounts of identity politics in two parts of Africa.

Both employ poststructural notions of multiple identity and the importance of signifiers, imagery and language. But both also relate the dynamics of identity to political economy: in southwest Zaire to the 'capitalist banditry' (76) of the frontier and the networks of dollar and diamond trade; in Cameroon to the emerging 'capitalist world-view' (194) and the tension it creates within communities and kinship. Relatedly, the morality produced by witchcraft practices throughout southern Africa relates to differentiation and forms of accumulation resulting from the impact of SAP and neoliberalism (Ferguson, 1995; Manson, 1998). This suggests a tension between the poststructural method and the recognition of a political economy with some 'systemic' traits. This chapter will argue that this tension is more apparent than real.

Postcolonial political identities and the notion of struggle

Does a concept of struggle have a role in this broad and diverse set of writings? It was noted earlier that poststructuralism has an innate hostility to an established idea of struggle (whether liberal or marxist). For poststructuralists, notions of struggle and liberation are based on metanarratives, or global and historical approaches to social change. No matter how ostensibly progressive an ideal liberation might appear, it is bound to end up *compelling* people to adhere to and comply with a social programme based on forms of absolute and transhistorical truth.

But, this does not necessarily remove struggle entirely from the analytical frame; rather, understandings of struggle are reconfigured to fit more easily with the poststructural approach. Struggle is not ordered, organized, progressive and purposive political action, but rather localized, ethnicized or 'parodic' and subversive of state power and other forms of authority. This focus opens up space for a more explicit ontology of postmodernism, into which 'games' and irony enter. The irony, according to Werbner, is that Africans conspire in their own oppression; now that the *leitmotif* of African politics is 'the wink', the game of postcolonial politics is a less-than-serious expression of the 'baroque style of political improvization in which everyone indulges' (Werbner, 1996). Struggle is really the subversion of – or play with – forms of oppressive political authority (Mbembe, 1992). The purpose is not liberation, but the innovation of complexity or self-reflexiveness. Often, these forms of resistance challenge authoritarian power through the unintended consequences that these struggles create, and the counter-strategies that this demands from ruling elites.

But, in many specific cases, irony and 'play' can relate to more 'concrete' forms of struggle: for example, Amadiume shows how market women in West Africa use 'satire and innuendo' as part of their struggle to maintain or wrest control of trade from men (1995: 61). The vibrant use of humour in Africa's *Radio Trottoir* (Ellis, 1989) often produces parodies of SAP from a class view. For example, after the 'IMF riots' in 1986 (Chapter 3) Zambian townships printed T-shirts reading: 'Looters Association of Zambia' (Ferguson, 1995: 139), inverting the morals of property and perhaps also sending up the urban and elite nature of civil society (Chapter 4) in which associations of one kind or another flourished at the same time as austerity measures were being imposed. Another example of parody as a response to neoliberal reform can be found outside of our geographical terms of reference, but it seems relevant to the point here. In South Africa, the neoliberal Growth Employment and Redistribution Programme was popularly dubbed 'reverse GEAR' to highlight the way that the ANC has abandoned its commitment to egalitarian economic reform. The various acronyms coined by the creation of numerous national SAPs have led to a whole series of new versions, for example Mozambique's Economic Reform Programme becomes the Exploiter's Rehabilitation Programme. One can see the same 'play' with language concerning corruption and its relationship with authoritarianism in Nigeria (Auwal,1987)

Nevertheless, the corollaries of the poststructural approach to political identity and struggle are a rejection of the possibility of social struggle, defined as organized resistance to the state, and a lack of utility of the concept of class within African societies. Sharp refers to the dangers of 'exposé analysis' (1997), that is a methodology which aims to reveal some form of essential social relation underlying the more complex facets of the appearance and events of politics. But what are the repercussions of this rejection of 'exposé analysis'? It is revealing that those who take a poststructural view on political identity are not fully prepared to face the repercussions, still making reference to some form of capitalist political economy as the framing condition of their analysis (Werbner, 1996: 5; De Boeck, 1996: 76, 89, 98). This implies that one can analyse the emergence of political identities such as ethnicity without abandoning a notion of oppression and struggle rooted in political economy although poststructuralist writers are less willing to address this explicitly. The alternative is to embrace a rejection of all liberation narratives as authoritarian and to concern oneself with transient struggles, based on parody or irony; or to celebrate acts of individual or diffuse political action for their 'complexing' effects. This alternative is also a rejection of development *tout court* (hence the associated epithet 'post-development').

What reasons might one have for rejecting liberation and development as useful concepts in understanding African politics?

1. *Liberation and development are authoritarian concepts based on Enlightenment metanarratives*. It is worth bearing in mind that only the most extreme postmodernism rejects the entirety of the Enlightenment philosophy and practice. In a world in which inequalities are increasing, it seems strange to reject notions of equality, progress, development, democracy and citizenship. It is also the case that metanarratives do not necessarily have to impose a strict iron cage upon all individuals, even if they do provide a fairly well-defined language within which different arguments are voiced.

2. *Liberation and development are intrinsically Western in origin, therefore their use in studying African politics can only be a form of cultural imperialism.* This is certainly the case to some degree, and it is something that all researchers need to be aware of. There have been some quite mechanistic transpositions of (for example) Western Marxism onto the African scene. But, this does not refute the use of these concepts in their entirety. Firstly, they can be used with a greater awareness of difference, cultural or otherwise. Secondly, as argued in Chapter 1, Africa is part of the modern capitalist system, and has been for at least a century (in many parts – southern Africa and the coasts – for a lot longer). Because the creation of markets, classes and states are a key part of Africa's history, to analyse them within a political economy perspective seems entirely appropriate – more a concern to address historic reality than to impose a foreign paradigm. Finally, it is worth bearing in mind that it is by no means self-evident that transposing Foucault is any better than transposing Marx or Weber into Africa.

So, there are both limitations to the poststructural approach to political identities and a set of robust reasons to maintain a political economy perspective, albeit one that listens to the warning of poststructural writers against ethnocentrism and the excesses of structuralism. It was mentioned earlier that it is possible to analyse political identity as a form of resistance that could provide insight for our understanding of liberation, based as it is in political economy. Let us investigate this further by taking some key aspects of political identity and their relation to political protest and struggle.

Culture, identity and class

Can one reconcile concepts of class with an interest in culture and political identity? One can investigate this question by looking at political identity and its role in the struggles of African workers. In the following section, we will tease out the associations between identity, broader processes of social change and class struggle. Subsequently, we will look at the dynamics of the formation of youth identities.

Migration and hybridity

African workers have (like all workers) never defined themselves in any corporate social form which does not include, in some fashion, a cultural identity. African workers' cultural identities are central to their 'classhood'. In this respect, a lot of attention has been paid to the fact that African workers have either recently arrived at the workplace from rural areas, or that they may intend to return to the village after a limited period of time. Thus, some have argued for the elaboration of a kind of hybrid class based on the 'dualistic' identity of the rural and urban: the worker-peasant, or even the 'peasantariat' (First, 1977). Some have looked at the way in which rural and urban social structures infuse an individual's identity (for example, Harries, 1994). These definitions raise the question of how rural social relations affect social relations in the workplace and vice versa.

In urban areas, relations of ethnic affiliation and the use of common African languages are actively reconstructed within the factory as part of a construction of class identity and solidarity. For example, Adesina, in examining the social community of the shop floor in an oil plant in Nigeria, finds 'lateral community work relations' which use cultural norms and symbols to galvanize worker solidarity, for example through the use (and transformation) of the Yoruba credit system, *Esusu*, to establish a credit cooperative which allowed workers autonomy from state and employer patronage (Adesina, 1990: 135–6). Another Yoruba concept works within both urban and rural areas: *Ilu*, meaning 'homeland' entreats those from the same place of origin to always relate back to the village of their birth and ancestry (Trager, 1995). In another article, Adesina explicitly outlines 'the understanding of work collectivities – as 'cultural' repositories of oppositional and protest activities' as follows:

> ... to the extent that work and non-work relations are bound up in workers' self-awareness, their self-identity is defined by and within specific cultural and experiential contexts. Work relations therefore acquire specific meaning: agrarian idioms, and ... allusion to chieftain relations are just two such cases ... The important thing is that consciousness is a process of constitution within definite socio-cultural contexts.
>
> (Adesina, 1989: 317–18)

Thus, we find that postcolonial innovations such as 'hybridity' (urban/rural, traditional/modern), often following the ideas of Homi Bhabha (1995: 34), or the fanfaring of the salience of culture and ethnicity, are themselves hardly innocent of political economy: of processes of proletarianization from the 1920s (Gutkind and Wallerstein, 1985) with a

most recent increase during the oil price hikes in 1973 in a few countries, for example in Nigeria, Algeria or Libya; or of the creation of a
system of migrant labour, principally to create a flexible and cheap
workforce for mining capital as in the case of southern Africa (Cohen,
1987: chapter 3; Amin, 1995). In other words, hybridization is not so
much suggestive of the indeterminacy of political identity and a sign
of the 'floating' nature of personality and perceptions of life vis à vis
'the social', rather it is a reflection of the 'hybridity' of African political
economy itself. Since the late 1880s, African political economies have
been rapidly, brutally and unevenly transformed into social systems of
migrant labour (Cooper, 1983; Baker and Aina, 1995; Baker and
Pedersen, 1992). This process has its own repercussions, but the experience of labour migration, seasonal or permanent, is often precarious.
The juxtaposition of rural and urban life, the experience of the city and
the possible subsequent return to the village, all provide the social conditions in which people internalize a whole range of diverse social rules
and relations. In this sense, there is a *real political economy of hybridization*: the real import of culture within the workplace can only be
understood within this defining context. This is the underlying argument of Berry's (1983) considerations of migration and class formation
in Western Nigeria: both class formation and lineage-based patronage
politics define and reinforce each other in a situation of constant
mobility and low levels of productivity.

Informalization and identity

In all independent African economies, the state has constituted a
major employer of wage labour: for example, within the civil service,
public provision (teachers, nurses, *inter alia*), and nationalized industries. The public waged sector has predominantly been analysed using
ideas of corporatism – that is the incorporation of (potentially oppositional) social groups within a broadly defined state project in order to
shore up state hegemony. As mentioned in Chapter 3, many African
states developed a panoply of party-affiliated organizations such as
unions, women's organizations and youth organizations shortly after
independence. Corporatism provided for the structuring of an urban
salaried class based in public service and parastatal firms, which generally grew precipitously after independence. During the 1980s, as most
African economies met with recession and implemented (parts of)
structural adjustment programmes, this state-funded urban 'salariat'
has declined as real wages have fallen (especially for those in the more

numerous lower positions), and retrenchment programmes been implemented. This has led researchers to pay more attention to the informalization of urban social life, in which fixed class identities forged during the corporatist dispensation are replaced by another kind of hybridity, this time a mixing of occupations and social roles (not residency) in order to elaborate new strategies of survival – or enrichment – in a more uncertain social milieu.

Informalization connotes a whole range of contingent social processes and relations which replace more rigid ideas of corporatism: informal social networks based on common religious or ethnic identity are emphasized; people's strategies of livelihood are portrayed as flexible, dynamic and interactive. But it is important to bear in mind that this rise in more fluid urban identities, situationally located in an infinitely complex web of ever-changing social relations, gains much of its salience as a manifestation of economic and state restructuring. In this respect, Mustapha (1992) has developed the idea of multiple modes of livelihood, in which families typically undertake a whole range of activities in order to scrape a subsistence: state employees become taxi drivers at night, women farm small gardens in urban areas, men and/or women trade goods in informal markets. Similar processes have been identified in other countries (Marshall, 1990; Lugalla, 1995a, 1995b). Barchiesi notes that since structural adjustment in Nigeria '[i]increasing numbers of unemployed, or employed workers whose salaries are insufficient as a source of maintenance, had to look for strategies of survival in the informal sector' (1996: 362). This was part of a broadening of working-class culture into the poor communities of urban Nigeria which made community-based working-class action more radical than organized workplace action.

In fact, wage employment is often central to these variegated survival strategies: state resources are used to support other 'private' activities or connections with other state personnel business contacts. This relation has been commonly referred to as 'straddling' (for example, Bayart, 1993: 69–70; Chapter 2). Thus, one can see the decline of corporatism and the increasing informalization of the urban economy not as a sign of the decay of the urban working class, but rather the *reformulation* of its political identities into a realm of fiscal austerity and speculation. Straddling is also the key process through which some African capitalists have endured or even flourished during structural adjustment (Harrison, 1999c; Gibbon, 1996a). From this perspective, the rise of identity politics has less to do with the end of class as an analytical concept and more to do with the unceasing attempts of the World Bank and the IMF to squeeze interest payments on debt from debtor states, and the class struggles which define the allocation of costs and benefits of structural adjustment. This can also relate back to the previous section on migration, and the dynamics of peasant identity. Bryceson shows how, in the face of economic collapse and SAP, peasants' production strategies have become ever more diverse, involving itinerant rather that regulated rural–urban migration, not based on wage labour but on involvement in multiple modes of livelihood more generally. This has given these migrants a 'neither here nor there' identity (Bryceson, 2000: 56), a combination of residential and occupational intermixing generated by the destabilizing influences of economic crisis and adjustment.

The central point in our consideration of culture and urban workers is that political identities *are* important and significant – all the more so for the role that they play in processes of broader social change. Hybridization is both a component of worker migration and the restructuring of livelihood strategies away from state employment and into various kinds of informal markets.

Youth, violence and urban protest

The social category of 'youth' has become the focus of increasing attention recently and constitutes another arena of identity politics. The term youth is concerned not so much with an age cohort as a sociological distinction: men who have left school but have not started families (Iordansky, 1994). Beneath this very broad socio-temporal categorization, one finds various subsets of youth: the urban unemployed, university students, employees and peasants. Here we are concerned with the first two categories, manifestly urban forms of youth identity. Two very insightful analyses of youth politics in rural areas are Geffray (1991) and Ellis (1995).

Growing academic attention given to youth politics in urban Africa is principally a result of the spectacular upheavals in African cities, driven by urban youth groups. It has been the youth who have often been at the forefront of anti-dictator street protests (see also Chapter 4) throughout the 1980s, for example in Mali (Turrittin, 1991; Kay Smith, 1997). In other cases, youth have been responsible for less evidently political uprisings, such as the looting and destruction of property in Mozambique's capital, Maputo, in October 1995. Each of these cases suggests an important part of youth identity in urban Africa: its association with – or even definition by – violence. Let us investigate this through a case study.

El-Kenz (1996: 42–4) begins his article on 'Youth and Violence' with a greatly revealing and sympathetic case study of Ibo, an 18 year old who lives near Dakar, the capital of Senegal. Ibo leaves his village in order to establish his independence and to find a more rewarding way of survival than the extremely austere conditions of agricultural production. In the city, he cannot find any stable employment. His only way of surviving is to take any kind of petty employment which is available. Criminality and violence become part of his life, as he subsidizes his income through theft and as he joins one of the street gangs who protect their trading patch from other hawkers (informal traders). He joins an organized urban protest, not fully understanding the nature of the political grievance, but gaining a sense of empowerment which he had never experienced before – 'His eyes are burning from the teargas, but he has never felt so dignified, or so much a man'. He finds a chance to destroy the wealth to which he had customarily to prostrate himself in order to earn a crust – 'Ibo finds himself with stones in his hands that he hurls with all his might at the cars ... he has so often cleaned and guarded'. This brings him to the forefront of the protest and into direct conflict with the police. He is shot in the leg, which later has to be amputated. Thus El-Kenz ends the short narrative: 'Ibo: a permanent victim of the violence in which he was an actor for one day.'

Youth has always been at the forefront of violent anti-state protest in Africa, and indeed elsewhere. So, why has the youth been so frequently on the streets of African capitals during the last ten years? The answer to this question also requires that we look at the broader social changes in Africa's cities and the specific impact of these changes on Africa's urban youth.

In order to deal with the first concern, we can look to the states of the Maghrib because they highlight particularly well a broader trend in African social change. The North African states have been through an extreme but not exceptional postcolonial history. Bromley (1993) notes the widespread revolutions which overthrew various forms of *ancien régime* and replaced them with secular republican regimes, whose central concern was of nationalist modernization, for example Tunisia, Algeria, Libya and Egypt. Secular modernization, and especially the provision of wage employment and social welfare by the state, was the foundation of the legitimacy of the revolutionary republican regimes. The relative wealth of the North African economies has facilitated a more extensive state-led modernization compared to most of sub-Saharan Africa, but the general social programme of authoritarian modernization, or developmental dictatorships in Hutchful's phrase (1991), has been a defining characteristic of the whole continent (and beyond), despite quite limited advances south of the Sahara.

Again, in common with Africa south of the Sahara, the Maghribian states have undergone severe crisis since the early 1980s. The fiscal crisis of the state has manifested itself as the collapse of the whole modernizing project upon which the state based its legitimacy or, minimally, its right to rule. The Maghribian states can no longer afford pre-existing levels of social provision and subsidy. Protests at the decline in standards of living which the collapse of modernization has created provokes an increasing recourse to authoritarianism, an authoritarianism which had in any case always accompanied the modernizing project (Seddon, 1986).

This, then, is the context in which the youth have expressed growing violent opposition to the state in Africa: the increasingly difficult conditions of life and the patent lack of capacity for the regime to address the concerns that economic crisis creates – in a word, the failure of the modernizing state. The repercussions of this on the urban youth are easily teased out of El-Kenz's narrative of Ibo, but consider the following passage on the roots of social protest in Algeria.

> From 1985–86, the social situation became explosive ... social inequalities were mounting... The core problem, however, was that Algerian society has been split into two distinct halves. The haves included those more or less integrated into the ... system. The have-nots were the outsiders. These outsiders live ... on the fringes of the city. Among them, the younger generation live the tragedy of exclusion in a particularly straightforward, brutal fashion. The overwhelming majority are out of school ... Their chances of getting into the productive work chain are slim, because urbanization no longer goes hand in hand with industrialization. These people are in 'social quarantine'. Unemployment rates climbed from 16 per cent in 1983 to ... 23.6 per cent in 1989. And these young people make up the overwhelming majority of those counted in these statistics.
>
> (Chikhi, 1995: 325–6)

This passage clearly argues the particular condition in which the youth find themselves during the fiscal crisis of the corporatist state. The social trajectory from school to wage employment which was the cornerstone of social stability during modernization has been cut. Urban school leavers, and increasingly graduates, leave the academic institution to face unemployment. The incorporative facets of authoritarian modernization have been destroyed as industrialization and the expansion of the state have come to a halt. It is the temporal manifestation of the rupture in this process which gives youth identity its contemporary salience. Many urban youths face a form of social truncation: cadets condemned not to graduate to adulthood which requires a basic financial stability – previously often provided by wage labour – in order to establish a family. Remaining with the example of Algeria, Salah Tahi (1995: 198) notes that the first twenty years of independence were dominated by the 'revolutionary generation', those whose political views were strongly influenced by the anti-colonial struggle and who were accustomed to the state-based modernization paradigm which, fuelled by oil revenues, prevailed until the mid-1980s. The collapse in this social regime and the impact this has had on the young 'post-revolutionary' generation has given a strong generational edge to the ongoing contestation and conflict over Algeria's future.

Two other themes are worth teasing out of the Chikhi quotation. Firstly, the economic crisis and the way it has been dealt with has led to a marked process of social differentiation: an increasingly stark division between the haves and have-nots. This differentiation is reinforced by the changing nature of work in urban areas. Recall Ibo's satisfaction in smashing the cars which he usually cleaned. In the absence of wage employment, the urban youth of many African cities often try to scrape a living by offering their services in some temporary casual way to the elites – as car washers, bag carriers, car guards or ambient traders of cigarettes and newspapers. This is, psycho-socially speaking, an extremely degrading way of life for young men whose ideal is to establish the independence and control which a full-time waged job would provide. This relates back to the decline in modernization, as Cruise O'Brien notes for West Africa: the 'independence generation' grew up in a period of (albeit slow and unstable) economic growth, but the present generation of youth have none of the prospects of economic security which their parents enjoyed. This moves Cruise O'Brien to talk of a 'lost generation... [which] marks the rupture from the relatively comfortable socialization procedures of the period from 1960 to the late 1970s' (1996: 57).

The second point emerges from the intriguing phrase 'social quarantine'. What Chikhi is alluding to is the fact that the youth are in a kind of social limbo: brought into the urban sphere with ideas of education, employment and independence, the impossibility of this future leads the youth to reject the order of urban life. But this is a highly ambivalent relation: it involves both an aspiration to integrate into the urban formal social system, and a violent attempt to destroy it. The same equivocation is evident in another category of urban youth: students.

Student protests have grown alongside the protests of the unemployed and underemployed youth. Students have been a strong force behind anti-government protests which have subsequently toppled dictatorships. But while challenging corrupt dictatorships, part of the politics of student protests has been to gain access to the very networks of patronage which dictatorships produce. Thus, in Mali, student protests were pivotal in the overthrow of the Traoré regime, but in 1993, after multi-party elections, students rioted and provoked the sacking of the now democratic Ministry of Education in pursuit of better scholarships (Cruise O'Brien, 1996: 65). Students' rejection of state politics can be a result of their marginalization within an existing state of affairs, democratic or otherwise: Mamdani's (1993) retrospective on the political role of the postcolonial African university eloquently outlines its frequent uncritical alliance with the regime of the day. This tendency towards protest for narrow self-interest is countered by more clearly politically motivated student action, as we shall see in the case of Burkina Faso in Chapter 6.

Broadly speaking, one can see that the collapse of authoritarian modernization has set in train a whole series of equivocal relations between society and the state, which challenge both the rigid differentiations between state and civil society and ideas of secular change and progress which were the stock-in-trade of most political science on Africa until recently. Young people, the unemployed, underemployed and students, are disillusioned by the apparent failure of modernization. They find themselves temporally (and unfortunately) situated in a longer-term process of economic decline and structural transformation.

Briefly to summarize, the salience of youth identities derives from a broader set of changes. Economic crisis has had a direct and negative impact on the postcolonial socio-political project of modernization. The ensuing ruptures to social life have impacted on the whole of urban society – notably they are part of the context in which the working class has become fractured and 'informalized', as discussed above. But the particular situation of youth, either leaving school to find employment, dignity and independence, or leaving university to join the middle classes, predominantly through linkages with the state, gives a peculiarly sharpened twist to the experience of Africa's recent economic decline. Without an understanding of these broader changes, youth identity politics remains an arena of description rather than analysis.

Towards a resolution of identity, class and struggle

How can we relate identity politics, derived from workers' cultures and their hybridization and youth protests and violence, to the approach taken generally within the book? At the start of the chapter, it was noted that Bayart (1993) ascribes to left-leaning scholars interested in structures and struggle a common approach of the 'paradigm of the yoke', that is a tendency to render Africans as hapless victims of powerful external forces. The examples given in the chapter reveal that African political identities and their political expression refute the paradigm of the yoke, but they do not refute the centrality of political economy and the presence of structures which constrain but do not demobilize, condition but do not ensnare.

Clearly, political identity is an important part of struggle, whether at the workplace or in the streets. It can and should be researched on its own merits. But an evaluation of its significance must involve an attempt flexibly to reconcile identity politics with political economy. The examples given above reveal how political identities are not innocent of capitalism, class or state. It is the interaction of the cultural resources of identity and structural change that account for the fact that in a particular location and time a certain kind of identity will become a salient political force, not another. After all, *pace* Lassiter (1999), there are no fixed and immutable identities in African societies; rather, a more fluid and contextualized set of norms and practices can be drawn on by certain social groups in order to engage with processes of change that are, in their origins, substantially outside of their control. Methodologically, there is a need to overcome the false distinction between class, culture and identity. Clearly one cannot have one without the other. Works by E. P. Thompson (1980) and Michael Burawoy et al. (1991) contribute to this methodology, showing that class identity is infused with norms and culture, and that struggle will make reference to culturally embedded norms, morals and idioms as much as positivist notions of exploitation.

Political identity and struggle introduce more complexity to our understanding of liberation, however. Working-class culture can elaborate the means to cope with alienating forms of labour, rather than the means to improve the conditions of work, and youth identities can elide the distinction between (formative) protest and (destructive) riot. Does this mean that these forms of political identity and action do not contribute to processes of liberation? Perhaps – even worse – they have more regressive effects? One response to these questions would be to evoke some form of empirically based checklist of criteria which separate out the liberation and regression in political identities. This would inevitably produce the kind of modernist Western methodology of *prescription* which one can easily agree does violence to African realities.

Another way to approach the dichotomy of liberation–regression is to historicize the analysis. Forms of collective political action based on identities are constructed over time; their visibility will be manifested through a series of events with repercussions for broader political economies; their repercussions will be felt in the following months and perhaps years. It is within this realm that one can meaningfully engage with judgement about the effects of political identity for our notion of liberation. Riots – which seem on the surface to be destructive forms of action – might be prosecuted after a series of other forms of political action have been brutally suppressed by a regime, and the effect of the riot might be to pose the possibility in a collective mind that resistance and (some form of) victory is possible. The violence of a riot might also highlight to a ruling elite the fragility of its position, evoking reformist tendencies. Judgements such as these are only feasible with attention to historical detail. Something of this methodology has been present in debates among Kenyan activists debating the utility or otherwise of engaging with Daniel Arap Moi's limited *abertura*, in which reference to recent Kenyan political history infuses concerns with political strategy (Ajulu, 1995).

This issue comes into closer focus in a consideration of ethnic identity. Ethnicity in sub-Saharan Africa poses a large range of questions concerning its historical construction, political conflict, relations with the state, and culture. Many of the most 'solid' ethnicities in sub-Saharan Africa are, in fact, constructions of the recent past and/or a result of distinctly 'un-traditional' agencies such as the *apartheid* state (South Africa: see, for example, Maré, 1989, 1993) or a collapsing authoritarian state in the midst of civil war (Rwanda: see, for example, *Africa Rights*, 1994; Prunier 1995; Newbury 1998). Ethnic difference does not connote ethnic conflict, and an ethnic identity can be as porous and fluid, prompting one leading anthropologist to reflect on the epistemology of ethnicity and conclude that the only valid starting point is a form of 'originary intermixing' (Amselle, 1998), that is to assume that all ethnic identities are fluid and defined as patterns within broader systems of production, migration and cultural intercourse. Some ethnic identities change with wealth (from Hutu to Tutsi or Senufo to Diola), or are profoundly moderated by region (for example the variety of Fulani identities in West Africa).

Consequently, analysis of ethnic politics should be open to a wide range of constructed identities. Relatedly, one should be open to the ways in which normative judgements can be made about ethnic identities. Clearly, all research on ethnic identity is full of normative analysis, mainly negative – ethnic chauvinism, conservatism, violence, oppression, ethnic 'false consciousness' – but also positive: ethnicized strategies of political and economic empowerment. Some have tried to distinguish between 'positive' and 'negative' ethnic identities. Positive ethnic identities might mobilize a collective set of idioms, morals or arguments to make a claim to justice or mere recognition. Doornbos argues that one can only understand ethnic political identities by looking at the moralities they produce in reference to the past and future (1991). Adam (1992) claims that one of the dynamics at work in Somalia outside of the dynamic of warlord clan conflict was a desire for justice and a claim for collective expression. An emerging Mbororo ethnic identity, expressed through a civic organization called *Mboscuda*, has made tentative steps in engaging some sections of Mbororo society with the process of democratization in Cameroon (Davis, 1995). These examples reveal that, with a complex and diffuse field of study such as ethnicity, it is necessary to make a judgement concerning the content of an ethnic identity, and the best way to do this is to look at the historical development and effects of its political form.

This chapter has understood political identity as an important component of our understanding of liberation. Political identity draws our attention to African agency in ways that other chapters have not, giving more space to innovation, adaptation, and formative responses to conventionally perceived 'top-down' and external phenomena such as globalization (Meyer and Geschiere, 1999b). Also, the importance of political identity – and its substance as a form of struggle – is inextricably interlinked with the nature of political and economic change and the relationship between structure and struggle. No political identity is innocent of changes in class relations, accumulation, and state action, but this does not require the crude reproduction of base-superstructure

epistemologies. Instead it requires more flexible and empathetic associations between identity and social context and a more open
approach to the normative aspect of evaluation which is embedded in
all analysis. It also demands an attentiveness to historical context, as
struggles and the identities that they dynamize are constructed over
time, not snapshots of events, so to speak. The next chapter will take
three case studies and reveal the threads of struggle that weave through
postcolonial politics in more detail.

Further reading

On poststructuralism and African politics, see Mbembe (1991, 1992)
and more generally Bayart (1993). Probably the most developed
attempt to analyse politics as discourse is Norval's (1996) analysis of
the collapse of apartheid. The best text on political identity is Werbner
and Ranger (1996). Sharp et al.'s (1997) special issue of the *Journal of
Contemporary African Studies* is well worth delving into. Literature on
migration is very diffuse, covering anthropology, sociology, politics
and economics. A brilliant case study is Harries (1994). Baker's work is
more sociological/geographical and comparative (Baker and Aina,
1995; Baker and Pedersen, 1992). On youth politics, see El-Kenz (1996)
and Cruise O'Brien (1996). The Centre for African Studies, University of Edinburgh, has published a set of fresh papers from a recent
conference on youth politics.

6
Political Struggle as History

This chapter will take three case studies in order to illustrate how it is vital to integrate the dynamics of struggle and liberation into modern historiographies of Africa. Each country's modern history can be written sketchily by highlighting the most prominent political events (regime changes, or war and peace), but it is also the case that these apparently 'top-down' or macropolitical changes often involve – and are shaped by – struggles by classes and other social groups which base their political action on some notion of liberation. This is how each of the case studies proceeds: from a general account of postcolonial politics to a 'writing in' of political struggle. The cases selected are: Mozambique, Nigeria and Burkina Faso. This means that the chapter covers anglophone, lusophone and francophone Africa. The case studies also reveal the tension between unity and diversity which was considered in Chapter 1: one can see both how each African country is different, and how there are important binding features between them as well.

Mozambique

Late decolonization (1962–74)

In the early 1960s, most of Africa went through a process of de-colonization. Portugal refused to make similar preparations for its colonies. As a result, a number of small African nationalist parties or organizations emerged, based in different regions of the country. Out of three of these small organizations, the *Frente de Libertação de Moçambique* (Mozambique Liberation Front, FRELIMO) was formed. FRELIMO fired the first shots of the liberation war in 1962 in the northern province of Cabo Delgado. We will go on to consider the development of the war itself later, but first we should recognize the indirect repercussions of the war. The liberation struggle forced the colonial state to undertake a limited liberalization: some Mozambican organizations were allowed to develop, more Mozambicans were allowed to establish themselves as commercial farmers, less coerced labour was extracted from peasants and workers, and the pass system in the cities was relaxed. All of these measures were designed to take the political wind out of the sails of FRELIMO's liberation struggle, which drew support from the south of the country as well as the north. It also created a limited class of small property-owning Mozambicans. The war boosted the Mozambican economy, rates of construction boomed in the 1960s, and the South African mining industry demanded increasing numbers of Mozambican migrant labourers. As a result of these factors, the Mozambican economy grew and industrialized at an unprecedented rate in the 1960s.

The war was a classic guerrilla war: large cumbersome Portuguese troop manoeuvres met with small and evasive groups of FRELIMO fighters who gained territory through a war of attrition. In 1968, when Frelimo held its second Party Congress, a particular faction emerged as hegemonic within FRELIMO which was more closely aligned to ideas of socialism as well as African nationalism. This gained FRELIMO an international legitimacy within leftist currents in Europe and America, as well as the ANC. Finally, the fascist nationalist regime of Salazar was overthrown in Portugal itself, in no small part as a result of the tensions produced by the liberation wars in lusophone (Portuguese speaking) Africa – not only in Mozambique, but also in Angola and Guinea-Bissau. The military officers who briefly replaced Salazar committed Portugal to negotiate Independence in the colonies. As a result, FRELIMO's leader, Samora Machel, signed the Lusaka Protocol in 1974 and, after a year's transition, FRELIMO took the reigns of power in an independent Mozambique.

Early independence (1975–80)

Frelimo (the convention is to put the acronym into lower case after independence to distinguish the liberation movement from the government) inherited the colonial state and, as a result, faced a bewildering array of challenges and problems (Wield, 1983; Saul, 1985). In the early 1970s, there was an exodus of Portuguese citizens from Mozambique, removing the skilled personnel from the economy. Many of those who left sabotaged infrastructure or destroyed machinery, vindictively undermining the new government before it came to power. The rural commercial networks, established by Portuguese farmer-shop owners, were abandoned. Furthermore, at least two-thirds of the country's territory was unknown to Frelimo and, although people were happy to see the back of the Portuguese, Frelimo had to replace old authoritarian structures of power with something else. In 1976, South Africa unilaterally reduced its demand for Mozambican migrant workers, reducing state revenues and creating economic crisis in the southern peasant societies which were constructed on labour remittances. Rhodesia, now under the 'Unilateral Declaration of Independence' rule of Ian Smith having seceded from the British colonial realm, waged an undeclared war on Mozambique which provided a safe haven for African liberation movements along their shared border. To top it all, in 1977, southern Mozambique suffered terrible flooding. It is worth bearing in mind that Frelimo was at this stage a small organization, based on the liberation struggle in the northern third of the country.

In 1977, Frelimo held its Third Party Congress and set out a more explicit ideological and programmatic agenda. The official ideology of the Party was to be Marxism-Leninism. The Party was to be a vanguard party, only accessible to workers and peasants, and its ideological guidance would ensure that the state promoted a transition to socialism. In effect, a Party-state was established, under the control of the Central Committee of Frelimo. Democratic centralism, another key aspect of Leninism, meant that a hierarchy of participatory organs would be established, all being accountable to the next highest echelon, and ending up at the National Assembly. The same pyramid-shaped hierarchy was established for the state administration. In this respect, the state remained quite similar to the form it took during Portuguese colonialism. The spontaneity of the Dynamizing Groups was replaced by Party control, and the same 'Party-ization' could be seen in respect of labour organization. Political opposition to Frelimo was banned.

Frelimo's development plans were extremely ambitious; at the end of the day Frelimo pinned its success to the legitimacy which would be afforded by a developing economy. The early successes of Frelimo, for example in terms of literacy and vaccination campaigns (Walt and Melamed, 1983; Marshall, 1993; Searle, 1981), led to a general atmosphere of hope, at least within the Frelimo cadres, that real changes could be achieved through popular mobilization and organization. Once Frelimo had managed to ride the storm of early independence and gained an ideological sense of purpose, it adopted an ambitious set of plans for the economy based on central planning. Agriculture was to be collectivized through the establishment of cooperatives and state farms; industry was to be developed by the state using large-scale technologies imported from other socialist countries. The keystones were the power of the state and the vision of the Plan. Industries were nationalized, at first as part of the 'firefighting' and subsequently as part of a strategy. Communal villages were encouraged, and the settler farms were consolidated into large-scale mechanized state farms, notably in the Limpopo valley (Hermele, 1988b).

Frelimo's vision of Mozambique's development was encapsulated in the Decade for the Victory Over Underdevelopment, from 1980 to 1990. This ambitious programme of state-based indicative investment foresaw investments at the 'commanding heights' which would allow Mozambique to achieve a developed economy within ten years. Great faith was put in the planning and administration process; Mozambicans were to be mobilized behind Frelimo's revolution; international solidarity with the eastern bloc (and, it was hoped, membership of the Council of Mutual Economic Assistance), and technological improvement were the foundations of Frelimo's bold plans. The 'mood' of the late 1970s gives us an idea of Frelimo's social vision: its desire to develop Mozambique, twinned with a top-down approach to governance and a great impatience to transform Mozambique's complex social tapestry. Looking closely at the politics of the time, one can identify key contradictions in Frelimo's socialism – not least the absence of a politicized working-class base – but in historical retrospect, the regional politics of the 1980s proved to be far more important.

Regional war and rural violence (1980–92)

Rhodesia gained independence as Zimbabwe in 1980. At the same time, the South African state began to take the threat of Mozambique more seriously – the Frelimo state espoused socialism and opposed *apartheid*. The main result of this was that the South African security apparatus (which gained increasing prominence within the *apartheid* state during the 1980s) undertook a programme of *destabilization* in Mozambique. Destabilization connotes a desire by the South African state to undermine any successes enjoyed by the Frelimo state on its borders. The main mechanism through which South Africa executed this strategy was the *Resistência Nacional Moçambicana*, or Renamo. Renamo was a rural insurgency made up of Mozambicans, but funded and controlled by the South African security services.

Thus Renamo, on the instructions of South Africa, terrorized the populations of Frelimo's communal villages, massacred Frelimo cadres in rural areas, destroyed rural infrastructure and forced peasants into its service as porters or fighters, using psychological techniques of fear and guilt. The story of Renamo's emergence and growth is a grim one, based on violence and destruction, and close links with *apartheid* (Fauvet, 1984; Cammack, 1988; Hall, 1990). By the mid-1980s, Renamo had expanded to infuse the whole of Mozambique's rural society with violence, refugees and food insecurity. The Renamo insurgency put an abrupt end to the sanguine aspirations of Frelimo, however problematic the latter's premises might have been.

However, it also became clear in the late 1980s that Renamo's insurgency had grown beyond any simple and direct relaying of South African aims to Renamo's actions. By the late 1980s, Renamo's presence in all provinces and the apartheid state's increasing concern to manage the transition towards a non-racial political dispensation meant that one could not explain Renamo's presence purely in terms of destabilization. It became clear that the insurgency was gaining local roots in the contradictions of Mozambique's rural societies. Some social groups used insurgency to remove themselves from Frelimo's influence; some used the context of general instability to pursue strategies of banditry; some bent to the authority of whoever wielded the guns at the time, hoping merely to stay alive (Geffray, 1991; Clarence-Smith, 1989). In particular, Renamo played on the resentment that peasants in some parts of the country felt towards Frelimo's anti-tradition sentiments. Some chiefs, and their lineages, actively supported Renamo, identifying Renamo with a political movement to bring back chieftaincy. And, as the war went on, Frelimo's actions in the countryside became more militarized and authoritarian, seeing peasants as possible Renamo supporters or as a strategic resource to keep out of Renamo's hands.

Overall, during this period, 'development' of any kind was abandoned. Mozambique's state-driven economy went into severe decline and indebtedness, while new forms of market and accumulation emerged within the informal sector or through strategies of straddling between the official and unofficial economies (Chingono, 1996). As the state's plans collapsed and the debt built up, Frelimo began negotiations with the World Bank and IMF.

Structural adjustment and peace (late 1980s–)

After a limited set of liberalization reforms from 1984, Mozambique commenced a structural adjustment programme (PRE) in 1987 with

World Bank funding. The key policies of PRE were similar to those in other African adjusting states:

- currency devaluation;
- removal of price subsidies;
- reduction in state expenditure (Hermele, 1988b, 1990).

Mozambique implemented structural adjustment at the height of the Renamo war's intensity. Little acknowledgement was made by the IFIs of the particular circumstances imposed by war; instead World Bank and IMF reports refer to 'external factors' or assumptions of a return to normality in the medium term. The wisdom of implementing SAP during war has been seriously questioned (Wuyts, 1991). Looking at the example of health care reveals the problems that PRE caused. In 1988, as part of Mozambique's SAP, health expenditure was cut to an average of $1 per person, compared to $5 in 1981 (Hermele, 1990: 27), despite the fact that there were a lot more starving, uprooted and injured people as a result of the war, and that Renamo had destroyed 31 per cent of the health care system in rural areas by 1987 (Hermele, 1990: 6). Small wonder, then, that some observers saw PRE as finishing off the remaining gains that Frelimo had achieved that had not been wiped out by Renamo. Concurrently with the social crisis, a large number of Western non-governmental organizations flooded into the country, each providing their own projects of social support as the state's social infrastructure collapsed.

PRE created a general fall in social well-being, especially in the cities. In Chapter 3, we mentioned how the removal of price subsidies had made it even more difficult for families to gain access to a basic subsistence. Furthermore, Mozambique's economy did not recover markedly during PRE. In 1990, Mozambique and the World Bank signed a new SAP known as the PRES, or Economic and *Social* Rehabilitation Programme. This involved an expenditure component given over to health and education. After the flooding of 1992, the economy began to recover and direct foreign investment in Mozambique began to increase markedly. The southern regions of the country, especially the capital Maputo, began to experience new construction, more cars and the rehabilitation of tourism. Agricultural production also began to rise. However, each of these positive developments comes with important caveats: growth has been regionally and socially concentrated in the south of the country, based on foreign investment and with little spread to the poorest sections of the population; agricultural recovery might be a 'one-off' phenomenon created by the stabilization of the countryside after the war; much of Mozambique's recovery depends on ongoing good relations with donors and creditors and Mozambique remains trapped in indebtedness, despite even Highly Indebted Poor Country status. In other words, Mozambique's recent positive economic developments can only be fully evaluated in a longer time frame.

The main positive development in Mozambique's recent history is the Rome Peace Agreement (RPA) of 1992. Despite much cynicism, the Peace Accord held, with a few small exceptions, bringing peace to a country which had been beset by instability in one part or another since 1962. Frelimo signed the RPA after a series of efforts by external institutions and individuals to convince the government to accept Renamo as a political party. Frelimo was generally convinced that elections held after the RPA would return a large Frelimo majority. Renamo signed the RPA after ensuring that it would be allowed to form a political party and contest the elections. It also faced a severe food shortage in the early 1990s, and received a series of financial inducements to sweeten the peace deal.

The RPA set out a schedule for demobilization, demining, the reintegration of Renamo zones into the national territorial administration and the preparations for multi-party elections. All of these processes were funded or coordinated by the United Nations Operation in Mozambique (ONUMOZ). ONUMOZ set up a series of commissions with Frelimo and Renamo representation and – with a few hiccups along the way – successfully left the country after generally free and fair elections in October 1994. ONUMOZ represents a rare success for the UN in post-Cold War Africa. Frelimo won the elections, but by less than it expected. Significantly, Renamo made a transition from guerrilla insurgency to political party (Cahen, 1997).

Writing in political struggle in Mozambique: violence and peace

In comparative terms, Mozambique has experienced a particularly turbulent history. War has been more common than peace, and the state has often failed to control all of its territory. These seem like particularly inauspicious circumstances for political struggle. Indeed, the extent to which struggle has impinged on Mozambique's grand course of events is limited but, taking into account the prevailing forces which developed over Mozambique's postcolonial history, these threads of struggle become all the more salient for existing at all.

Liberation war

Let us begin during the liberation struggle. During the 12 years of guerrilla war, FRELIMO managed to establish liberated zones in the northern third of the country. The ideological currents which ran through FRELIMO were diverse: socialism, Maoism, African national-ism and various ethnic-political undercurrents (Opello, 1975; De Brito, 1988; Munslow, 1983). In general the liberation war only succeeded because it enjoyed the support of the peasants of northern Mozam-bique, who provided troops, intelligence and food for FRELIMO. The liberation struggle was a struggle prosecuted by peasants who wished to gain a greater degree of freedom – political and economic – out of independence.

FRELIMO provided the opportunity for peasants to struggle against the oppressive chieftaincy system – known as the *regulado* – imposed by the Portuguese. The liberation war also provided peasants with an opportunity to get rid of the day-to-day racism of colonial culture, and the economic discrimination that the colonial state subjected them to. So, although there is no clearly distilled praxis of struggle, peasant par-ticipation in the war clearly related to a desire to overthrow colonial-ism and replace it with a political form which would be non-racist and more sensitive to the developmental needs of peasant communities.

Unlike their French and English counterparts, the Portuguese did not wish to decolonize. Mozambique, Angola and Guinea-Bissau all remained colonies throughout the 1960s. The nationalist elites of each country found that they had to raise an insurgency with some popular appeal in order to force the state from the colonizer's hands (although Angola's story is considerably more complicated). Mozambique won its independence as a result of a rural insurgency prosecuted by peasants. In fact, one might argue that the peasant struggles of Lusophone Africa attained world-historic proportions: it was the colonial question which centrally provoked the revolution in Portugal itself, overthrowing the Salazar dictatorship with a progressive military coup which assured lusophone Africa of its independence and brought Portugal itself out of the grips of authoritarian rule. So, it would be difficult to write about Portugal's modern history without a consideration of the struggles of Mozambique's peasants.

Mozambican socialism

Although Frelimo enjoyed widespread legitimacy by virtue of its libera-tion struggle, and it received increasing numbers of members in the urban areas after independence, it had to reconcile itself to work with a bureaucracy staffed by some whites, incumbent African lower-level officials from the Portuguese period and its own cadres. Consequently, Frelimo's first few years were characterized by emergency responses and 'firefighting': trying to keep the economy working, and establishing the bare bones of an administration. Notable during this period was the emergence of local popular self-organization in the form of Dynamizing Groups (*Grupos Dinamizadores*) which established forms of collective labour, self-help and participation (Davidson, 1979). In this early period, when 'the revolution' enjoyed widespread legitimacy, Mozambicans organized and struggled to recover from the shock imposed by decolonization and crisis.

Much of this popular dynamic to the early years of Mozambique's postcolonial rule has been lost in a general critique of Frelimo's postcolonial rule. Incisive critiques (Cahen, 1993) have produced a less discriminating cynicism to all claims of popular participation or struggle during the early Frelimo years. But it is clearly wrong to write history in such a simple way, using a kind of reverse teleology, writing backwards from the sorry denouement of Frelimo's socialism. Dynamizing Groups did provide people with a level of political participation which was historically unprecedented, and political meetings and rallies generally were attended with enthusiasm. This did change over the years, and in fact did not exist at all in some parts of the country, but it did infuse Frelimo's early postcolonial rule with a popular content, and it did contribute to the tenacious way Mozambique survived the terrible circumstances left by the Portuguese. Unfortunately, it also raised the hackles of Mozambique's powerful apartheid neighbour.

The Renamo war

As the war of destabilization rooted itself in Mozambique's rural social fabric (Geffray, 1991), notions of peasant spiritual and lineage authority were integrated into Renamo's war strategy. In particular, certain chiefs proactively removed themselves from Frelimo zones and relocated in Renamo zones; also Renamo's image of military prowess was tied up in a notion of ethnic Ndau military identity. But symbols of spiritual power and the morals of the ancestors could be mobilized to produce what Wilson (1992) calls 'cults of counterviolence'. Wilson's term deserves some explanation. It is not just that Renamo's cults of violence were being met with cults of violence mobilized by Frelimo, producing a 'war of the spirits'. This was partly the case, but also local spiritual authorities succeeded in articulating cults of non violence, challenging the prevalence of coercion, torture and death that pervaded Mozambique's rural areas through the 1980s. Wilson gives detailed examples of this process, and quotes approvingly from Vines that 'the peasants themselves [have] been able to mobilise the resources of religion to distance or tame Renamo, enlisting their ancestors to achieve for them what Frelimo has too often been unable to do' (1992: 554).

A growing popular resistance to violence consolidated itself after 1992. The success of the peace process was underpinned by a powerful and popular anti-war sentiment, what Wilson has called 'the people's peace' (1994). Without this popular feeling – which made mobilizing troops on either side unthinkable, and which produced a 'ratchet effect' in which all moves towards peace soon became consolidated within popular political culture – the peace process might not have been the success that it was.

Contemporary struggle in Mozambique

Mozambique held its second multi-party elections in 1999. Again, they were generally seen as 'free and fair' by the international observers, although there were far fewer observers than in 1994, and Renamo boycotted the Assembly of the Republic in protest at what it saw as irregularities and fraud. During the 1990s, there had also been a national census and the establishment of locally elected municipal authorities. The economy was the fastest growing in the world in 1999, with an increase in GNP of 19 per cent. One might imagine, then, that Mozambique has successfully stabilized itself after the war and is now on the way to 'normality' or even 'recovery'. But political issues and struggles remain which behove us to take a more critical view of Mozambique's contemporary politics.

Mozambique relies on the export of cashew and prawns for the bulk of its export revenue. As part of PRE, state-owned cashew nut processing factories were privatized. In contrast to the general trend in privatization in Mozambique (which has been radical and far-reaching compared with the rest of Africa), the factories stayed under national control, bought by Mozambican capitalists, often of Asian origin. Many factories were re-equipped with new machinery after their private owners had taken out loans to secure productivity. Cashew privatization was seen as one of the few successful cases of national development, after many state enterprises sold off to foreign concerns faced problems as productive units were changed into trading centres, there was widespread retrenchment and allegations of racist labour relations emerged.

In 1995, the World Bank, supported by a consultancy it had funded, conditioned further loans on the removal of an export tariff on raw cashew nuts. The export tariff ensured a price structure which allowed Mozambican factories to gain access to cashew nuts (a peasant crop) rather than face shortages as nuts were exported to India for processing and re-export. The government protested, arguing that removing the export tariff would damage the embryonic Mozambican cashew processing sector, and succeeded in ensuring a phasing out of the tariff rather than its abolition. However, pressure was maintained to get rid of the tariff, and the cashew processing industry had to lay off workers as a result of the changes in the cashew price structure. Later on, almost all cashew processing factories were forced to close as the nuts went abroad unprocessed, leaving Mozambican capitalists with large debts and no means to pay interest or principal. A second consultancy, undertaken by the international auditors Deloitte & Touche, found that – contrary to World Bank arguments – removal of the tariff had damaged Mozambican cashew processing and that the policy had had an overall detrimental effect (Hanlon, 2000).

Much of the controversy concerning cashew nut processing has been generated by Mozambican organizations. The cashew industry's representative body, AICAJU, as well as the cashew workers' union, SINTIC, have lobbied the government to replace the tariff and to demand 'reparations' from the World Bank. In 1997, AICAJU demanded that the World Bank pay compensation for the damage it had imposed. SINTIC also claimed that the World Bank was liable to pay compensation to retrenched cashew workers. The Bank agreed to consider this proposal in 1997, while not changing its liberalization policy in spite of the Deloitte report. The activity of AICAJU and SINTIC have defined the controversy over cashews. It has also highlighted the complex contours of political struggle in an indebted country: a need to engage with IFIs as well as the national government, and a situation in which it is not entirely clear that the government represents the 'national interest' articulated through the cashew organizations, as it has a great deal tied up in its good relations with the World Bank and IMF. As a result of political mobilization through these bodies, the IMF finally agreed in December 2000 that tariffs and protective measures could be reinstated for Mozambique's cashew processing industry.

Other specific policies enforced by the IFIs have also met with resistance. The removal of staple food subsidies created sporadic urban protests in the early 1990s. The draconian statements of the IMF concerning small general increases in the minimum wage led to outrage within Mozambique's urban civil society which in turn generated a defence of the wage increases by bilateral donors and a volte-face on behalf of the IMF. The imposition of VAT, again at the behest of the IMF, created a backlash from small and medium-sized businesses protesting at the cost of administering the new form of tax, this leading to a more phased implementation. All of these individual struggles highlight the complexity of Mozambique's political disposition: as IFIs become more intimately involved in Mozambique's political economy (through the articulation of notions of governance and so on), and as the Mozambican government becomes more closely aligned with the IFIs through constant meetings and negotiations to arrange loans, debt relief and further rescheduling, old ideas of government representing the 'national interest' seem inappropriate.

At all stages in Mozambique's history, struggle constitutes a key component of political change. Mozambique's independence was won through the armed struggle of peasant troops, organized by Frelimo. The limited but significant success of Frelimo's 'early days' owed itself to the popular mobilization and participation of ordinary people and Party cadres, who built drainage channels in the cities, worked energetically to provide education and vaccinations to the population, and kept a skeleton of administration and production going. Peasant culture elaborated innovative forms of spiritual authority which provided a minimal space outside of the widespread violence and insecurity brought by the Renamo war. The nature of the implementation of structural adjustment policy has been contested by a range of Mozambican organizations – based in capital and labour, as well as the independent media – which has meant that, now, the main adversary of the IFIs is Mozambican civil society as much as a residual nationalism or egalitarian commitment within the state. One final example would be the Mozambican Debt Group, which joined in the 'Drop the Debt' campaign on the streets of Maputo simultaneously with Jubilee 2000 organizations throughout the world, and protested at the opaque fashion in which Mozambique's Country Strategy Documents have been devised. It is perhaps the thread of struggle interwoven throughout Mozambique's history which explains the persistence of the phrase '*a luta continua*', or the struggle continues, in Mozambican studies.

Nigeria

Nigeria presents us with an example which is in many substantial ways very different to Mozambique. In terms of basic geography, it is located in West Africa, is much larger than Mozambique and contains a far greater population. It exists in a different regional subsystem and, if one conceives of Mozambique and Nigeria as components of a region, Mozambique is very much a peripheral state and Nigeria something of a regional 'superpower'. We will make a schematic review of Nigeria's political history, highlighting similarities and differences with the general patterns identified in previous chapters, before looking more closely at the struggles of Nigerians to influence political change.

Independence

Nigeria's early postcolonial polity was strongly influenced by post-1945 British colonial policy. Generally, after the Second World War, Britain attempted to promote capitalist development in its colonies, albeit always subject to the dilemma of the political repercussions of increasingly powerful African groups based in trade, chieftaincy and administration. In Nigeria, the British administration created the bones of a political infrastructure which was to constitute the foundation of much political division and violence in the coming decades. In 1954, Nigeria was separated into three regions: North, East and West. Each of these reflected a form of corporate ethnic geography (simplified and politicized as all ethnic geographies were by colonialism): a Hausa-Fulani northern region, an Igbo east and a Yoruba west. As independence approached, each of these regions developed forms of patronage and political party identities based in their respective regions so that, by 1959 when general elections took place, three parties representing the hegemonic regional ethnic groups vied for federal (central) power. Coalitions there were, but the fundamental ethno-regional template remained.

Early postcolonial Nigerian politics is fascinating for its interplay between parties, ideologies, ethnic rivalries and strong personalities. It is also intriguing because of the struggles that took place within the regions to secure political power as a base for personal accumulation and enrichment – a kind of decentralized politics of the belly, as described in Chapter 1. In each region, a ruling clique consolidated its power via the state, marginalizing smaller ethnic groups, and the poor and powerless more generally. The early independence period also saw an increasing keenness in the struggle for federal power.

A general feature of Nigeria's political geography is that the North maintains a hold over political power, and the south retains the most wealth, education and capital. The North's jealousy of political power was a reflection of an insecurity and resentment concerning the monopoly of 'development' in the south, especially the high levels of education in the Yoruba west. The tension between an inconsistent geography of political power and economic power were distilled in the attempts to carry out a national census in 1962 and 1963. The fundamental controversy concerning the census was the size of the Northern population: the larger the population, the greater the claim to power – and federal resources – the North could make. It is generally believed that the census of 1963 was substantially 'cooked' to yield a large majority in the North (Osaghae, 1998b: 41 et seq.).

The controversy of census taking (which continued during the 1970s) highlights a central theme in Nigeria's postcolonial politics: the tension between the state and federal governments. During the First Republic, the macro-regional tensions between North, East and West infused the party system, leading to a situation of unstable alliances and conflicts, and producing a degree of territorialism, that is a sense that one region belonged to a particular party and others were not welcome to operate there. The ongoing dominance of the Northern People's Congress (NPC) during the 1964 federal elections created substantial resentment in the East, creating the conditions for the first of many military regimes in 1966.

The first military period (1966–79)

The coup of 1996 brought Major-General Ironsi to power. Ironsi was an Igbo, and his accession to power served to heighten the regional sensitivities of the North, where the military elite felt that they had 'lost' their grip on federal power previously secured through the northern party, the NPC. The coup set in train a series of ethnic tensions in the north, as Igbo working in the north were subject to violence. Later in the same year, a 'counter-coup' was effected, bringing (northern) Lieutenant-Colonel Yakubu Gowon to power. This recapture of federal power by the northern military elite was coupled by an intensifying pogrom against Igbos in northern states, which led to the deaths of perhaps 10 000. It was these two key processes: the 'restorative' coup and the ethnic cleansing in the north that provoked the secession of the east in 1967, when Lieutenant-Colonel Ojukwu declared the independence of Biafra. The Biafran civil war followed, claiming 500 000 to 2 million lives (Osaghae, 1998a: 6 et seq.). In 1970 the eastern region was reintegrated back into the Nigerian nation-state.

The Biafran war not only highlighted the sensitivities of Nigeria's federal system (Nixon, 1972); it also threw into relief the difficulties of uneven development (Forrest, 1995). It is the Igbo east that detains the bulk of Nigeria's onshore oil reserves. After the war, Nigeria's oil reserves came on line, and oil revenues rocketed, making the entire economy substantially dependent on dollar revenues from oil exports (Khan, 1994).

Oil production had a number of effects on Nigeria's political development. In the first place, it provided for an increase in public revenues. This meant that the Gowon administration could implement ambitious social programmes, notably a programme of Universal Primary Education. Also, the sudden increase in revenues created large amounts of fungible money which provided lucrative opportunities for politicians to enrich themselves. Oil provided the means for some to import Mercedes-Benz or even personal jets, as well as to construct luxury houses and set up foreign bank accounts. The prominence of oil also increased the power of the federal (central) government over the states, which had, under the First Republic, been relatively unencumbered by the centre. Now, all state governments focused their attention keenly on the federal state as a source of funds, as it detained the duties, taxes and sales revenues of the oil industry (through a set of contracts involving oil transnationals).

Thus the politics of oil patronage became the key issue of Nigeria's politics. One result of this was a series of rounds of state creation. This provided more intricate patterns of patronage distribution, as new states received monies to build public offices, universities, airports and highways. This was still seen in terms of the enduring tripolar geography: new states in the north meant more power for the northern elite and so on. But the creation of new states also challenged the 'macro-ethnicity' embedded in the existing state system. Previously, the three corporate ethnic groups had dominated state governments, leaving little scope for political expression or access to power for the thousands of smaller ethnic groups, scattered around within the states. Smaller and more numerous states allowed smaller ethno-regional groups a greater access to state power. Gowon reinforced this rebalancing by introducing a derivation principal to the distribution of oil revenues. This meant that the eastern Rivers states received a substantial proportion of the oil revenues generated in their territories.

The Gowon regime progressively lost its stability as a result of the broader structural disposition of postcolonial Nigeria, outlined above, and its own decisions and authoritarianism. Another census in 1973 revived controversies over the demographic distribution between north, east and west, and the regime increasingly became perceived as 'northern' rather than national, despite the initially meticulous efforts of Gowon to promote reconciliation after the Biafra war. Furthermore, oil revenues created substantial corruption, both at the centre and in the states. In 1975, Gowon was ousted in a bloodless coup by Murtala

Mohamed, who was succeeded in the same year by Brigadier Olusegun Obasanjo (the current Nigerian president). Obasanjo pledged that the military would take more concerted steps to usher in a Second Republic with multi-party elections.

The second republic (1979–83)

As the military regime progressively lost stability, a new constitution was written in 1979, establishing the structures for a multi-party system with a strong presidency. Presidential and legislative elections took place in 1979 with a fair degree of success, although not without accusations of foul play. Shegu Shagari and his National Party of Nigeria (NPN) gained power, beginning a period of political decline and contributing to a popular Nigerian sentiment that civilian rule was as venal – if not more so – than military regimes. The NPN won the elections as a political patronage machine rather than as an ideologically informed party. Once it had gained control of the federal state, it proceeded to shore up a patronage system based around the party and the President. The oil price hikes of 1979 and 1983 only exacerbated this civilian patronage politics. As such, there was little ideology or substantial political change during the Second Republic as much as the reconfiguration and intensification of the logic of clientelism. Governors often administered their states as fiefs, distributing patronage, salting away revenues and making increasingly intense demands of federal resources. Contractors and state officials colluded and inflated contracting, leaving state and federal governments with growing debts. Finally, the clientelist logic of civilian politics also increased the intensity of factionalism *within* the ruling party.

The new civilian government, perhaps wary of the proclivity of the military to intervene in politics, tried to remove political power from established military officers. It also built up a more intrusive and politicized police force which came to be increasingly resented by Nigerians facing road blocks, extortions and oppression. As such, the Second Republic is not remembered well and, after the second elections of the Second Republic generated widespread (and often justified) accusations of bribery, political machinations and intrigue, the military stepped in once more.

The second military period (1983–99)

Major-General Muhammad Buhari came to power in a coup in 1983. There was only limited protest concerning the coup, and the military regime was afforded a certain reserved legitimacy (as had previous ones) as a result of two factors: firstly a declaration that the military would prepare the Nigerian state for a return to civilian rule in the right circumstances; secondly that it would implement necessary reforms which the self-regarding and short-term politicians were unable to do.

Consequently, the Buhari regime installed a relatively authoritarian austerity, top-down and populist in form. The clearest characterization of the Buhari regime was the War Against Indiscipline (WAI), which aimed to purge not just the state, but society in general, of its corruption, lack of order and generally poorly developed sense of national-civic duty. The WAI resembles other populist military regimes in West Africa in some senses: the campaigns to clear up urban areas remind one of the Rawlings or Sankara regimes in Ghana and Burkina Faso respectively. Some progress was made in exposing corruption – not just at the level of 'small fry' or even contemporary political enemies – but also in respect of existing 'big fish'. All of this was accompanied by a 'home-grown' regime of economic austerity, although no meaningful dialogue with the IMF existed at this time. Buhari's regime's conditional legitimacy was eroded by the patrician way in which decisions were made. Buhari entertained practically no consultation with other groups concerning policy, and he ruled through the Presidential directive. The President's staff and administration expanded, eroding the civil service and creating increasingly complex forms of administration. The general direction of reform did not give the impression of a concerted attempt to return the country to some form of democratic rule. It was within these circumstances that a further coup took place in 1985, bringing Ibrahim Babangida to power.

Babangida proved to be a relatively imaginative and open military President, winning an exceptional degree of support from Nigeria's academic community (for example, Ate, 1991). Former political detainees were released, a Political Bureau was created with civilian representation, and a clear intention to move towards some form of political transition away from military rule was visible. Okoye dubs the Babangida period one of 'liberal reformism' (1999: 160) to capture the distinction between Babangida and his predecessor.

A limited political liberalization took place (the official ban on organized politics was lifted in 1989), simultaneously with the implementation of a structural adjustment programme from 1986. This conjuncture created a period of unstable but 'lively' politics in Nigeria: a profusion of independent media, the contestation of parties and individuals to contest the elections, debates about a new constitution (a new Constitutional Assembly was created) and debates about the merits of structural adjustment. However, Babangida wished to maintain control of the political trajectory. After a period of political party disputes, dirty tricks and a failure of the Electoral Commission to ensure transparency, it was declared that the government would *create* two parties to contest the elections: the National Republican Party (NRP) and the Social Democratic Party (SDP), the former 'a little to the right' and the latter 'a little to the left', in Babangida's now infamous formulation. There were also strong suspicions that Babangida himself was preparing to 'civilianize', in the style of Jerry Rawlings. The other key piece of evidence of an overriding imperative to control the transition was the banning of the powerful Nigeria Labour Congress in 1988, as it had become a central actor opposing SAP and supporting the democratic struggle in general (for example supporting students).

In 1990, it was declared that national party and presidential elections would take place in 1992; in 1992, a year-long delay was announced. Throughout this period, analyses of Nigeria highlighted the instability of Babangida's transition process: there were uncertainties about the military's (and Babangida's) motives, corruption was increasing precipitously, there was an attempted coup in 1990 and the selection of the presidents for the NRP and SDP was confused and opaque. But, on 12 June 1993, 'unexpectedly sound' presidential elections did take place (Lewis, 1999: 144), returning a victory for the Yoruba millionaire businessman Moshood Abiola of the SDP. Abiola and his party were perceived as (to some extent) 'southern', but, significantly (and in accordance with electoral law), Abiola won considerable support in the north as well. As a result of a complicated series of events (which are still analysed and discussed), the full results were not announced by the National Elections Commission and, in the political vacuum, the military stepped in once again. Babangida was ousted in 1993 and, after a brief interregnum, Sani Abacha installed himself as another Nigerian President in military uniform.

In response to these events, a powerful pro-democracy movement emerged, centred mainly in the south of the country. Abacha crushed the 'June 12 movement' (named after the date of the annulled elections) and implemented a form of government more authoritarian than any previously, military or civilian. The military clique around Abacha had probably forced the annulment of the elections as 'their' candidate, Bashir Tofa, lost to a 'southern' candidate – something which the entrenched ethno-regional power within the military could not accept. The extent of Abacha's brutality is well known internationally: Abiola was imprisoned, along with many other media editors, politicians and military men. Most famously, Ken Saro-Wiwa and eight other members of the Movement for the Survival of the Ogoni People (MOSOP) were hanged in 1995 after a politically controlled trial. It is estimated that $6 bn was taken out of the state coffers in Abacha's short (and reclusive) period of rule. Abacha died in mysterious circumstances in June 1998 (*Africa Confidential,* 12, June 1998), giving way to General Abdulsalami Abubakar, who immediately announced a programme to remove the military from direct political control by May 1999 (Lewis, 1999: 141).

Abiola died in prison, probably of a heart attack which must have been exacerbated by dire prison conditions. Abubakar released political detainees, including the former military president Obasanjo. Obasanjo went on to win the presidential elections in 1999, not without some controversy concerning the extent to which they were free and fair, and Nigeria entered the Third Republic.

Writing in political struggle in Nigeria: identity, rights and a 'New Social Movement'

Nigeria's turbulent political history is reflected in a history of struggle. Political action to promote democracy is one important component of this (Olukoshi, 1993b; Ihonvbere and Vaughan, 1995); labour politics is another (Adesina, 1989, 1990; Bangura and Beckman, 1993; Ibrahim, 1986, 1993). The fact is that all regimes have been challenged to live up to social and political expectations articulated by a variety of social groups. In Chapters 3 and 4, some aspects of these struggles were reviewed. Here, we return to Nigeria consider the politics of ethnic identity, struggle and federalism.

The historical account above revealed two fundamental contra-dictions in Nigeria's ethnic politics. First there were the difficulties of articulating a central state with an expansive and diverse set of societies, defined by religious, linguistic, regional, cultural and chiefly structures of authority. The mere fact of diversity does not automatic-ally connote a 'problem', but the relationship between ethnic groups and the central state raises questions of access to power and, of course, access to resources – mainly generated from oil. Secondly, there was the dominance of the three macro-ethnicities (Hausa-Fulani, Yoruba, and Igbo) over the two hundred plus smaller ethnic groups which often find that their access to political power is limited by the 'big three'. In Chapter 5, a distinction was made between 'positive' and 'negative' ethnic mobilization, the former of which involves ethnic mobilization to promote some notion of collective empowerment, rather than violence, chauvinism or revanchism. Nigeria's postcolonial history is full of small-scale examples of ethnic or regional organizations promoting collective development or empowerment of this kind (Ihonvbere and Vaughan, 1995; Adedeji and Otite, 1997), but we will look at a better known (and researched) example: MOSOP.

MOSOP was created in 1990, establishing itself by issuing a charter-like Ogoni Bill of Rights. The Ogoni make up part of the complex social tapestry of the Niger delta area, numbering about 500 000 and divided into six chieftaincies. Like many small ethnic groups, the Ogoni have suffered from the monopolization of power by the three macro-ethnic groups: in this case Igbo dominance of the east. Nevertheless, an Ogoni elite has consolidated itself throughout the postcolonial period, and one can identify other ethnic groups which have had less access to power than the Ogoni. Ken Saro-Wiwa, MOSOP's president until his death, was the best example of this, occupying positions in state governments and having a base in private enterprise.

What made the Ogoni struggle particularly sharp was the combination of popular powerlessness and oil. The land and rivers farmed and fished by the Ogoni are in Rivers State, producer of most of Nigeria's onshore oil, with six oilfields on Ogoni land. Shell, Chevron and the Nigerian National Petroleum Corporation (in partnership with the former two) had established a network of extraction plants and pipeline from the 1960s onwards. The political effects of this are twofold (Frynas, 1998; Detheridge and Pepple, 1998):

1. Negative externalities of oil extraction have been imposed on Ogoni peasants. Oil leaks have polluted land and estuaries and flaring has polluted the atmosphere (Frynas, 2000: 160 et seq.; Ejobowah, 2000: 39–40). Osaghae describes the effects of oil extraction as a 'permanent scorched earth regime' (1995a: 330).
2. Oil has produced massive revenues for the oil companies, but little of that wealth had been put into the region: for example, despite producing tens of billions of dollars of oil, the region has no water or electricity infrastructure. Furthermore, the 'derivation principle' which introduced some proportionality in the distribution of state revenues was all but moribund by the time of the Babangida regime: from 20 per cent in 1975 to 3 per cent in 1993 (Ejobowah, 2000: 36; Frynas, 2001: 32–3).

Culturally, land is central to Ogoni ethnic identity. The fact that Ogoni land yields great wealth for the oil companies, but produces mainly environmental damage for the Ogoni, produced a powerful moral politics of injustice within Ogoniland. Naanen neatly summarizes the conjuncture which led to the formation of MOSOP:

> First, ethnic-based political domination, which is used to expropriate the resources of the oil communities ... second the alliance between the oil companies and the state enterprises, which restricts the minorities' access to the modern and more rewarding sectors of the oil economy; and third, oil-based environmental degradation, which undermines the traditional peasant or fishing economy of the oil-producing areas without providing a viable economic alternative.
>
> (1995: 50)

MOSOP harnessed this sense of injustice (and, of course, of real suffering) that this conjuncture produced to articulate a programme of ethnic self-determination (within a more confederal Nigerian constitution), a demand to compensate the Ogoni for the oil revenue that has been extracted from their land over the last thirty years, and a concern to ensure that environmental issues are taken more seriously.

MOSOP succeeded in mobilizing a range of organizations in support of its general cause. MOSOP began by writing letters to Babangida and the oil companies, and holding protests outside oil plants. These actions met with little or no response. Consequently, political action became more effective: on 4 January 1993, the UN Year of World Indigenous People, a protest march was held which attracted about 300 000 people (that is, three-fifths of the entire Ogoni population!). This raised the profile of the Ogoni struggle not just in Nigeria but also throughout the world (Naanen, 1995: 70 et seq.). Ken Saro-Wiwa's understanding of publicity allowed MOSOP to become a legitimate representative of a threatened indigenous people, mobilizing support from Greenpeace (who protested outside Shell's headquarters), and gaining them representation in international fora such as the Unrepresented Nations and Peoples Forum (Welch, 1995: 644). In 1992, Saro-Wiwa made a presentation to the UN Commission on Human Rights in Geneva.

Babangida's response was a mixture of force and limited concession. The Oil Mineral Producing Areas Development Commission was established to manage oil revenues and implement development projects in the oil regions (Osaghae, 1998a: 13). Also, President Abacha and the Rivers State government seemed to prosecute a campaign of suppression and dirty tricks against MOSOP. For example, conflicts with neighbouring ethnic groups occurred, with evidence pointing to Internal Security Task Force involvement, for example in the high-tech nature of the violence from the Andoni community in 1993, a community which had no history of enmity with the Ogoni.

The MOSOP leadership were constantly detained. Once Sani Abacha came to power, the relationship between MOSOP and the government became increasingly conflictual. After the aborted 1993 elections, which the Ogoni boycotted *en masse*, the nine leading members were detained under the accusation that they had been responsible for the murder of four Ogoni chiefs. After a trial that can uncontroversially be likened to a kangaroo court, the nine Ogoni members were hanged in 1995 (Welch, 1995: 649). Later evidence revealed that the bodies were not given a proper burial but were covered with acid and buried in unmarked sites.

During the period that Saro-Wiwa and the others were detained (1994–95), a concerted international campaign for their release was effected. So forceful was the campaign that, in Rivers State, the oil companies significantly reduced their operations and, internationally, 'the Ogoni question' became an important issue. The 'judicial murder' of the Ogoni nine led to the suspension of Nigeria's membership of the Commonwealth for two years, and it contributed to the emerging international consensus that Nigeria could only establish formal political relations with the rest of the world once Abacha had gone. As with Mozambique, a local African struggle attained global significance.

Burkina Faso

Our final case study is Burkina Faso, a francophone country in West-Central Africa. Compared with Nigeria and Mozambique, it has greater resemblance with the latter. It is a small and extremely poor country that has experimented with a form of socialism with some similarities to that of Frelimo in Mozambique. However, Burkina Faso (formerly Upper Volta until 1984) is also very much part of a regional system, formed out of the migration and trade of pre-colonial Africa and the regional relations of colonial nation-states established by the French. We will sketch out Burkina Faso's postcolonial political history, before bringing out the importance of democracy and the struggle for development as themes embedded in that history.

Before the revolution (1960–83)

Burkina Faso, like most of francophone Africa, gained its independence in 1960. Maurice Yameogo, Upper Volta's first president, oversaw a clearly neocolonial political economy, pressured by the French into taking his position, and backed by a cadre of civil servants from the colonial period. Upper Volta's external dependence worked along two axes: firstly, a massive aid dependency on France, to an extent that puts the early post-independence period on a par with the extreme aid dependency experienced by the poorest of the debt-riven states of Africa today. Secondly, the regional system of labour migration, implemented by French colonial rule in the region, remained untouched, meaning that *millions* of Upper Volta citizens worked in neighbouring states, especially Côte d'Ivoire, the economic centre of francophone West Africa. Consequently, Upper Volta was dependent on two external sources of income: migrant remittances and French aid.

Politically, Upper Volta's first civilian government maintained a political conservatism that left little trace in the country's history. The First Republic saw the emergence of a small clique of businessmen and politicians, integrated around common regional and ethnic (Mossi) backgrounds. Yameogo was re-elected in 1965, but the state had run up unsustainable debts, exacerbated by a planned reduction in the all-important French aid programme (Saul, 1986: 137).

As a result, in 1966, Lieutenant Colonel Sangoule Lamizana overthrew the civilian government in a coup that led to the abolition of the National Assembly and an authoritarian military regime which aimed to impose a more disciplined and monetarist economic policy. In 1970, the military regime liberalized its rule slightly by installing a new National Assembly (under its control) and instituting a new constitution, although incremental liberalization was stopped in the mid-1970s. The military coup was conservative and did not significantly worry France which, during the 1970s and 1980s, was happy to maintain close relations with authoritarian and military regimes in 'its' region. From 1960 to 1972, Upper Volta received US$2 billion in French aid, that is five times the government budget for 1972 (Boudon, 1997: 129). The political elite of Upper Volta relied on aid to maintain its social privileges, resulting in a prevalence of corruption. In the countryside, the 90 per cent or so of Upper Volta's people maintained difficult livelihoods in ecologically challenging circumstances: Upper Volta suffered from the 1972–3 Sahelian famine, as it is located on the margins of the Sahara desert. In 1977, a new constitution was written, ushering in another attempt to add a civilian façade to the regime.

The 1980 coup by Colonel Saye Zerbo introduced a new instability to Upper Volta's politics, although the coups themselves were, until the next one, remarkably violence-free. Zerbo's rule was short-lived, as he was ousted by Major Jean-Baptiste Ouedraogo in 1982, the first coup which shed blood. This coup was significant because it was effected with the support of young and ideologically motivated officers, including Thomas Sankara and Blaise Compaoré (both subsequently president), who saw the changes of regime as the beginning of more fundamental change. Nevertheless, the frequent succession of coups highlighted the fact that Upper Volta's political economy was weak and unstable after 20 years of independence. Popular indifference or discontent rose during Ouedraogo's rule. Ouedraogo, like Zerbo before him, tried to incorporate members of opposition groups into his regime and, like Zerbo again, this involved offering Thomas Sankara a place in government, this time as Prime Minister.

In May 1983, after likely consultations with France, Sankara was arrested and detained, along with two of Sankara's allies with similar radical nationalist views. This only served to sharpen popular discontent with the regime, as Sankara made a relatively popular politician-soldier (famously, he rode a bicycle to work when Prime Minister, giving himself a populist image based on an ascetic lifestyle). Sankara's ally, Captain Blaise Compaoré, who evaded detention, led a coup from the military barracks at Po, marching 250 soldiers to the capital and releasing Sankara and his allies. This coup ushered in a very different regime to those that preceded it (Brittain, 1985).

Revolution (1983–87)

Sankara's radical politics were set out during the year he came to power, most clearly in his Political Orientation Speech. The key features of Sankara's politics were (Sankara, 1985; Skinner, 1988):

- a general asceticism and hostility to opulence, based on notions of equality, development and anti-corruption;
- a 'rural bias' (quite unlike the standard 'urban bias' politics mentioned in Chapter 3) which has even led some commentators to

suggest that Sankara's politics were not so far from the World Bank's! (Fontaine, in Speirs, 1996: 83);

- a lack of sympathy with public employees (who were relatively well-off) and merchants (who speculated while most peasants went hungry) (Saul, 1986);
- an assertive anti-imperialist foreign policy, which disturbed for the first time the cosy Franco–Burkinabé relationship;
- a strongly modernizing economic policy, based on rapid, state-led development.

Although Sankara's intellectual background shows affinities with Marxism, one might better describe the policies and programmes implemented during his regime as radical nationalism, based more on ideas of national pride, modernization and discipline. This explains the change in the country's name to Burkina Faso, which means 'land of the people with integrity'. Let us look in a little more detail at the evolution of Sankara's radical nationalism.

In 1983, the Sankara regime consolidated itself in the National Council of the Revolution, an executive body made up of Sankara and his close allies, notably those who were detained with him under Ouedraogo, and Blaise Compaoré. The strong desire to modernize Burkina Faso was predicated on the mobilization and participation of the population, and the vehicle to ensure that this mobilization was effected was the Committee for the Defence of the Revolution (CDR). These Committees were established at all levels in all parts of society, from the villages to the urban neighbourhood and the workplace. Committees were elected in Leninist democratic centralist fashion, from local level, through delegates to higher levels, finally to a CDR national conference. CDRs were supposed to transmit the revolutionary ethos to the grassroots, mobilize people to build 'bottom-up' development, and provide an organizational device to invigilate against corruption and anti-revolutionary activity. Popular Tribunals of Conciliation provided local fora for conflict resolution.

In 1984, a Popular Development Programme (PDP) was implemented, principally based on social provision and rural development projects. The PDP reinforced Sankara's central concern with the peasantry of Burkina Faso, although its effects were complicated by two factors: firstly the marginalization of chiefs and secondly the growing resentment of the salaried classes in the urban areas, notably civil servants (who took a real pay cut) and wage labour (whose unions were suppressed by Sankara). The gains in social provision did allow the revolution real legitimacy in rural areas, although the ways in which 'the revolution' translated into local village societies was not straightforward. For example, during Sankara's rule, 3 million children were vaccinated against yellow fever, measles and meningitis (Baxter and Somerville, 1988). Fifteen months after Sankara came to power, 334 primary schools, 184 clinics, 78 pharmacies and 962 wells and boreholes were constructed, relying substantially on mobilized labour through the CDRs (Atampugre, 1997: 58); by 1987 7500 primary health posts had been set up (Harsch, 1998: 628). But the CDRs sometimes became mechanisms to victimize certain groups at the local level, groups or individuals who were declared 'anti-revolutionary' (Skinner, 1988: 444, 449).

Land was nationalized, which meant that the systems of chief-based tenure were abolished (again, this was the official policy, not necessarily the reality on the ground) and effective control of land placed under the CDRs (Speirs, 1996: 113). The PDP also set in motion a series of large-scale infrastructural developments, necessarily with external funding, which was less centred on France. In the urban areas, Sankara restricted luxury consumer goods imports, decreed that civil servants should wear cotton clothes made by indigenous tailors, abolished the customary Ministerial fleet of Mercedes-Benz and forced all Ministers to travel in Renault 5 cars. In 1986, a Five Year Plan set out indicative targets for the PDP, which foresaw Burkina Faso becoming substantially modernized in an extremely short period of time under a strategically devised 'state capitalism' which would usher in the social conditions for a more progressive politics. One can identify in this approach all the signs of the essentially statist and top-down modernization that featured in many postcolonial African countries' histories (not least Mozambique).

'Rectification' of the revolution (1987–)

Sankara's overthrow and death have not been clearly explained. It appears that, after a tense meeting in October 1987, Sankara stormed out, leaving Compaoré and others strongly alienated from the President. Retrospective accounts from Compaoré and others argue that they resolved to remove Sankara because they feared for their lives and the 'revolution'. In any case, Sankara was either shot or blown up in October, and Compaoré took the helm, declaring that Sankara had betrayed the revolution and that his ascent to power would ensure its rectification.

Much of the rhetoric of the revolution was maintained by Compaoré, with quotations from Sankara's founding Political Orientation Speech and talk of imperialism. The CDRs were replaced by Revolutionary Committees in 1988, but – like much of the early Compaoré period – the name change was in style more than substance. One could say the same about the Programme of Action which was not radically different from the Popular Development Programme. However, in contrast to Sankara's stark hostility to elites and vested interests, Compaoré's regime gradually opened up to Mossi ethnic authorities and merchants. Later, Compaoré explicitly compared his regime to the glasnost regime of Gorbachev (Boudon, 1997: 132). In 1989, he opened up his Popular Front to a wider gamut of political forces than would have been entertained by Sankara. In the same year opposition parties were legalized, and a stronger independent media began to emerge.

The year 1991 can be seen as a key turning point. In that year a new constitution, ushering in a multi-party polity, was created. Land reform legislation was also introduced, privatizing ownership administered through modern and 'traditional' agencies. Also, the government signed a Structural Adjustment Loan with the World Bank, starting a longer-term relationship between the World Bank, IMF and Burkinabé state (Englebert, 1992/4: B18). In 1991–92, Compaoré and his party, *Organisation pour la Démocratie Populaire/Mouvement de Travail* won the elections. Opposition parties boycotted these elections, as they wished to install a *Conférence National* in the same vein as many Francophone neighbours, and there remained an authoritarian and corporatist tendency behind Compaoré's liberalization (Boudon, 1997). This authoritarianism became more apparent as the 1990s progressed: Compaoré was re-elected in 1998 after a rigged election, but his regime became increasingly unstable. *Africa Confidential* notes that 'two states in the [West Africa] region which are not at war – Burkina Faso and Togo – have been highlighted by Amnesty International as having some of the worst human rights records in the world' (10 November 2000: 7; see also *Africa Confidential*, 24 November 2000).

Writing in political struggle in Burkina Faso: democracy and development

Burkina Faso's political fortunes and misfortunes have been influenced by a constant background of political agitation, often based around ideological mobilizations from the left. Baxter and Somerville summarize this general dispensation:

From the earliest days of independence it was clear that Burkina Faso was going to be a political hornet's nest. In spite of a very low literacy rate... there has always been a small number of highly educated and motivated people organised in heady and highly active political groups, mostly adhering to leftist doctrines.

(1988: 247)

Unions' political rights

A key part of this political backdrop has been the actions of the labour unions. Lamizana faced a string of strikes in the late 1980s carried out in pursuit of gains for labour and more profound political change, and the instability that this generated contributed to the circumstances of the subsequent coup by Zerbo (Baxter and Somerville, 1988: 248). Zerbo's rule was opposed by the Patriotic League for Development (LIPAD), a left-wing political organization supported by various unions and led by Soumane Touré.

Burkina Faso's political pluralism up until 1980 – exceptional in the region – was substantially a result of constantly defended plural and independent union activity, as well as the complex cross-currents from labour unions to political parties (Otayek, 1989: 14). The ideological sway of leftist and revolutionary ideals gripped a younger cadre of the army as well, including Sankara, Compaoré and others. The next regime, that of Ouedraogo, immediately had to reconcile itself with these politicized groups incorporating radical elements from the military who were linked to LIPAD. In fact, 'trade unions have opposed virtually every regime and have been battered by almost as many' (Englebert, 1998: 43). During Sankara's rule, unions remained a force to be reckoned with. Sankara's relationship with the unions, as an alternative source of power, was one of increasing hostility. Famously, 2500 striking teachers were dismissed en masse in 1984, and the Sankara period was characterized by the constant detention of union and party leaders in 1986. The core dynamic of the state–labour relationship was both a political struggle over pay, and a tension between a desire by the state to incorporate the social power of the unions and the latter's desire to maintain political independence. This led the unions not only to struggle to protect their own corporate activities, but to denounce Sankara's creeping authoritarianism and its repercussions for democracy more generally (Otayek, 1989: 27). Compaoré immediately tried to ensure a *rapprochement* with the unions, releasing Touré from prison and giving him employment, but he was not permitted to retake his position as head of the Confederation of Burkinabé

Trade Unions. But the state–union relationship has remained difficult. Otayek sees Burkina Faso as a unique example of a persistent pluralist politics throughout the postcolonial period, substantially a result of union plurality and activism.

Structural adjustment

As has been argued in Chapter 4, structural adjustment imposes deleterious social effects on domestic societies that can generate organized struggle and provoke instability and authoritarianism within the state. Since implementing SAP in Burkina Faso, the Compaoré regime has had to contend with organized opposition from labour unions and students (Harsch, 1998, 1999). These organizations, which have been a force influencing Burkina Faso's politics from independence, have proved quite durable, even in the face of regimes which have tried to marginalize or incorporate opposition:

> The consolidation of the Compaoré regime proceeded over the period under consideration, 1992–94, behind a smokescreen of democratization... With the opposition parties marginalized, the only significant challenge to the regime came from the trade unions and student organizations who actively opposed the government's austerity policies.
>
> (Englebert, 1992/4: B13)

Unions have carried out a number of political activities to shape the course of structural adjustment in Burkina Faso. A series of strikes throughout the 1990s forced the government to increase public sector wages in the face of real wage declines. Failure to ensure industrial peace after the devaluation of the CFA franc in 1994 led the Prime Minister to resign. At the same time, unions mobilized in support of a Social Charter, to fence off certain entitlements from the austerity measures of the SAP. These broke down in 1994 (Englebert, 1992/4: B16).

Burkina Faso's 'vibrant' democracy

The activities of small leftist associations and unions jealous of their independence have been a constant theme in Burkina Faso's politics, and have contributed to the emergence of a relatively vibrant civil society in the present day. In rural areas, the mobilizational and empowerment aspect of the CDR has left a legacy in contemporary Burkina Faso and its peasant organizations (Atampugre, 1997: 60, 63).

The regional union of village groups, CRUS, regularly raises issues of central concern to peasants, and has lobbied the European Union concerning dumping practices, with some success (ibid.: 68). In 1996, students commenced a year-long strike against the declining conditions on campus and the increasing authoritarianism of the Compaoré government. The strike enjoyed widespread support (Wise, 1998). More recently, only weeks after Compaoré's re-election (again in dubious circumstances) in 1998, the murder of Norbert Zongo (*Africa Confidential*, 8 October 1999), a popular investigative journalist, triggered a year-long period of broad social protest and unrest. A democratic coalition was formed out of the student organizations, labour unions, human rights groups, women's groups, professional associations and others. Fifteen thousand attended Zongo's funeral, strikes rendered towns 'villes mortes', and the resurgence of civil opposition galvanized opposition parties into some action (Harsch, 1999).

Boudon concludes that:

> Civil society is comparatively dynamic and active. Unions, associations, and religious groups abound and express themselves regularly through strikes and demonstrations.
>
> (1997: 141)

Conclusion

The three cases outlined above demonstrate that political struggle is intrinsic to African politics. It may well be the case that political organizations and mobilizations are not centre-stage, and that ruling elites or powerful external forces provide the main conduits through which political change takes place. But it is also the case that each regime change, change in economic policy, new constitution or international intervention has to consider its effects on organized groups rooted in some ideal of struggle and liberation based on notions of justice and social equality: no structure of power can be entirely removed from struggles from below. Mozambique shows how peasants can struggle for decolonization or an end to war; Nigeria shows how ethnic groups can organize to promote a fairer redistribution of resources and political accountability within a diverse nation-state; and Burkina Faso shows how unions and other groups can pressure governments to take consideration of social welfare during adjustment. One could easily add other historiographies of struggle to this list: a consideration of union activity in Zambia (Mufune, 1996; Simutanyi, 1996);

pro-democracy movements in Nigeria (Ihonvbere and Vaughan, 1995); 'social mobilizations' in Benin (Banégas, 1995), and so on.

Further reading

A good introduction to Mozambique is Hanlon (1991) and his previous *Mozambique: Revolution Under Fire* (1990). On war in Mozambique, see Hall (1990), Fauvet (1984) and Wilson (1992). Forrest (1995) provides an excellent political economy of Nigeria. On MOSOP, see Frynas (1998) and his exchange with Detheridge and Pepple in *Third World Quarterly*. Ejobowah (2000) provides a readable overview. The best (and one of only two!) introduction to Burkina Faso is Englebert (1998). Otayek (1989) provides a critical assessment of revolution in Burkina Faso. See also Boudon (1997) and Harsch (1998, 1999).

7
Defending the Ideal of Struggle

Chapter 1 set out a fairly open conceptualization of political struggle, based on considerations of equality and participation and with an awareness of the powerful shaping forces of historical capitalism. Having reviewed a number of themes and issues of contemporary African politics, one gets a sense of how *contested* structures of domination are. Peasants subvert or ignore the regulations of states and market their goods in semi- or non-licit ways; structural adjustment has been implemented on an uneven and unstable landscape of resistance and mobilization, leading states to suppress and co-opt political organizations simultaneously with attempts to democratize. Democratization itself has provided opportunities for new forms of political expression and mobilization. Finally, new forms of identity politics have mobilized images and moralities of ethnic, religious and other identities to raise a wide variety of social–political agendas. Chapter 6 takes three country cases to reveal that the threads of political struggle are often present and play important roles in postcolonial history more generally. If this narrative is convincing, then we need to return to an issue raised in Chapter 1, namely the lack of interest in political struggle in most studies of contemporary African politics. A substantial part of the answer to this question can be found in contemporary academic approaches to African politics.

The death of political struggle?

It is easy to understand how political struggle has not enjoyed great prominence recently. The end of the Cold War (or at least the way the 'victory' of the West has been represented) and the neoliberal 'revolution' entrenched throughout many societies in the 1980s has yielded (and been promoted by) an intellectual climate which is increasingly hostile to the idea – and certainly the *ideal* – of struggle. The key features of this intellectual climate are the more nihilistic strains of post-structuralism, the triumphalism of a schematic liberalism (articulated with increasing power as the World Bank consolidates a greater intellectual presence), a tendency towards eschatology (with telling cross-overs into the media of the intelligentsia), and a revived interest in the epistemology of cultural relativism. Each of these approaches has written into it a hostility towards a serious consideration of the role of political struggle in African political economy. Let us briefly review these approaches in order to get a sense of the decline of struggle as an analytical concept.

Poststructuralism and the end of 'heroic narratives'

Poststructuralism as a general rubric contains within it a significant amount of diversity in terms of both epistemology and normative approach. The postmodern desire to reject all 'foundational' political beliefs, and to concern oneself with a supposedly agnostic analysis of discourse and signifiers can reasonably be rejected while taking on board the increasing cynicism with grand constructions of nationalism and progress, and accepting an increasing awareness of the complexity and local specificity of political formations. Furthermore, the increasing interest with 'new social movements', very much the progeny of a poststructuralism and post-marxist tendency, has provided important insights into contemporary forms of struggle (most often seen as new forms of resistance to globalization).

More specifically in respect to analyses of political struggle (and not only encompassing poststructuralism), there has certainly been an increased – and healthy – cynicism concerning previously fairly well-established 'heroic' narratives of national liberation which, when subject to detailed historical investigation, reveal aspects of oppression, and ideologies of liberation which hide the fact that, during struggle and after liberation, some are more equal than others. One might reasonably draw a trajectory here from de Brito's (1988) revisionist work on FRELIMO's liberation war, to Leys and Saul's (1995) balanced evaluation of SWAPO, and finally Clapham's (1988) edited volume on present-day guerrilla warfare, in which struggle is perhaps driven by popular aspirations and ideology (one could make this case in respect of the NRM/A in Uganda) or concerns of institutional control and power, as well as control over resources.

Liberalism and positive-sum politics

Concurrent with all of this interesting work has been a growth in the significantly more vacuous and stultifying work produced by the World Bank's dalliance into the field of 'political science'. Since it became apparent that economic liberalization in sub-Saharan Africa produces considerable political and social disturbance (perhaps over-lain on already existing social and political instability), the Bank has elaborated a strategy of external relations based on engagement with – and the selective incorporation of – important alternative sources of information and evaluation concerning the Bank's activities. Thus, we see the Bank's attempts to engage with non-governmental organiza-tions, to create a political lexicon for Bank interventions (governance, partnership, participation and so on), and to produce large amounts of academic work on issues such as corruption, ownership and culture. Also, within academe, the increasing importance of consultancies and the profusion of workshops and other forms of funding by the Bank and intergovernmental organizations has ensured that the Bank's polit-ical ideology has 'rippled' into the university (Schmitz, 1995). The broad contours of the Bank's work defines an image of African politics based on a bland liberalism, or neoliberal populism (Harrison, 2001a), portraying political change, or more accurately political 'progress', in terms of rational dialogue, positive-sum games, mutual concessions between different interest groups, and a conceptual separation of politics from economics. Reading the Bank's literature, there is no room for a notion of political struggle, unless one uses this term to encompass the three strategies of voice, exit and control (Paul, 1992). The problematic for the Bank is to avoid exit and, in doing so, to render political action delimited by narrow liberal boundaries.

Eschatology and the end of hope

Since the early 1990s, some observers – especially diplomats and jour-nalists – have come to the conclusion that, even if political struggle once existed as a significant presence in African politics, it has now been replaced – destroyed? – by an overwhelming wave of self-destruc-tion. The best-known example here is Kaplan's *Atlantic Monthly* article (1994), which was reviewed with great insight by Englund (1998). The tenor of this viewpoint – as Westerners stand aghast at the genocide in Rwanda or the war economies of Sierra Leone or Angola – is that the West would be best off disengaging as much as is practically possible from Africa, constructing a wall of defence in their wake. Clearly it would not be surprising to learn that, if he has read anything on

Africa, George 'Dubya' W. Bush has read Kaplan. Political struggle in this sense merely connotes a struggle for rapidly declining resources – not only minerals (the 'blood diamonds' of Angola or Sierra Leone, or even the tropical hardwoods of Liberia), but also livestock and people.

Functional chaos and the end of progress

A strong argument has emerged which portrays notions of political struggle as prescribing, in authoritarian fashion, a culturally and historically embedded set of ideals on Africa's non-Western societies and cultures. Rejecting this Western liberal notion of struggle has led some to analyse contemporary African politics through a relativist lens. As with poststructuralism (with which there are some affinities here), there is no good reason to reject all of this work – Williams (1996) has provided much insight into the supposedly neutral term 'development', especially as articulated by the World Bank. But, in other forms, cultural relativism appears to have a complex affinity with Kaplan et al. Chabal and Deloz's *Africa Works* (1999) takes disorder as its starting point, portraying African politics in essentially the same vein as Kaplan but without the journalistic salacity. Chabal and Deloz then identify the ways in which chaos, disorder and the collapse of all things 'official' work to reproduce forms of authority. Corruption, civil war and so on are actually signs of a functioning African polity, not a collapsing one. It follows that struggles for peace, democracy and social progress are actually dysfunctional – almost retrograde.

Political struggle and 'liberation'?

So much for political struggle: the victim of our neoliberal historical conjuncture and a profusion of epistemologies which write struggle out of the picture. Furthermore, the undeniably upsetting and extremely costly emergence of conflict and economic collapse in much (but not all) of Africa give even those who have a normative sympathy with the notion of struggle little more than a kind of 'hope against hope' approach to struggle: a reference to struggle as an act of faith, a coda of *a luta continua* at the end of otherwise dour narratives.

In light of the approaches above, it should be clear that one argument of this book is to chart a way through contemporary events, avoiding either the bland utopias of liberalism or the dystopias of what is generally known as 'Afropessimism', in which unreachable powers determine future possibilities. The book has been modest in its representations of struggle – there is no incipient 'revolution' afoot – but, in insisting on the persistence of political struggle and resistance, it allows a reasonable space for measured hope and aspiration in the study of African politics against formulations of Afropessimism. If writing is partly a political act then not to provide space for and consideration of struggle and resistance may be partly a result of the weakness of these phenomena in a certain place and time, but it is also to conspire in the production of images of the absence of struggle which reinforce constraining structures and support arguments that all images of liberation are ill-advised. While this author would not wish to prescribe a definitive notion of liberation, an awareness of the importance of struggle does allow for a consideration of ideals of liberation which – in light of Africa's general economic and political instability during the last 15 years or so – seems as necessary today as ever before.

Bibliography

Adam, H. (1992) 'Somalia: Militarism, Warlordism, or Democracy?' *Review of African Political Economy* 19, 54: 11–26.

Adedeji, A. and Otite, O. et al. (1997) *Nigeria: Renewal from the Roots: the Struggle for Democratic Development*. London: Zed Press.

Adepojou, A. (ed.) (1993) *The Impact of Structural Adjustment on the Population of Africa: the Implications for Education, Health and Employment*. London: James Currey.

Adesina, J. (1989) 'Worker Consciousness and Shopfloor Struggles: a Case Study of Nigerian Refinery Workers', *LABOUR Capital and Society*, 22, 2: 288–345.

Adesina, J. (1990) 'The Construction of Social Communities in Word: the Case of a Nigerian Factory', *Capital and Class*, 40: 115–49.

Africa Rights (1994) *Rwanda: Death, Despair, and Defiance*. London: Africa Rights.

Agbu, O. (1998) 'Political Opposition and Democratic Transitions in Nigeria, 1985–1996', in Olukoshi, A. (ed.), *The Politics of Opposition in Contemporary Africa*. Uppsala: Nordiska Afrikainstitutet, 242–64.

Ajulu, R. (1992) 'Kenya: the Road to democracy', *Review of African Political Economy*, 19, 53: 79–87.

Ajulu, R. (1993) 'The Kenyan Elections', *Review of African Political Economy*, 20, 56: 98–102.

Ajulu, R. (1995) 'The Left and the Question of Democratic Transition in Kenya: a Reply to Mwakenya', *Review of African Political Economy*, 22, 64: 229–35.

Aké, C. (1995) 'The Democratization of Disempowerment in Africa', in Hippler, J. (ed.), *The Democratization of Disempowerment. The Problem of Democracy in the Third World*. London: Pluto Press, 70–90.

Alavi, H. (1972) 'The State in Post-Colonial Societies: Pakistan and Bangladesh', *New Left Review*, 74: 59–81.

Alexander, P. (2000) 'Zimbabwean Workers, the MDC, and the 2000 Election', *Review of African Political Economy*, 85, 27: 385–406.

Allen, C. (1992) 'Restructuring an Authoritarian State: Democratic Renewal in Benin', *Review of African Political Economy*, 54: 43–59.

Allen, C. (1995) 'Understanding African Politics', *Review of African Political Economy*, 22, 65: 301–20.

Allen, M. (1999) 'Women, Bargaining and Change in Seven Structures of the World Political Economy', *Review of International Studies*, 25, 3: 453–74.

Alpers, E. A. (1975) *Ivory and Slaves in East Central Africa: Changing Patterns of International Trade to the Later Nineteenth Century*. London: Heinemann.

Amadiume, I. (1995) 'Gender, Political Systems, and Social Movements: a West African Experience', in Mamdani, M. and Wamba-dia-Wamba, E. (eds), *African Studies in Social Movements and Democracy*. Dakar: CODESRIA, 35–68.

Amadiume, I. (1997) *Reinventing Africa: Matriarchy, Religion, and Culture*. London: Zed Press.

Amin, S. (1987) 'Democracy and National Strategy in the Periphery', *Third World Quarterly*, 9, 4: 1129–56.

Amin, S. (1990) *Delinking: Towards a Polycentric World*. London: Zed Press.

Amin, S. (1995) 'Migrations in Contemporary Africa: a Retrospective View', in Baker, J. and Aina, T. (eds), *The Migration Experience in Africa*. Uppsala: Nordiska Afrikainstitutet, 29–40.

Amselle, J. L. (1998) *Mestizo Logics. Anthropology of Identity in Africa and Elsewhere*. Stanford, CA: Stanford University Press.

Anglin, D. (1998) 'International Election Monitoring: the African Experience', *African Affairs*, 97, 389: 471–97

Anstee, M. (1996) *Angola: An Orphan of the Cold War* London: Macmillan, now Palgrave.

Anyang' Nyong'o, P. (ed.) (1987) *Popular Struggles for Democracy in Africa*. London: Zed.

Appaiah, K. A. (1992) *In My Father's House: Africa in the Philosophy of Culture*. Oxford: Oxford University Press.

Arrighi, G. (1966) 'The Political Economy of Rhodesia', *New Left Review*, 39: 35–65.

Atampugre, N. (1997) 'Aid, NGOs and Grassroots Development: Northern Burkina Faso', *Review of African Political Economy*, 24, 71: 57–73.

Ate, B. (1991) 'The Political Imperative of Structural Adjustment in Nigeria', in Deng, L., Kostner, M. and Young, C. (eds), *Democratization and Structural Adjustment in the 1990s*. Madison, WI: University of Wisconsin-Madison, 162–71.

Auwal, N. (1987) 'A Hausa Vocabulary on Corruption and Political Oppression', *Corruption and Reform*, 2, 3: 293–6.

Baker, B. (1998) 'The Class of 1990: how have the Autocratic Leaders of Sub-Saharan Africa Fared under Democratization?', *Third World Quarterly*, 19, 1: 115–27.

Baker, B. (2000) 'Who Should be Called to Account for Good Governance in Africa?', *Democratization*, 7, 2: 186–210.

Baker, J. and Aina, T. (eds) (1995) *The Migration Experience in Africa*. Uppsala: Nordiska Afrikainstitutet.

Baker, J. and Pedersen, P. (eds) (1992) *The Rural–Urban Interface in Africa: Expansion and Adaptation*. Uppsala: Nordiska Afrikainstitutet.

Banégas, R. (1995) 'Mobilizations Socialies et Oppositions sous Kérékou', *Politique Africaine*, 59: 25–44.

Bangura, Y. and Beckman, B. (1993) 'African Workers and Structural Adjustment: a Nigerian Case Study', in Olukoshi, A. (ed), *The Politics of Structural Adjustment in Nigeria*. London: James Currey, 75–96.

Barchiesi, F. (1996) 'The Social Construction of Labour in the Struggle for Democracy: the Case of Post-Independence Nigeria', *Review of African Political Economy*, 23, 69: 349–69.

Barengu, M. (1997) 'Political Culture and the Party-State in Tanzania', in REDET, *Political Culture and Popular Participation*, Dar es Salaam: REDET.

Barratt-Brown, M. (1995) *Africa's Choices*. London: Penguin.

Barrington-Moore, M. (1966) *Social Origins of Dictatorship and Democracy*. London: Penguin.

Bartlett, D. (2000) 'Civil Society and Democracy: a Zambian Case Study', *Journal of Southern African Studies*, 26, 3: 429–46.

Bassett, T. (1988) 'Development Theory and Reality: the World Bank in Northern Ivory Coast', *Review of African Political Economy*, 41: 45–59.

Bates, R. (1981) *Markets and States in Tropical Africa: the Political basis of Agricultural Policies* Berkeley: University of California Press.

Bates, R. (1987) 'The Regulation of Rural Markets in Africa', in Commins, S., Lofchie, M. and Payne, R. (eds), *Africa's Agrarian Crisis: the Roots of Famine*. Boulder CO: Lynne Rienner, 37–53.

Baxter, J. and Somerville, K. (1988) 'Burkina Faso', in Allen, C. et al., *Benin, The Congo, and Burkina Faso. Politics, Economics, and Society*. London: Pinter, 247–285.

Bayart, J. F. (1993) *The State in Africa: the Politics of the Belly*. London: Heinemann.

Bayart, J. F. (2000) 'Africa in the World: a History of Extroversion', *African Affairs*, 99, 395: 217–69.

Bayart, J., Ellis, S. and Hibou, B. (2000) *The Criminalization of the State*. Oxford: James Currey.

Baylies, C. (1995) '"Political Conditionality", and Democratization' *Review Of African Political Economy*, 22, 65: 321–37.

Baylies, C. and Szeftel, M. (1982) 'Zambia's Economic Reforms and their Aftermath: the State and the Growth of Indigenous Capital', *Journal of Commonwealth and Comparative Politics*, XX, 3: 235–64.

Baylies, C. and Szeftel, M. (1997) 'The 1996 Zambian Elections: Still Awaiting Democratic Consolidation', *Review of African Political Economy*, 24, 71: 113–28.

Beckman, B. (1995) 'The Politics of Labour and Adjustment: The Experience of the Nigeria Labour Congress', in Mkandawire, T. and Olukoshi, A. (eds), *Between Liberalization and Oppression: The Politics of Structural Adjustment in Africa*. Dakar: CODESRIA, 281–324.

Beer, C. and Williams, G. (1975) 'The Politics of the Ibadan Peasantry' *African Review*, 5, 3: 235–57.

Beinart, W. and Bundy, C. (1987) *Hidden Struggles in Rural South Africa,* London: James Currey.

Berman, B. (1998) 'Ethnicity, Patronage, and the African State: the Politics of Uncivil Nationalism', *African Affairs*, 97, 388: 305–43.

Berman, B. and Leys, C. (eds) (1994) *African Capitalists in African Development*. London: Lynne Rienner.

Berman, B. and Lonsdale, J. (1991) *Unhappy Valley: Conflict in Kenya and Africa*, 2 vols. London: James Currey.

Bernstein, H. (1977) 'Notes on Capital and the Peasantry', *Review of African Political Economy*, 10: 60–74.

Bernstein, H. (1981) 'Notes on the State and the Peasantry: the Tanzanian Case', *Review of African Political Economy*, 21, 44–63.

Bernstein, H. (1990) 'Taking the Part of Peasants?', in Bernstein, H., Crow, B., Mackintosh, M. and Martin, C. (eds), *The Food Question*. London: Earthscan, 69–80.

Bernstein, H. (1996) 'South Africa's Agrarian Question: Extreme and Exceptional?', *Journal of Peasant Studies*, 23, 2/3: 1–53.

Bernstein, H. (2001) 'The Peasantry in Global Capitalism: Who, Where, and Why?', in Pantich, L. and Leys, C. (eds), *Socialist Register*: 25–52.

Bernstein, H., Crow, B., Mackintosh, M. and Martin, C. (eds) (1990) *The Food Question*. London: Earthscan.

Berry, S. (1983) 'Work Migration and Class in Western Nigeria: A Reinterpretation', in Cooper, F. (ed.), *Struggle for the City: Migrant Labor, Capital and the State in Urban Africa*. Beverly Hills: Sage, 111–34.

Berry, S. (1985) *Fathers Work for their Sons: Accumulation, Mobility, and Class Formation in an Extended Yoruba Community*. Berkeley: University of California Press.

Berry, S. (1993) *No Condition is Permanent. The Social Dynamics of Agrarian Change in Sub-Saharan Africa*. Madison: University of Wisconsin Press.

Berry, S. (1997) 'Tomatoes, Land and Hearsay: Property and History in Asante in the Time of Structural Adjustment', *World Development*, 25, 8: 1225–41.

Bhabha, H. (1995) 'Signs Taken for Wonders', in Ashcroft, B., Griffith, G. and Tiffin, H. (eds), *The Post-Colonial Studies Reader*. London: Routledge, 29–35.

Bierman, W. and Campbell, J. (1989) 'The Chronology of Crisis in Tanzania, 1974–86', in Onimode, B. (eds), *The IMF the World Bank and African Debt*, Vol 1. London: Zed Press, 69–87.

Biermann, W. and Wagao, J. (1986) 'The IMF and Tanzania: a Solution to the Crisis?', in Lawrence, P. (ed.), *World Recession and the Food Crisis in Africa*. London: James Currey, 140–8.

Bigsten, A. and Kayizzi-Mugerwa, S. (1999) *Crisis, Adjustment and Growth in Uganda: A Study of Adaptation in an African Economy*. London: Macmillan, now Palgrave.

Blackburn, R. (1997) *The making of New World Slavery: from the Baroque to the Modern*. London: Verso.

Bloom, (1998) *Identity and Ethnic Relations in Africa*. Aldershot: Ashgate.

Blunt, P. (1995) 'Cultural Relativism, "Good Governance" and Sustainable Human Development', *Public Administration and Development*, 15, 1: 1–9.

Bond, P. (1999) 'Political Reawakening in Zimbabwe', *Monthly Review*, 50, 11: 1–18.

Bond, P. and Mayekiso, M. (1996) 'Developing Resistance and resisting "Development"', in Panich, L. and Leys, C. (eds) *Socialist Register*: 33–61.

Boone, C. (1994) 'Accumulation, Wealth, Consolidating Power: Rentierism in Senegal', in Berman, B. and Leys, C. (eds), *African Capitalists in African Development*. London: Lynne Rienner, 163–89.

Boone, C. (1998) 'State Building in the African Countryside: Structure and Politics at the Grassroots', *Journal of Development Studies*, 34, 4: 1–31.

Boudon, L. (1997) 'Burkina Faso: the Rectification of the Revolution', in Clark, J. and Gardiner, D. (eds), *Political reform in Francophone Africa*. Boulder, CO: Westview Press, 127–44.

Bowen, M. (2000) *The State Against the Peasantry*. London: University Press of Virginia.

Brand, V., Mupedziswa, R. and Gumbo, P. (1993) 'Women Informal Sector Workers and Structural Adjustment in Zimbabwe', in Gibbon, P. (ed.), *Social Change and Economic Reform in Africa*. Uppsala: SIAS, 270–306.

Brass, T. (1997) 'The Agrarian Myth, the "New" Populism and the "New" Right', *Journal of Peasant Studies*, 24, 4: 201–46.

Bratton, M. and Posner, D. (1999) 'A First Look at Second Elections in Africa with Illustrations from Zambia', in Joseph, R. (ed.), *State, Conflict, and Democracy in Africa*. Boulder, CO and London: Lynne Rienner: 377–407.

Bratton, M. and van de Walle, N. (1992) 'Popular Protest and Political Reform in Africa', *Comparative Politics*, 24, 4: 419–41.

Bratton, M. and van de Walle, N. (1997) *Democratic Experiments in Africa. Regime Transitions in Comparative Perspective*. Cambridge: Cambridge University Press.

Brenner, L. (ed.) (1993) *Muslim Identity and Social Change in Sub-Saharan Africa* London: Hurst.

Brett, E. (1973) *Colonialism and Underdevelopment in East Africa: the Politics of Economic Change, 1919–1939*. London: Heinemann.

Brett, E. A. (1997) 'A Case for Structural Adjustment', *New Political Economy*, 2, 2: 322–5.

Brittain, V. (1985) 'Introduction to Sankara and Burkina Faso', *Review of African Political Economy*, 32: 25–39.

Brittain, V. (1998) *Death of Dignity: Angola's Civil War*. London: Pluto Press.

Bromley, S. (1993) 'Prospects for Democracy in the Middle East', in Held, D. (ed.) *Prospects for Democracy*. Cambridge: Polity, 380–407.

Bryceson, D. (1999) 'African Rural Labour, Income Diversification and Livelihood Approaches: A Long Term Development Perspective', *Review of African Political Economy*, 80, 26: 171–89.

Bryceson, D. (2000) 'African Peasants' Centrality and Marginality: Rural Labour Transformations', in Bryceson, D., Kay, C. and Mooij, J. (eds), *Disappearing Peasantries? Rural Labour in Africa, Asia, and Latin America*. London: Intermediate Technology Publications, 37–64.

Bryceson, D., Kay, C. and Mooij, J. (eds) (2000) *Disappearing Peasantries? Rural Labour in Africa, Asia, and Latin America*. London: Intermediate Technology Publications.

Bundy, C. (1979) *The Rise and Fall of the South African Peasantry*. London: Heinemann.

Bunker, S. (1984) 'Ideologies of Intervention: the Ugandan State and Local Organization in Bugisu', *Africa*, 54, 3: 50–72.

Burawoy, M. et al. (1991) *Ethnography Unbound: Power and Resistance in the Modern Metropolis*. Berkeley: University of California Press.

Burnell, P. (1995) 'The Politics of Poverty and the Poverty of Politics in Zambia's Third Republic', *Third World Quarterly*, 16, 4: 675–90.

Bush, R. (1994) 'Crisis in Egypt: Structural Adjustment, Food Security and the Politics of USAID', *Capital and Class*, 53: 15–37.

Byres, T. J. (1982) 'Agrarian Transition and the Agrarian Question', in Harriss, J. (ed.), *Rural Development: Theories of Peasant Economy and Agrarian Change*. London: Hutchinson, 82–94.

Cahen, M. (1990) 'Le Mozambique: une Nation africaine de langue oficielle portugaise?', *Canadian Journal of African Studies*, 24, 3: 315–47.

Cahen, M. (1993) 'Check on Socialism in Mozambique: What Check? What Socialism?', *Review of African Political Economy*, 57: 46–59.

Cahen, M. (1997) '"Entrons dans la nation" Notes por une étude du discours politique de la marginalité: le cas de la RENAMO du Mozambique', *Politique Africaine*, 67: 70–88.

Cammack, D. (1988) 'The "Human Face" of Destabilization: the War in Mozambique', *Review of African Political Economy*, 40: 65–75.

Cammack, D. (1999) 'The Democratic Transition in Malawi: from Single Party Rule to a Multi Party State', in Daniel, J., Southall, R. and Szeftel, M. (eds),

Voting for Democracy: Watershed Elections in Contemporary Anglophone Africa.
Aldershot: Ashgate, 183–205.

Campbell, B. (1989) 'Indebtedness in Africa: Consequence, Cause, or Symptom of Crisis?', in Onimode, B. (ed.), *The IMF, World Bank, and African Debt.* London: Zed Press, 44–65.

Campbell, B. and Clapp, J. (1995) 'Guinea's Economic Performance under Structural Adjustment: Importance of Mining and Agriculture', *Journal of Modern African Studies,* 33, 3: 425–51.

Campbell, H. and Stein, H. (eds.) (1992) *Tanzania and the IMF: The Dynamics of Liberalization,* Boulder, CO: Westview Press.

Carmody, P. (1998) 'Constructing Alternatives to Structural Adjustment in Africa', *Review of African Political Economy,* 25, 75: 25–47.

Caufield, C. (1998) *Masters of Illusion: The World Bank and the Poverty of Nations.* London: Macmillan, now Palgrave.

Chabal, P. and Deloz, J.-P. (1999) *Africa Works: Disorder as a Political Instrument* Oxford: James Currey.

Chambers, R. (1983) *Putting the Last First.* London: Longman.

Charlton, R. and May, R. (1995) 'NGOs, Politics, Projects, and Probity: a Policy Implementation Perspective', *Third World Quarterly,* 16, 2: 237–56.

Charney, C. (1987) 'Political Power and Social Class in the Neo-Colonial African State', *Review of African Political Economy,* 38: 48–65.

Chikhi, S. (1995) 'The Working Class, The Social Nexus and Democracy in Algeria', in Mamdani, M. and Wamba-dia-Wamba, E., eds), *African Studies in Social Movements and Democracy.* Daker: CODESRIA, 325–6.

Chingono, M. (1996) *The State, Violence, and Development. The Political Economy of War in Mozambique, 1975–1992.* Aldershot: Avebury.

Clapham, C. (1983) *Third World Politics.* London: Croom Helm.

Clapham, C. (1993) 'Democratization in Africa: Obstacles and Prospects', *Third World Quarterly,* 14, 3: 423–38.

Clapham, C. (1996) *Africa and the International System.* Cambridge: Cambridge University Press.

Clapham, C. (ed.) (1998) *African Guerrillas.* Oxford: James Currey.

Clarence-Smith, G. (1989) 'The Roots of the Mozambican Counter-revolution', *Southern African Review of Books,* April/May: 7–10.

Clark, D. (1991) *Democratizing Development.* London: Earthscan.

Cleaver, F. 1999 'Paradoxes of Participation: Questioning Participatory Approaches to Development', *Journal of International Development,* 11, 4: 597–612.

Cliffe, L. (1987) 'The Debate on African Peasantries', *Development and Change* 18, 4: 625–35.

Cliffe, L., Bush, R., Pankhurst, D. and Littlejohn, G. (1988) 'Southern Africa after the Drought: a Breakdown of Social Reproduction', *Leeds Southern African Studies,* No. 1.

Cliffe, L. and Davidson, B. (1988) *The Long Struggle of Eritrea.* London: Spokesman.

Cohen, R. (1980) 'Resistance and Hidden Forms of Consciousness Among African Workers', *Review of African Political Economy,* 7: 8–22.

Cohen, R. (1987) *The New Helots: Migrants in the International Division of Labour.* Aldershot: Avebury.

Cohen, R. and Goulbourne, H. (eds) (1991) *Democracy and Socialism in Africa*. Boulder, CO: Westview Press.

Cooper, F. (ed.) (1983) *Struggle for the City: Migrant Labour, Capital and the State in Africa*. Beverly Hills, CA: Sage.

Cooper, F. (1987) *On the African Waterfront: Urban Disorder and the Transformation of Work in Colonial Mombasa*. London: Yale University Press.

Coquery-Vidrovitch, C. (1976) 'The Political Economy of the African Peasantry and Modes of Production', in Gutkind, P. and Wallerstein, I. (eds), *The Political Economy of Contemporary Africa*. Beverly Hills, CA: Sage, 90–110.

Coquery-Vidrovitch, C. (1988) *Africa: Endurance and Change of the Sahara*, trans. David Maisel. London: University of California Press, 1988.

Corbridge, S. (1982) 'Urban Bias, Rural Bias, and Industrialization: an Appraisal of the Work of Michael Lipton and Terry Byres', in Harriss, J. (ed.) *Rural Development: Theories of Peasant Economy and Agrarian Change*. London: Hutchinson, 66–89.

Cornia, G., Jolly, R. and Stewart, F. (1987) *Adjustment with a Human Face. Vol.1, Protecting the Vulnerable and Promoting Growth*. Oxford: Clarendon Press.

Coulson, A. (1981) 'Agricultural Policies in Mainland Tanzania 1946–76', in Heyer, J., Roberts, P. and Williams, G. (eds), *Rural Development in Tropical Africa*. London: Macmillan, 52–89.

Coulson, A. (1982) *Tanzania: a Political Economy*. Oxford: Clarendon Press.

Cowen, M. (1981) 'Commodity Production in Kenya's Central Province', in Heyer, J., Roberts, P. and Williams, G. (eds), *Rural Development in Tropical Africa*. London: Macmillan, 121–42.

Cowen, N. and Shenton, R. (1998) *Doctrines of Development*. London: Routledge.

Crehan, K. (1997) '"Tribes" and the People who Read Books: Managing History in Colonial Zambia', *Journal of Southern African Studies*, 23, 2: 203–18.

Crook, R. (1988) 'Farmers and the State', in Rimmer, D. (ed.), *Rural Transformation in Tropical Africa*. London: Belhaven Press, 116–37.

Crook, R. (1997) 'Winning Coalitions and Ethno-regional Politics: the Failure of the Opposition in the 1990 and 1995 Elections in Côte d'Ivoire' *African Affairs*, 96, 383: 215–43.

Cruise O'Brien, D. (1971) 'Co-operators and Bureaucrats: Class Formation in a Senegalese Peasant Society', *Africa*, XLI, 4: 263–77.

Cruise O'Brien, D. (1991) 'The Show of the State in a Neo-Colonial Twilight: Francophone Africa', in Manor, J. (ed.), *Rethinking Third World Politics*. London: Longman, 145–65.

Cruise O'Brien, D. (1994) 'Democracy and Africa', *Economy and Society*, 23, 2: 247–53.

Cruise O'Brien, D. (1996) 'A Lost Generation? Youth Identity and State Decay in West Africa', in Werbner, R. and Ranger, T. (eds), *Postcolonial Identities in Africa*. London: Zed Press, 55–75.

Crummey, D. (ed.) (1986) *Banditry Rebellion and Social Protest in Africa*. London: James Currey.

Danaher, K. (ed.) (1994) *50 Years is Enough: The Case Against the World Bank and the International Monetary Fund*, Boston, MA: South End Press.

Davidson, B. (1978) *Let Freedom Come*. New York: Little, Brown.

Davidson, B. (1979) 'The Revolution of People's Power: Notes on Mozambique 1979', *Race and Class*, XXI, 2: 127–43.

Davidson, B. (1992) *The Black Man's Burden: the Curse of the Nation State*. London: James Currey.

Davis, L. (1995) 'Opening Political Space in Cameroon: the Ambiguous Response of the Mbororo', *Review of African Political Economy*, 22, 64: 213–28.

De Boeck, P. (1996) 'Postcolonialism, Power, and Identity: Local and Global Perspectives from Zaire', in Werbner, R. and Ranger, T. (eds), *Postcolonial Identities in Africa*. London: Zed Press, 75–107.

De Boeck, P. (1999) 'Domesticating Diamonds and Dollars: Identity, Expenditure, and Sharing in Southwestern Zaire (1984–1997)', in Meyer, B. and Geschiere, P. (eds), *Globalization and Identity: Dialectics of Flow and Closure*. Oxford: Blackwell, 177–211.

De Brito, L. (1988) 'Une relecture nécessaire: la genèse du parti-État FRELIMO' *Politique Africaine*, 29: 15–27.

Decalo, S. (1997) 'Benin: First of the New Democracies', in Clark, J. and Gardiner, D. (eds), *Political Reform in Francophone Africa*. Boulder, CO: Westview Press, 43–61.

Detheridge, A. and Pepple, N. (1998) 'A Response to Frynas', *Third World Quarterly*, 19, 3: 479–86.

Dia, M. (1996) *Africa's Management in the 1990s and Beyond. Reconciling Indigenous and Transplanted Institutions*. Washington, DC: World Bank.

Diamond, L., Linz, J. and Lipset, S. (1988) *Democracy in Developing Countries: Africa*. London: Adamantine.

Dieng, A. (1995) 'The Political Context of Structural Adjustment in Africa', in Mkandawire, T. and Olukoshi, A. (eds), *Between Liberalisation and Oppression: the Politics of Structural Adjustment in Africa*. Dakar: CODESRIA, 104–16.

Doom, R. and Vlassenroot, K. (1999) 'Kony's Message: a new *koine*? The Lord's Resistance Army in Northern Uganda', *African Affairs*, 98, 390: 5–37.

Doornbos, M. (1991) 'Linking the Future with the Past: Ethnicity and Pluralism', *Review of African Political Economy*, 19, 52: 53–65.

Doornbos, M. (1995) 'State Formation Processes under External Supervision: Reflections on "Good Governance"', in Stokke, O. (ed.), *Aid and Political Conditionality*. London: Frank Cass, 377–91.

Economic Commission for Africa (1989) *African Alternative Framework to Structural Adjustment Programmes for Socio-economic Recovery and Transformation*. Addis Ababa: UNECA.

Ejobowah, J. (2000) 'Who Owns the Oil? The Politics of Ethnicity in the Niger Delta of Nigeria', *Africa Today*. 47, 1: 29–47.

El-Kenz, A. (1996) 'Youth and Violence', in Ellis, S. (ed.), *Africa Now: People, Policies, and Institutions*. London: James Currey, 42–58.

Ellis, F. (1982) 'Agricultural Marketing and Peasant–State Transfers in Tanzania', *Journal of Peasant Studies*, 10, 4: 214–43.

Ellis, S. (1989) 'Tuning into Pavement Radio', *African Affairs*, 88, 352: 321–31.

Ellis, S. (1995) 'Liberia 1989–1994: a Study of Ethnic and Spiritual Violence', *African Affairs*, 94, 375: 165–99.

Elson, D. (1991) *Male Bias in the Development Process*, Manchester: Manchester University Press.

Elson, D. (1994) 'People, Development, and International Financial Institutions: an Interpretation of the Bretton Woods System', *Review of African Political Economy*, 62, 21: 511–24.

Engberg-Pedersen, P., Gibbon, P., Raikes, P. and Udsholt, L. (1996a) 'Structural Adjustment in Africa: a Survey of the Experience', in Engberg-Pedersen, P., Gibbon, P., Raikes, P. and Udsholt, L. (eds), *Limits of Adjustment in Africa.* London: James Currey, 1–78.

Engberg-Pedersen, P., Gibbon, P., Raikes, P. and Udsholt, L. (eds) (1996b) *Limits of Adjustment in Africa.* London: James Currey.

Englebert, P. (1992/4) 'Burkina Faso', in Legum, C. (ed.), *African Contemporary Record* Vol. 24. London: Africana, B13–B20.

Englebert, P. (1998) *Burkina Faso: Unsteady Statehood in West Africa.* Boulder, CO: Westview Press.

Englund, H. (1998) 'Culture, Environment and the Enemies of Complexity', *Review of African Political Economy*, 25, 76: 195–88.

Falola, T. (1999) *The History of Nigeria.* Westport, CT: Greenwood Press.

Fauvet, P. (1984) 'Roots of the Counter-Revolution: the MNR', *Review of African Political Economy*, 29: 108–21.

Feierman, S. (1990) *Peasant Intellectuals. Anthropology and History in Tanzania* Madison: University of Wisconsin Press.

Feinberg, R. (1988) 'The Changing Relationship Between the World Bank and the International Monetary Fund', *International Organization*, 42, 3: 545–560.

Ferguson, J. (1995) 'From African Socialism to Scientific Capitalism: Reflections on the Legitimation Crisis in IMF-Ruled Africa', in Moore, D. and Schmitz, G. (ed.), *Debating Development Discourse: Institutional and Popular Perspectives.* London: Macmillan, now Palgrave, 129–48.

Ferraz, B. and Munslow, B. (eds) (1999) *Sustainable Development in Mozambique.* Oxford: James Currey.

Fine, B. (1989) 'The Antinomies of Nationalism and Democracy in the South African Liberation Struggle', *Review of African Political Economy*, 16, 45/46: 98–106.

Fine, B. and Rustomjee, Z. (1996) *The Political Economy of South Africa.* London: Hurst.

First, R. (1970) *The Barrel of a Gun.* London: Allen.

First, R. (1977) *Black Gold.* Brighton: Harvester.

Fisiy, C. and Geschiere, P. (1996) 'Witchcraft, Violence, and Identity: Different Trajectories in Postcolonial Cameroon', in Werbner, R. and Ranger, T. (eds), *Postcolonial Identities in Africa.* London: Zed Press, 193–222.

Forrest, T. (1995) *Politics and Economic Development in Nigeria.* Boulder, CO: Westview Press.

Foster-Carter, A. (1978) 'The Modes of Production Controversy', *New Left Review*, 107: 47–77.

Fowler, A. (1992) 'Distant Obligations: Speculations on NGO Funding and the Global Market', *Review of African Political Economy*. 55: 9–29.

Freund, B. (1988) *The Making of Contemporary Africa.* London: Macmillan.

Frynas, J. (1998) 'Political Instability and Business: Focus on Shell in Nigeria', *Third World Quarterly*, 19, 3: 457–78.

Frynas, J. (2000) 'Shell in Nigeria: a Further Contribution', *Third World Quarterly*, 21, 1: 157–64.

Frynas, J. (2001) 'Corporate and State Responses to Anti-Oil Protests in the Niger Delta', *African Affairs*, 100, 398: 27–54.

Fukuyama, F. (1992) *The End of History and the Last Man*. London: Hamish Hamilton.

Galli, R. (1990) 'Liberalization is not Enough: Structural Adjustment and Peasants in Guinea-Bissau', *Review of African Political Economy*, 49: 52–68.

Gary, I. (1996) 'Confrontation, Co-operation, or Co-optation: NGOs and the Ghanaian State during Structural Adjustment', *Review of African Political Economy*, 23, 66: 169–95.

Geest, W. van der (1994a) 'The Bargaining Process of Police Based Lending', in van der Geest, W. (ed.), *Negotiating Structural Adjustment in Africa*. London: James Currey, 186–97.

Geest, W. van der (ed.) (1994b) *Negotiating Structural Adjustment in Africa*. London: James Currey.

Geffray, C. (1991) *A Causa das Armas: Antropologia da Guerra em Moçambique*. Porto: Afrontamento.

Geisler, G. (1993) 'Fair? What Has Fair Got to Do with It? Vagaries of Elections Observations and Democratic Standards', *Journal of Modern African Studies*, 31, 4: 21–34.

George, S. and Sabelli, F. (1994) *Faith and Credit: the World Bank's Secular Empire* London: Penguin.

Geras, N. (1990) 'Seven Types of Obloquy. Travesties of Marxism', *Socialist Register*: 1–34.

Gervais, M. (1995) 'Structural Adjustment in Niger: Implementations, Effects, and Determining Political Factors', *Review of African Political Economy* 22, 63: 27–43.

Ghai, D. (ed.) (1991) *The IMF and the South: The Social Impact of Crisis and Adjustment*. London: Zed Press.

Gibbon, P. (1992) 'The World Bank and African Poverty, 1973–91', *Journal of Modern African Studies*, 30, 2: 193–221.

Gibbon, P. (1996a) 'Structural Adjustment and Structural Change in Sub-Saharan Africa: Some Provisional Conclusions', *Development and Change*, 27, 4: 751–85.

Gibbon, P. (1996b) 'Zimbabwe', in Engberg-Pedersen, P., Gibbon, P., Raikes, P. and Udsholt, L. (eds), *Limits of Adjustment. in Africa*. London: James Currey, 347–93.

Gibbon, P. et al. (eds) (1992) *Authoritarianism Democracy and Adjustment: The Politics of Economic Reform in Africa*. Uppsala: SIAS.

Giddens, A. (1995) *A Contemporary Critique of Historical Materialism* London: Macmillan, now Palgrave.

Gill, S. (1993) 'Epistemology, Ontology, and the Italian School', in Gill, S. (ed.), *Gramsci, Historical Materialism and International Relations* Cambridge: Cambridge University Press, 21–49.

Gilroy, P. (1993) *The Black Atlantic: Modernity and Double Consciousness*. London: Verso.

Goulbourne, H. (1987) 'The State, Development, and the Need for Participatory Development in Africa', in Anyang' Nyong'o, P. (ed.), *Popular Struggles for Democracy in Africa*. London: Zed, 26–47.

Gutkind, P. and Wallerstein, I. (eds.) (1985) *The Political Economy of Contemporary Africa*. Beverly Hills, CA: Sage.

Guyer, J. (1992) 'Representation without Taxation: an Essay on Democracy in Rural Nigeria', *African Studies Review*, 35, 1: 41–81.

Hall, M. (1990) 'The Mozambican National Resistance Movement (RENAMO): a Study in the Destruction of an African Country', *Africa*, 60, 1: 39–67.

Halliday, F. (1989) *Cold War, Third World: an Essay on US–Soviet Relations*. London: Hutchinson.

Halliday, F. (1997) *Rethinking International Relations* London: Macmillan, now Palgrave.

Hanlon, J. (1986) *Beggar Your Neighbours: Apartheid Power in Southern Africa*. London: James Currey.

Hanlon, J. (1991) *Mozambique: Who Calls the Shots?* London: James Currey.

Hanlon, J. (1999) *Peace without Profit: How the IMF Blocks Rebuilding in Mozambique*. Oxford: James Currey.

Hanlon, J. (2000) 'Power without Responsibility: the World Bank and Mozambican Cashew Nuts', *Review of African Political Economy*, 27, 83: 29–45.

Harries, P. (1994) *Work, Culture and Identity*. Oxford: James Currey.

Harris, L. (1980) 'Agricultural Co-operatives and Development Policy in Mozambique', *Journal of Peasant Studies*, 7, 2: 338–52.

Harrison, G. (1994) 'Mozambique: an Unsustainable Democracy', *Review of African Political Economy*, 21, 61: 429–40.

Harrison, G. (1998) 'Marketing Legitimacy in Rural Mozambique: the Case of Mecúfi District, Northern Mozambique', *Journal of Modern African Studies*, 36, 4: 569–93.

Harrison, G. (1999a) 'Corruption, Development Theory, and the Boundaries of Social Change', *Contemporary Politics*, 5, 3: 207–20.

Harrison, G. (1999b) 'Conflict in a "Non Conflict Situation". Tensions and Reconciliation in Northern Mozambique', *Review of African Political Economy*, 26, 81: 407–14.

Harrison, G. (1999c) 'Corruption as "Boundary Politics": the State, Democratization, and Mozambique's Unstable Liberalization', *Third World Quarterly*, 20, 3: 537–51.

Harrison, G. (1999d) 'Mozambique Between Two Elections: A Political Economy of Transition', *Democratization*, 6, 4: 166–80.

Harrison, G. (2000) *Grassroots Governance: The Politics of Rural Democratization in Mozambique*. Lampeter: Edwin Mellen.

Harrison, G. (2001a) 'Administering Market Friendly Growth? Liberal Populism and the World Bank's Involvement in Administrative Reform in Sub-Saharan Africa', *Review of International Political Economy*, 8: 3.

Harrison, G. (2001b) 'Post-Adjustment Politics and Administrative Reform: Reflections on the Cases of Uganda and Tanzania', *Development and Change*, 32: 4.

Harrison, G. (2002) 'The Absence of Tradition in Rural Mozambique', *Journal of Contemporary African Studies*, forthcoming.

Harrison, G. and Riley, S. (1999) *The Evolution of Corruption in Mozambique*, MS. Paris: OECD Development Centre.

Harriss, J. (ed.) (1982) *Rural Development: Theories of Peasant Economy and Agrarian Change*. London: Hutchinson.

Harsch, E. (1998) 'Burkina Faso in the Winds of Liberalization', *Review of African Political Economy*, 78, 25: 625–41.

Harsch, E. (1999) 'Trop, c'est trop! Civil Insurgence in Burkina Faso 1998–99', *Review of African Political Economy*, 26, 81: 394–406.

Havnevik, K. (1993) *Tanzania: The Limits to Development from Above*. Uppsala: Nordiska Afrikainstitutet.

Hawthorn, G. (1993) 'Sub Saharan Africa', in Held, D., (ed.) *Democracy: North, South, East, West*. Oxford: Polity, 330–55.

Hay, M. and Stichter, S. (1984) *African Women South of the Sahara*. London: Longman.

Helleiner, D. (1966) *Peasant Agriculture, Government, and Economic Growth in Nigeria*. Homewood, IL: Richard D. Irwin.

Herbold Green, R. and Mavie, M. (1994) 'From Survival to Livelihood in Mozambique', *IDS Bulletin* 25, 4: 77–84.

Herbst, J. (1991) 'Labour in Ghana under Structural Adjustment: The Politics of Acquiescence', in Rothchild, D. (ed.), *Ghana: the Political Economy of Recovery*. Boulder, CO: Lynne Rienner, 173–92.

Hermele, K. (1988) 'Guerra e Estabilização. Uma análise a médio prazo do Programa de Recuperação Económica de Moçambique (PRE)', *Revista Internacional de Estudos Africanos*, 8/9: 339–49.

Hermele, K. (1990) *Mozambican Crossroads: Economic and Politics in the Era of Structural Adjustment*. Bergen: Chr. Michelsen Report No. 3.

Heyer, J. (1981) 'Agricultural Development Policy in Kenya from the Colonial Period to 1975', in Heyer, J., Roberts, P. and Williams, G. (eds), *Rural Development in Tropical Africa*. London: Macmillan, 90–120.

Heyer, J., Roberts, P. and Williams, G. (eds) (1981) *Rural Development in Tropical Africa*. London: Macmillan.

Holmquist, F. (1984) 'Self-Help: the State and Peasant Leverage in Kenya', *Africa*, 54, 3: 72–91.

Hook, S. (1998) 'Building Democracy through Foreign Aid: the Limitations of United States Political Conditionalities, 1992–1996', *Democratization*, 5, 3: 156–80.

Hope, K. and Chikulo, B. (eds) (2000) *Corruption and Development in Africa: Lessons from Country Case Studies*. London: Macmillan, now Palgrave.

Hopgood, S. (2000) 'Reading the Small Print in Global Civil Society: The Inexorable Hegemony of the Liberal Self', *Millennium: Journal of International Studies*, 29, 1: 1–25.

Howe, J. (1998) *Afrocentrism*. London: Verso.

Howell, J. (2000) 'Making Civil Society from the Outside: Challenges for the Donors', *European Journal of Development Research*, 12, 1: 3–22.

Huntington, S. (1991) *The Third Wave: Democratization in the Late Twentieth Century*. London: University of Oklahoma Press.

Huntington, S. (1996) *The Clash of Civilizations and the Remaking of World Order*. New York: Simon & Schuster.

Hutchful, E. (1989) 'From "Revolution" to Monetarism: the Economics and Politics of the Adjustment Programme in Ghana', in Campbell, B. and Loxley, J. (eds), *Structural Adjustment in Africa*. London: Macmillan, 92–131.

Hutchful, E. (1991) 'Eastern Europe: Consequences for Africa', *Review of African Political Economy*. 18, 50: 51–9.

Hutchful, E. (1994) '"Smoke and Mirrors": The World Bank's Social Dimensions of Adjustment (SDA) Programme', *Review of African Political Economy,* 21, 62: 569–84.

Hutchful, E. (1995) 'Adjustment, Regimes and Politics in Africa', in Mkandawire, T. and Olukoshi, A. (eds), *Between Liberalization and Oppression: The Politics of Structural Adjustment in Africa.* Dakar: CODESRIA, 52–77.

Hutchful, E. (1996) 'Ghana', in Engberg-Pedersen, P., Gibbon, P., Raikes, P. and Udsholt, L. (eds), *Limits of Adjustment in Africa.* London: James Currey.

Hyden, G. (1980) *Beyond Ujamaa in Tanzania: Underdevelopment and an Uncaptured Peasantry.* Berkeley, California: University of California Press.

Hyden, G. (1983) *No Shortcuts to Progress: African Development Management in Perspective.* Berkeley: University of California Press.

Hyden, G. (1992) 'Governance and the Study of Politics', in Hyden, G. and Bratton, M. (eds), *Governance and Politics in Africa.* Boulder, CO and London: Lynne Rienner, 1–26.

Hyden, G. and Bratton, M. (eds) (1992) *Governance and Politics in Africa.* Boulder, CO and London: Lynne Rienner, 141–206.

Ibrahim, J. (1986) 'The Political Debate and the Struggle for Democracy in Nigeria' *Review of African Political Economy,* 37: 38–48.

Ibrahim, J. (1993) 'The Transition to Civil Rule: Sapping Democracy', in Olukoshi, A. (ed.), *The Politics of Structural Adjustment in Nigeria.* London: James Currey, 129–39.

Ibrahim, J. and Souley, A. (1998) 'The Rise to Power of an Opposition Party: the MNSD in Niger Republic', in Olukoshi, A. (ed), *The Politics of Opposition in Contemporary Africa.* Uppsala: Nordiska Afrikainstitutet, 144–70.

Ihonvbere, J. (1993) 'Economic Crisis, Structural Adjustment and Social Crisis in Nigeria', *World Development,* 21, 1: 141–53.

Ihonvbere, J. (1995) 'From Movement to Government: the Movement for Multi Party Democracy and the Crisis of Democratic Consolidation in Zambia', *Canadian Journal of African Studies,* 29, 1: 1–25.

Ihonvbere, J. (1997) 'From Despotism to Democracy: the Rise of Multiparty Politics in Malawi', *Third World Quarterly,* 18, 2: 225–49.

Ihonvbere, J. and Vaughan, O. (1995) 'Nigeria: Democracy and Civil Society: the Nigerian Transition Programme 1985–1993', in Wiseman, J. (ed.), *Democracy and Political Change in Sub Saharan Africa.* London: Routledge, 71–91.

Iliffe, J. (1983) *The Emergence of African Capitalism.* London: Macmillan.

Iliffe, J. (1996) *Africans: The History of a Continent.* Cambridge: Cambridge University Press.

Iordansky, V. (1994) 'Youth in Sub Saharan Africa', in Legum, C. (ed.), *Africa Contemporary Record,* Vol. 24. New York and London: Africana, A159–A166.

Isaacman, A. (1990) 'Peasants and Rural Social Protest in Africa', *African Studies Review,* 33, 2: 1–121.

Isaacman, A. (1996) *Cotton is the Mother of Poverty.* London: James Currey.

Isaacman, A. and Roberts, R. (ed.) (1995) *Cotton Colonialism and Social History in Sub-Saharan Africa.* London: James Currey

Jackson, R. and Rosberg, C. (1982) 'Why Africa's Weak States persist: the Empirical and the Judicial in Statehood', *World Politics* 35, 1: 1–24.

Jeffries, R. (1991) 'Leadership Commitment and Political Opposition to Structural Adjustment in Ghana', in Rothchild, D. (ed.), *Ghana: the Political Economy of Recovery*. Boulder, CO: Lynne Rienner, 157–71.

Jeffries, R. (1993) 'The State, Structural Adjustment and Good Government in Africa', *Journal of Commonwealth and Comparative Politics*, 31, 1: 20–35.

Jeffries, R. (1998) 'The Ghanaian Elections of 1996: Towards the Consolidation of Democracy?', *African Affairs*, 97, 387: 189–209.

Jewsiewicki, B. (1980) 'Political Consciousness among the African Peasants in the Belgian Congo', *Review of African Political Economy*, 19: 23–32.

Jones, P. (2000). 'Individuals, Communities, and Human Rights' *Review of International Studies*, 26 (special issue): 199–216.

Joseph, R. (1987) *Democracy and Prebendal Politics in Nigeria*. Cambridge: Cambridge University Press.

Joseph, R. (1998) 'Africa, 1990–1997: From Abertura to Closure', *Journal of Democracy*, 9, 2: 3–17.

Kaiser, P. (1996) 'Structural Adjustment and the Fragile Nation: the Demise of Social Unity in Tanzania', *Journal of Modern African Studies* 34, 2, 227–37.

Kanyinga, K. (1998) 'Contestation over Political Space: The State and the demobilization of Opposition Politics in Kenya', in Olukoshi, A. (ed.), *The Politics of Opposition in Contemporary Africa*. Uppsala: Nordiska Afrikainstitutet, 39–91.

Kaplan, R. (1994) 'The Coming Anarchy', *Atlantic Monthly*, February, 44–66.

Kapur, D., Lewis, J. and Webb, R. (eds) (1997) *The World Bank: Its First Half Century* Vol. 1. Washington: Brookings Institution Press.

Karikari, K. (1993) 'Africa: the Press and Democracy', *Race and Class*, 34, 3: 55–66.

Karnick, N. (1998) 'Rwanda and the Media: Imagery, War, and Refuge', *Review of African Political Economy*, 25, 78: 611–25.

Kasfir, N. (1986) 'Are Peasants Self-sufficient?', *Development and Change*, 17, 4: 335–57.

Kasfir, N. (ed.) (1998a) *Civil Society and Democracy in Africa. Critical Perspectives* London: Frank Cass.

Kasfir, N. (1998b) 'The Conventional Notion of Civil Society: A Critique' in Kasfir, N. (ed.), *Civil Society and Democracy in Africa. Critical Perspectives*. London: Frank Cass, 1–20.

Kay Smith, Z. (1997) '"From Demons to Democrats": Mali's Student Movement 1991–1996', *Review of African Political Economy*, 24, 72: 249–63.

Kelsall, T. (2000) 'Governance, Local Politics, and Districtization in Tanzania: the 1998 Arumeru Tax Revolt', *African Affairs*, 99, 396: 533–52.

Kennedy, P. (1988) *African Capitalism: the Struggle for Ascendancy*. Cambridge: Cambridge University Press.

Khan, S. (1994) *Nigeria: the Political Economy of Oil*. Oxford: Oxford University Press.

Kirschke, L. (2000) 'Informal Repression, Zero Sum Politics and Late Third Wave Transitions', *Journal of Modern African Studies*, 38, 3: 383–407.

Kitching, G. (1980) *Class and Economic Change in Kenya. The Making of an African Petite Bourgeoisie*. London: Yale University Press.

Kitching, G. (1982) *Development and Underdevelopment in Historical Perspective*. London: Methuen.

Kraus, J. (1991) 'The Political Economy of Stabilization and Structural Adjustment in Ghana', in Rothchild, D. (ed.), *Ghana: the Political Economy of Recovery.* Boulder, CO: Lynne Rienner, 119–55.

Krieger, M. (1994) 'Cameroon's Democratic Crossroads', *Journal of Modern African Studies,* 32, 4: 605–28.

Krieger, N. (2000) 'Zimbabwe Today: Hope against Grim Realities', *Review of African Political Economy,* 27, 85: 443–50.

Labazée, P. (1985) 'Réorganization Économique et Résistances Sociales: la Question des Alliances au Burkina', *Politique Africaine,* 20: 10–29.

Lall, S. (1983) *The Poverty of Development Economics.* London: Institute for Economic Affairs.

Landell-Mills, P. (1992) 'Governance, Cultural Change and Empowerment', *Journal of Modern African Studies,* 30, 4: 543–569.

Lassiter, J. (1999) 'African Culture and Personality: Bad Social Science, Effective Social Activism, or a Call to Reinvent Ethnology?', *African Studies Quarterly,* 3, 3 [no page numbers].

Lawson, L. (1999) 'External Democracy Promotion in Africa: Another False Start?' *Commonwealth and Comparative Politics,* 37, 1: 1–30.

Leach, M. and Mearns, R. (eds.) (1996) *The Lie of the Land: Challenging Received Wisdom on the African Environment.* Oxford: James Currey.

Lele, U. (1975) *The Design of Rural Development. Lessons from Africa.* Baltimore, MD: Johns Hopkins University Press/World Bank.

Lemelle, S. and Kelley, R. (1994) *Imagining Home: Class, Culture and Nationalism in the African Diaspora.* London: Verso.

Lewis, P. (1999) 'Nigeria: an End to the Permanent Transition?', *Journal of Democracy,* 10, 1: 141–56.

Leys, C. (1996) *The Rise and Fall of Development Theory.* London: James Currey.

Leys, C. and Saul, J. (eds) (1995) *Namibia's Liberation Struggle: the Two Edged Sword.* London: James Currey.

Lipton, M. (1982a) 'Why Poor People Stay Poor', in Harriss, J. (ed.), *Rural Development: Theories of Peasant Economy and Agrarian Change.* London: Hutchinson, 66–81.

Lipton, M. (1982b) 'Game against Nature: Theories of Peasant Decision-Making', in Harriss, J. (ed.), *Rural Development: Theories of Peasant Economy and Agrarian Change.* London: Hutchinson, 258–68.

Lonsdale, J. (1986) 'Political Accountability in African History', in Chabal, P. (ed.), *Political Domination in Africa.* Cambridge: Cambridge University Press, 129–40.

Loxley, J. (1989) 'The Devaluation Debate in Tanzania', in Campbell, B. and Loxley, J. (eds.), *Structural Adjustment in Africa.* London: Macmillan, 13–36.

Loxley, J. (1990) 'Structural Adjustment in Africa: Reflections on Ghana and Zambia', *Review of African Political Economy,* 47: 8–27.

Luckham, R. (1982) 'French Militarism in Africa', *Review of African Political Economy,* 9, 24: 55–84.

Luckham, R. and Bekele, D. (1984) 'Foreign Powers and Militarism in the Horn of Africa', *Review of African Political Economy,* 30: 8–20 and 31: 7–28.

Lugalla, J. (1995a) 'The Impact of SAP on Women and Children's Health in Tanzania', *Review of African Political Economy,* 22, 63: 43–55.

Lugalla, J. (1995b) *Adjustment and Poverty in Tanzania*. Bremen: Information-szentrum Afrika.

MacGaffey, J. (1991) *The Real Economy of Zaire*. London: James Currey.

MacGaffey, J. (1994) 'State Deterioration and Capitalist Development: the Case of Zaire', in Berman, B. and Leys, C. (eds), *African Capitalists in African Development*. London: Lynne Rienner, 189–205.

Mackintosh, M. (1987) 'Agricultural Marketing and Socialist Accumulation: a Case Study of Maize Marketing in Mozambique', *Journal of Peasant Studies*, 14, 2: 243–67.

Magnusson, B. (1999) 'Testing Democracy in Benin: Experiments in Institutional Reform', in Joseph, R. (ed.), *State, Conflict, and Democracy in Africa*. Boulder, CO and London: Lynne Rienner, 217–37.

Malima, K. (1986) 'The IMF and World Bank Conditionality: the Tanzanian Case', in Lawrence, P. (ed.), *World Recession and the Food Crisis in Africa*. London: James Currey, 129–40.

Maliyamkono, T. and Bagachwa, M. (1990) *The Second Economy in Tanzania* London: James Currey.

Mamdani, M. (1976) *Politics and Class Formation in Uganda*. Kampala: Fountain Press.

Mamdani, M. (1983) *Imperialism and Fascism in Uganda*. London: Heinemann.

Mamdani, M. (1987) 'Contradictory Class Perspectives on the Question of Democracy: the Case of Uganda', in Anyang' Nyong'o, P. (ed.), *Popular Struggles from Democracy in Africa*. London: Zed, 78–93.

Mamdani, M. (1990) 'Uganda: Contradictions of the IMF Programme and Perspective', *Third World Quarterly*, 21, 3: 427–69.

Mamdani, M. (1993) 'University Crisis and Reform', *Review of African Political Economy*, 20, 58: 7–20.

Mamdani, M. (1995a) 'The Politics of Democratic Reform in Uganda', in Langseth, P., Katorobo, J., Brett, E. and Munene, J. (eds), *Uganda: Landmarks in Rebuilding a Nation*. Kampala: Fountain Press, 229–40.

Mamdani, M. (1995b) 'Democratization and Marketization', in Mengisteab, K. and Logan, B. (eds), *Beyond Economic Liberalization in Africa*. London: Zed Press, 17–21.

Mamdani, M. (1996) *Citizen and Subject*. London: James Currey.

Manson, A. (1998) '"Money Breaks Blood Ties": Chiefs' Courts and the Transition from Lineage', *Journal of Southern African Studies*, 24, 3: 485–508.

Marcus, T. (1980) *Modernising Superexploitation*. London: Zed Press.

Maré, G. (1989) 'Inkatha and Regional Control: Policing Liberation Politics', *Review of African Political Economy*, 16, 45/46: 179–190.

Maré, G. (1993) *Ethnicity and Politics in South Africa*. London: Zed Press.

Mari Tripp, A. (1998) 'Expanding "civil society": Women and Political Space in Contemporary Uganda', *Commonwealth and Comparative Politics* 36, 2: 84–107.

Marshall, J. (1990) 'Structural Adjustment and Social Policy in Mozambique', *Review of African Political Economy*, 17, 47: 28–43.

Marshall, J. (1993) *Literacy, Power and Democracy in Mozambique: the Governance of Learning from Colonization to the Present*. Boulder, CO: Westview.

Martin, M. (1994) 'Negotiating External Finance for Adjustment', in Geest, W. van der (ed.), *Negotiating Structural Adjustment in Africa*. London: James Currey, 197–223.

Marx, K. (1978) 'The Eighteenth Brumaire of Louis Bonaparte', in Tucker, R., *The Marx-Engels Reader*. London: Norton.

Mayoux, L. (1995) 'Beyond Naivety: Women, Gender Inequality and Participatory Development', *Development and Change*, 26, 2: 235–59.

Mbembe, A. (1991) 'Power and Obscenity in the Post-Colonial Period: the Case of Cameroon', in Manor, J. (ed.), *Rethinking Third World Politics*. London: Longman, 166–82.

Mbembe, A. (1992) 'Provisional Notes on the Postcolony', *Africa*, 62, 1: 2–23.

McMichael, P. (1997) 'Rethinking Globalization: the Agrarian Question Revisited' *Review of International Political Economy* 4, 4, 663–8.

Meillassoux, C. (1981) *Maidens, Meal and Money*. Cambridge: Cambridge University Press.

Mengisteab, K. (1995) 'A Partnership of the State, the Market in African Development: What Is the Appropriate Strategy Mix?', in Mengisteab, K. and Logan, I. (eds), *Beyond Economic Liberalization in Africa*. London: Zed Press, 163–75.

Mengisteab, K. and Logan, I. (eds) (1995) *Beyond Economic Liberalization in Africa*. London: Zed Press.

Messkoub, M. (1996) 'The Social Impact of Adjustment in Tanzania in the 1980s: Economic Crisis and Household Survival', *Internet Journal of African Studies*, 1.

Meyer, B. (1999) 'Commodities and the Power of Prayer: Pentecostalist Attitudes towards Consumption in Contemporary Ghana', in Meyer, B. and Geschiere, P. (eds), *Globalization and Identity: Dialectics of Flow and Closure*. Oxford: Blackwell, 151–77.

Meyer, B. and Geschiere, P. (1999a) 'Globalization and Identity: Dialectics of Flow and Closure', in Meyer, B. and Geschiere, P. (eds), *Globalization and Identity: Dialectics of Flow and Closure*. Oxford: Blackwell, 1–16.

Meyer, B. and Geschiere, P. (eds) (1999b) *Globalization and Identity: Dialectics of Flow and Closure*. Oxford: Blackwell.

Meyns, P. (1981) 'Liberation Ideology and National Development Strategy in Mozambique', *Review of African Political Economy*, 22: 42–64.

Mikell, G. (1991) 'Equity Issues in Ghana's Rural Development', in Rothchild, D. (ed.), *Ghana: the Political Economy of Recovery*. Boulder, CO: Lynne Rienner, 85–99.

Minter, W. (1988) *Operation Timber: Pages from the Savimbi Dossier*. Trenton, NJ: Africa World Press.

Minter, W. (1991) 'The US and the War in Angola', *Review of African Political Economy*, 18, 50: 135–44.

Mkandawire, T. (1992) 'Adjustment, Political Conditionality and Democratization in Africa', paper on *Democratization Processes in Africa*. Dakar.

Mkandawire, T. (1999) 'Crisis Management and the Making of "Choiceless Democracies"', in Joseph, R. (ed.), *State, Conflict, and Democracy in Africa*. Boulder, CO London: Lynne Rienner, 119–36.

Mkandawire, T. and Olukoshi, A. (eds) (1995) *Between Liberalization and Oppression: the Politics of Structural Adjustment in Africa*. Dakar: CODESRIA.

Mkandawire, T. and Soludo, C. (2000) *Our Continent, Our Future: African Perspectives in Structural Adjustment*. Trenton, NJ and Asmara, Eritrea: Africa World Press.

Mohan, G., Brown, E., Milward, B. and Zack–Williams, A. (2000) *Structural Adjustment: Theory, Practice and Impacts*. London: Routledge.

Moody Stuart, G. (1997) *Grand Corruption*. Oxford: World View.

Mosley, P., Harrigan, J. and Toye, J. (1995a) *Aid and power: the World Bank and Policy-Based Lending*. London: Routledge.

Mosley, P., Subasat, T. and Weeks, J. (1995b) 'Assessing Adjustment in Africa', *World Development*, 23, 9: 1459–73.

Mosley, P. and Weeks, J. (1993) 'Has Recovery Begun? Africa's Adjustment in the 1980s Revisited', *World Development* 21, 10: 1583–606.

Mudimbe, Y. V. (1998) *The Invention of Africa: Gnosis, Philosophy, and the Order of Knowledge*. London: James Currey.

Mufune, P. (1996) 'Industrial Strike Patterns in Zambia: towards Institutionalization?', in Sichone, O. and Chikulo, B. (eds), *Democratization in Zambia: Challenges for the Third Republic*. Harare: SAPES Books, 129–49.

Mundt, R. (1997) 'Côte d'Ivoire: Continuity and Change in a Semi-Democracy', in Clark, J. and Gardiner, D. (eds), *Political Reform in Francophone Africa*. Boulder, CO: Westview Press, 182–203.

Munslow, B. (1981) *The Fly and the Spider's Web: Mozambique in the Southern African Regional Subsystem*, Manchester Discussion Papers in Development Studies.

Munslow, B. (1983a) 'Why Has the Parliamentary Model Failed in Africa?' *Parliamentary Affairs*, 36, 2: 1–15.

Munslow, B. (1983b) *Mozambique: the Revolution and its Origins*. London: Longman.

Munslow, B. (1993) 'Democratization in Africa', *Parliamentary Affairs*, 46, 4: 478–92.

Murray, C. (1992) *Black Mountain: Land, Class and Power in the Eastern Orange Free State, 1880s to 1980s*. Edinburgh: Edinburgh University Press.

Mustapha, A. R. (1992) 'Structural Adjustment and Multiple Modes of Livelihood in Nigeria', in Gibbon, P., Bangura, Y. and Ofstad, A. (eds), *Authoritarianism Democracy and Adjustment*. Uppsala: SIAS, 188–217.

Musyoki, A. and Orodho, J. (1993) 'Urban Women Workers in the Informal Sector and Economic Change in Kenya in the Late 1980s', in Gibbon, P. (ed.), *Social Change and Economic Reform in Africa*. Uppsala: SIAS, 106–34.

Naanen, B. (1995) 'Oil Producing Minorities and the Restructuring of Nigerian Federalism: the Case of the Ogoni People', *Journal of Commonwealth and Comparative Politics*. 33, 1: 46–78.

Nabuguzi, E. (1993) 'Peasant Responses to Crisis in Uganda', *Review of African Political Economy*, 56: 53–68.

Neimeijer, D. (1996) 'The Dynamics of African Agricultural History: Is It Time for a New Development Paradigm?', *Development and Change*, 27, 1: 87–111.

Nelson, J. (ed.) (1990) *Economic Crisis and Policy Choice: the Politics of Adjustment in Developing Countries*. Princetown, NJ: Princetown University Press.

Nesbitt, P. (1988) 'Terminators, Crusaders and Gladiators: Western (Private and Public) Support for Renamo and Unita', *Review of African Political Economy*, 43: 111–24.

New African (2000) 'Reporting Africa', July/August.

Newbury, C. (1998) 'Ethnicity and the Politics of History in Rwanda', *Africa Today*, 45, 1: 7–25.

Nixon, C. (1972) 'Self-Determination: the Nigeria/Biafra Case', *World Politics,* 24, 4: 473–97.

Nkiwane, T. (1998) 'Opposition Politics in Zimbabwe: the Struggle within the Struggle', in Olukoshi, A. (ed.), *The Politics of Opposition in Contemporary Africa.* Uppsala: Nordiska Afrikainstitutet, 91–113.

Norval, A. (1996) *Deconstructing Apartheid.* London: Verso.

Nwajiaku, K. (1994) 'The National Conferences in Benin and Togo Revisited', *Journal of Modern African Studies,* 32, 3: 429–47.

Obasi, E. (1997) 'Structural Adjustment and Gender Access to Education in Nigeria', *Gender and Education,* 9, 2: 161–77.

Ohlson, and Stedman, S. (1994) *The New Is Not Yet Born: Conflict Resolution in Southern Africa.* Washington, DC: Brookings Institution.

O'Keefe, P. and Kirkby, J. (1997) 'Relief and Rehabilitation in Complex Emergencies', *Review of African Political Economy,* 24, 74: 567–82.

Okoye, C. (1999) 'Blocked Transition in Nigeria: Democracy and the Power of Oligarchy', in Daniel, J., Southall, R. and Szeftel, M. (eds), *Voting for Democracy: Watershed Elections in Contemporary Anglophone Africa.* Aldershot: Avebury, 158–81.

Olsen, G. R. (1998) 'Europe and the Promotion of Democracy in Post Cold War Africa: How Serious Is Europe and for What Reason?', *African Affairs,* 97, 388: 343–69.

Olukoshi, A. (1993a) 'Structural Adjustment and Nigerian Industry', in Olukoshi, A. (ed.), *The Politics of Structural Adjustment in Nigeria* London: James Currey, 54–74.

Olukoshi, A. (ed.) (1993b) *The Politics of Structural Adjustment in Nigeria.* London: James Currey.

Olukoshi, A. (1995) 'The Politics of Structural Adjustment in Nigeria', in Mkandawire, T. and Olukoshi, A. (eds), *Between Liberalization and Oppression: the Politics of Structural Adjustment in Africa.* Dakar: CODESRIA, 157–86.

Olukoshi, A. (ed.) (1998) *The Politics of Opposition in Contemporary Africa* Uppsala: Nordiska Afrikainstitutet.

Onimode, B. (ed.) (1989) *The IMF, World Bank and African Debt,* Vols 1 and 2. London: Zed Press.

Opello, W. (1975) 'Pluralism and Elite Conflict in an Independence Movement: FRELIMO in the 1960s', *Journal of Southern African Studies,* 2, 1: 66–83.

Oquaye, M. (2000) 'The Process of Democratization in Contemporary Ghana', *Commonwealth and Comparative Politics,* 38, 3: 53–78.

Orvis, S. (1993) 'The Kenyan Agrarian Debate: a Reappraisal', *African Studies Review,* 36, 3: 23–49.

Osaghae, E. (1995a) 'The Ogoni Uprising: Oil Politics, Minority Agitation and the Future of the Nigerian State', *African Affairs,* 94, 376: 325–44.

Osaghae, E. (1995b) 'The Study of Political Transitions in Africa', *Review of African Political Economy,* 22, 64: 183–97.

Osaghae, E. (1998a) 'Managing Multiple Minority Problems in a Divided Society: the Nigerian Experience', *Journal of Modern African Studies,* 36, 1: 1–24.

Osaghae, E. (1998b) *Crippled Giant: Nigeria since Independence.* London: Hurst.

Otayek, R. (1989) 'Burkina Faso: Between Feeble State and Total State, the Swing Continues', in Cruise O'Brien, D., Dunn, J. and Rathbone, R. eds.

Contemporary West African States. Cambridge: Cambridge University Press, 13–30.

Otayek, R. (1992) 'The Democratic "Rectification" in Burkina Faso', in Hughes, A. (ed.), *Marxism's Retreat from Africa*. London: Frank Cass, 82–104.

Owusu, M. (1992) 'Democracy and Africa – a View from the Village', *Journal of Modern African Studies*, 30, 3: 369–96.

Pankhurst, D. (1995) 'Towards Reconciliation of the Land Issue in Namibia: Identifying the Possible, Assessing the Probable', *Development and Change*, 26, 3: 551–85.

Parfitt, T. (1990) 'Lies, Damned Lies and Statistics: the World Bank/ECA Structural Adjustment Controversy', *Review of African Political Economy*, 17, 47: 128–44.

Paul, S. (1992) 'Accountability in Public Services: Exit, Voice and Control', *World Development*, 20, 7: 1047–60.

Pearson, R. (1992) 'Gender Matters in Development', in Allen, T. and Thomas, A. (eds), *Poverty and Development in the 1990s*. Oxford: Oxford University Press, 291–312.

Petras, J. and Morley, M. (1984) 'The Ethiopian Military State and Soviet–US Involvement in the Horn of Africa', *Review of African Political Economy*, 30: 21–31.

Plank, D. (1993) 'Aid, Debt, and the End of Sovereignty: Mozambique and its Donors', *Journal of Modern African Studies*, 31, 3: 407–30.

Ponte, S. (1998) 'Fast Crops, Fast Cash: Market Liberalization and Rural Livelihoods in Songea and Morogoro Districts, Tanzania', *Canadian Journal of African Studies*, 32, 2: 316–49.

Prunier, G. (1995) *The Rwanda Crisis*. London: Hurst.

Raikes, P. (1982) 'The State and the Peasantry in Tanzania', in Harriss, J. (ed.), *Rural Development: Theories of Peasant Economy and Agrarian Change*. London: Hutchinson, 350–80.

Raikes, P. (2000) 'Modernization and Adjustment in African Peasant Agriculture' in Bryceson, D., and Kay, C. and Mooij, J. (eds), *Disappearing Peasantries? Rural Labour in Africa, Asia, and Latin America*. London: Intermediate Technology Publications, 64–81.

Raikes, P. and Gibbon, P. (1996) 'Tanzania', in Engberg-Pedersen, P., Gibbon, P., Raikes, P. and Udsholt, L. (eds), *Limits of Adjustment in Africa*. London: James Currey, 215–301.

Raikes, P. and Gibbon, P. (2000) '"Globalization" and African Export Agriculture', *Journal of Peasant Studies*, 27, 2: 50–93.

Ranger T. (1980) 'Tradition and Travesty: Chiefs and the Administration in Makoni District, Zimbabwe, 1960–1980', *Africa*, 52, 3: 20–42.

Ranger, T. (1985) *The Invention of Tribalism in Zimbabwe*. Harare: Ravan Press.

Rapley, J. (1994) 'The Ivorien Bourgeoisie', in Berman, B. and Leys, C. (eds), *African Capitalists in African Development*. London: Lynne Rienner, 39–69.

Richards, P. (1996) *Fighting for the Rainforest: War, Youth, and Resources in Sierra Leone*. Oxford: James Currey.

Riddell, B. (1992) 'Things Fall Apart Again: Structural Adjustment Programmes in Sub-Saharan Africa', *Journal of Modern African Studies*, 30, 1: 53–68.

Riley, S. and Parfitt, T. (1987) 'Party or Masquerade? The All-Peoples Congress of Sierra Leone', *Journal of Commonwealth and Comparative Politics* XXV, 2: 161–79.

Riley, S. and Parfitt, T. (1994) 'Economic Adjustment and Democratization in Africa', in Walton, J. and Seddon, D. (eds), *Free Markets and Food Riots: the Politics of Global Adjustment*. Oxford: Basil Blackwell, 135–70.

Rimmer, D. (ed.) (1988) *Rural Transformation in Tropical Africa*. London: Belhaven Press.

Rodney, W. (1972) *How Europe Underdeveloped Africa*. London: Bogle l'Ouverture.

Rosenburg, J. (1996) 'Isaac Deutsche and the Lost History of International Relations', *New Left Review*, 215: 3–15.

Rothchild, D. (ed.) (1991) *Ghana: the Political Economy of Recovery*. Boulder, CO: Lynne Rienner.

Rothchild, D. and Chazan, N. (eds) (1988) *The Precarious Balance: State and Society in Africa*. Bolder, CO: Westview Press.

Rudebeck, L. (1990) 'The Effects of Structural Adjustment on Kandjadja, Guinea Bissau', *Review of African Political Economy*, 17, 49: 34–51.

Rudebeck, L. (1997) '"To Seek Happiness": Development in a West African Village in the Era of Democratization', *Review of African Political Economy*, 24, 71: 75–86.

Rueschmeyer, D., Stephens, E. and Stephens, J. (1992) *Capitalist Development and Democracy*. Oxford: Polity.

Sachikonye, L. (1993) 'Structural Adjustment, the State, and Organised Labour in Zimbabwe', in Gibbon, P. (ed.) *Social Change and Economic Reform in Africa*. Uppsala: SIAS, 244–76.

Sahn, D., Dorosh, P. and Younger, S. (1999) *Structural Adjustment Reconsidered: Economic Policy and Poverty in Africa*. Cambridge: Cambridge University Press.

Said, E. (1995) *Orientalism*. Harmondsworth: Penguin.

Salah Tahi, M. (1995) 'Algeria's Democratisation Process: a Frustrated Hope', *Third World Quarterly*, 16, 2: 197–221.

Sandbrook, R. (1996a) 'Transitions without Consolidation: Democratization in Six African Cases', *Third World Quarterly*, 17, 1: 69–87.

Sandbrook, R. (1996b) 'Democratization and the Implementation of Economic Reform in Africa', *Journal of International Development*, 8, 1: 1–21.

Sankara, T. (1985) 'The Political Orientation of Burkina Faso', *Review of African Political Economy*, 32: 39–48.

Saul, J. (1974) 'The State in Postcolonial Societies: Tanzania', *Socialist Register*, 349–72.

Saul, J. (1990) 'From Thaw to Flood: the End of the Cold War in Southern Africa', *Review of African Political Economy*, 18, 50: 145–58.

Saul, J. (1991) 'South Africa: Between Barbarism and Structural Reform', *New Left Review*, 188: 3–44.

Saul, J. (1997) 'For Fear of Being Condemned as Old Fashioned: Liberal Democracy vs. Popular Democracy in Sub-Saharan Africa', *Review of African Political Economy*, 24, 73: 339–53.

Saul, J. S. (ed.) (1985) *A Difficult Road: the Transition to Socialism in Mozambique*. New York: Monthly Review Press.

Saul, M. (1986) 'Development of the Grain Market and Merchants in Burkina Faso', *Journal of Modern African Studies*, 24, 1: 127–53.

Schatz, S. (1994) 'Structural Adjustment in Africa: a Failing Grade so Far', *Journal of Modern African Studies*, 32, 4: 679–92.

Schatz, S. (1996) 'The World Bank's Fundamental Misconception in Africa', *Journal of Modern African Studies*, 34, 2: 239–47.

Schatzberg, M. (1990) *Mobutu or Chaos? The United States and Zaire, 1960–1990*. London: University Press of America.

Schmitz, G. (1995) 'Democratization and Demystification: Deconstructing "Governance" as Development Paradigm', in Moore, D. and Schmitz, G. (eds), *Debating Development Discourse*. London: Macmillan, now Palgrave, 54–91.

Schraeder, P. (1995) 'Political Elites and the Process of Democratization in Africa', in Hippler, J. (ed.), *The Democratization of Disempowerment. The Problem of Democracy in the Third World*. London: Pluto Press, 44–70.

Schraeder, P. (1996) *United States Foreign Policy Toward Africa*. Cambridge: Cambridge University Press.

Scott, J. (1985) *Weapons of the Weak: Everyday Forms of Peasant Resistance*. London: Yale University Press.

Searle, C. (1981) *We're Building the New School: Diary of a Teacher in Mozambique*. London: Zed Press.

Seddon, D. (1978) *Relations of Production – Marxist Approaches to Economic Anthropology*. London: Cass.

Seddon, D. (1986) 'Bread Riots in North Africa: Economic Policy and Social Unrest in Tunisia and Morocco', in Lawrence, P. (ed.), *World Recession and the Food Crisis in Africa*. London: James Currey, 177–193.

Sender, J. and Smith, S. (1986) *The Development of Capitalism in Africa*. London: Methuen.

Sharp, J. (ed.) (1997) 'The Politics of Identity', special number, *Journal of Contemporary African Studies*, 15, 1.

Sharp, J. (1997) 'Beyond Exposé Analysis', *Journal of Contemporary African Studies*, 15, 1: 7–23.

Shivji, I. (1978) *Class Struggles in Tanzania*. London: Heinemann.

Sichone, O. (1996) 'Democracy and Crisis in Zambia', in Sichone, O. and Chikulo, B. (eds), *Democratization in Zambia: Challenges for the Third Republic* Harare: SAPES Books, 109–28.

Simon, D., van Spengen, W., Dixon, C. and Närman, A. (eds) (1995) *Structurally Adjusted Africa: Poverty, Debt, and Basic Needs*. London: Pluto.

Simutanyi, N. (1996) 'Organised Labour, Economic Crisis and Structural Adjustment in Africa: the Case of Zambia', in Sichone, O. and Chikulo, B. (eds), *Democratization in Zambia: Challenges for the Third Republic*. Harare: SAPES Books, 151–72.

Singh, A. (1986) 'A Commentary on the IMF and World Bank Policy Programme', in Lawrence, P. (ed.), *World Recession and the Food Crisis in Africa*. London: James Currey, 104–14.

Skalnes, T. (1993) 'The State, Interest Groups, and Structural Adjustment in Zimbabwe', *Journal of Development Studies*, 29, 3: 401–28.

Skinner, E. (1988) 'Sankara and the Burkinabé Revolution: Charisma and Power, Local and External Dimensions', *Journal of Modern African Studies*, 26, 3: 437–55.

Smith, A. K. (1991) The Idea of Mozambique and its Enemies c. 1890–1930', *Journal of Southern African Studies*, 17, 3: 496–524.

Sogge, D. (ed.) (1996) *Compassion and Calculation*. London: Pluto.

Sparr, P. (ed.)(1994) *Mortgaging Women's Lives: Feminist Critiques of Structural Adjustment*. London: Zed.

Speirs, M. (1991) 'Agrarian Change and the Revolution in Burkina Faso', *African Affairs*, 90: 89–110.

Speirs, M. (1996) 'Burkina Faso', in Engberg-Pedersen, P., Gibbon, P., Raikes, P. and Udsholt, L. (eds), *Limits of Adjustment in Africa*. London: James Currey, 81–133.

Spivak, G. (1988) 'Can the Subaltern Speak?', in Nelson, C. and Grossberg, L. (eds), *Marxism and the Interpretation of Culture*. London: Macmillan, 311–57.

Stockwell, J. (1978) *In Search of Enemies: How the CIA Lost Angola*. London: Deutsch.

Stoneman, C. (ed.) (1988) *Zimbabwe's Prospects*. London: Macmillan.

Stoneman, C. (1992) 'The World Bank Demands its Pound of Zimbabwe's Flesh', *Review of African Political Economy*, 19, 53: 94–6.

Suberu, R. (1993) 'The Travails of Federalism in Nigeria', *Journal of Democracy*, 4, 4: 39–53.

Sutcliffe, P. (1986) 'Africa and the World Economic Crisis', in Lawrence, P. (ed.), *World Recession and the Food Crisis in Africa*. London: James Currey, 18–29.

Swantz, M. and Mari Tripp, A., eds (1996) *What Went Right in Tanzania: People's Response to Directed Development*. Dar es Salaam: Dar es Salaam University Press.

Szeftel, M. (1987) 'The Crisis in the Third World', in Bush, R., Johnston, G. and Coates, D. (eds), *The World Order: Socialist Perspectives*. Oxford: Polity Press, 87–141.

Szeftel, M. (2000) '"Eat with Us": Managing Corruption and Patronage under Zambia's Three Republics, 1964–99', *Journal of Contemporary African Studies*, 18, 2: 207–25.

Tarp, F. (1993) *Stabilization and Structural Adjustment: Macroeconomic Frameworks for Analysing the Crisis in Sub Saharan Africa*. London: Routledge.

Therborn, G. (1977) 'The Rule of Capital and the Rise of Democracy', *New Left Review*, 103: 3–41.

Therborn, G. (2001) 'Into the 21st. Century: New Parameters of Global Politics', *New Left Review*, 2, 10: 87–110.

Thompson, C. (1991) *Harvests Under Fire*. London: Zed Press.

Thompson, E. P. (1980) *The Making of the English Working Class*. London: Penguin.

Thornton, R. (1996) 'The Potentials of Boundaries in South Africa: Steps towards a Theory of the Social Edge', in Werbner, R. and Ranger, T. (eds), *Postcolonial Identities in Africa*. London: Zed Press, pp. 136–63.

Throup, D. (1993) 'Elections and Political Legitimacy in Kenya', *Africa*, 63, 3: 371–96.

Tiffen, P. and Barratt-Brown, M. (1992) *Short Changed*. London: Pluto Press.

Trager, L. (1995) 'Women Migrants and Rural–Urban Linkages in Southwestern Nigeria', in Baker, J. and Aina, T. (eds), *The Migration Experience in Africa*. Uppsala: SIAS, 269–89.

Turrittin, J. (1991) 'Mali: People Topple Traoré', *Review of African Political Economy*, 19, 52: 97–103.

Vail, L. and White, L. (1978) '"*Tawani Machambero!*" Forced Cotton and Rice Growing on the Zambezi', *Journal of African History*, XIX, 2: 239–63.

Van den Berg, J. (1987) 'A Peasant Form of Production: Wage-Dependent Agriculture in Southern Mozambique', *Canadian Journal of African Studies*, XXI, 3: 375–89.

Van Onselen, C. (1980) *Chibaro: African Mine Labour in Southern Rhodesia, 1900–1933*. Johannesburg: Ravan Press.

Vengroff, R. and Kone, M. (1995) 'Mali: Democracy and Political Change', in Wiseman, J. (ed.), *Democracy and Political Change in Sub Saharan Africa* London: Routledge, 45–70.

Venter, D. (1995) 'Malawi: the Transition to Multiparty Politics', in Wiseman, J. (ed.), *Democracy and Political Change in Sub Saharan Africa*. London: Routledge, 152–92.

Wallerstein, I. (1997) 'Eurocentricism and Its Avatars: the Dilemmas of Social Science', *New Left Review*, 226: 93–107.

Walt, G. and Melamed, A. (1983) *Mozambique: Towards a People's Health Service*. London: Zed Press.

Walton, J. and Seddon, D. (eds) (1994) *Free Markets and Food Riots: the Politics of Global Adjustment*. Oxford: Basil Blackwell.

Welch, C. (1995) 'The Ogoni and Self Determination: Increasing Violence in Nigeria', *Journal of Modern African Studies*, 33, 4: 635–49.

Werbner, R. (1996) 'Multiple Identities, Plural Arenas', in Werbner, R. and Ranger, T. (eds), *Postcolonial Identities in Africa*. London: Zed Press, 1–27.

Werbner, R. and Ranger, T. (eds) (1996) *Postcolonial Identities in Africa*. London: Zed Press.

White, L. (1993) *Bridging the Zambesi: a Colonial Folly*. London: Macmillan, now Palgrave.

Wieland, C. (1998) 'Economic Policy Reform and Political Transitions in Sub-Saharan Africa', *Democratization*, 5, 3: 127–55.

Wield, D. (1983) 'Mozambique – Late Colonialism and Early Problems of Transition', in White, G., Murray, R. and White, C. (eds), *Revolutionary Socialist Development in the Third World*. Brighton: Wheatsheaf, 75–113.

Wilkins, M. (1990/1) 'The Death of Thomas Sankara and the Rectification of the People's Revolution in Burkina Faso', *African Affairs*, 88, 352: 375–88.

Williams, D. (1996) 'Governance and the Discipline of Development', *European Journal of Development Research*, 8, 2: 157–77.

Williams, D. (1999) 'Constructing the Economic Space: the World Bank and the Making of Homo Oeconomicus', *Millennium: Journal of International Studies*, 28, 1: 79–101.

Williams, G. (1976) 'Taking the Part of the Peasants: Rural Development in Nigeria and Tanzania', in Gutkind, P. and Wallerstein, I. (eds), *The Political Economy of Contemporary Africa*. Beverly Hills, CA: Sage, 131–54.

Williams, G. (1981) 'The World Bank and the Peasant Problem', in Heyer, J., Roberts, P. and Williams, G. (eds), *Rural Development in Tropical Africa*. London: Macmillan, 16–52.

Williams, G. (1985) 'Marketing Boards in Nigeria', *Review of African Political Economy*, 34: 4–15.

Williams, G. (1987) 'Primitive Accumulation: the Way to Progress?', *Development and Change*, 18, 4: 637–59.

Williams, G. (1994) 'Why Structural Adjustment Is Necessary and Why It Doesn't Work', *Review of African Political Economy*, 60, 21: 214–25.

Wilson, K. B. (1992) 'Cults of Violence and Counter-violence in Mozambique', *Journal of Southern African Studies*, 18, 3: 527–82.

Wilson, K. B. (1994) 'The People's Peace in Mozambique', *Southern Africa Report*, 9, 4: 22–5.

Winchester, N. B. (1995) 'African Politics since Independence', in Martin, P. and O'Meara, D. (eds), *Africa*. London: James Currey, 247–359.

Wise, C. (1998) 'Chronicle of a Student Strike in Africa: the Case of Burkina Faso, 1996–1997', *African Studies Review*, 41, 2: 19–36.

Wiseman, J. (ed.) (1995) *Democracy and Political Change in Sub Saharan Africa*. London: Routledge.

Wolpe, H. (1972) 'Capitalism and Cheap Labour-power in South Africa: from Segregation to *Apartheid*', *Economy and Society*, 1, 4: 2–30.

Wolpe, H. (1980) *The Articulation of Modes of Production*. London: Routledge.

Wood, E. M. (1995) *Democracy against Capitalism*. Cambridge: Cambridge University Press.

Worby, E. (1998) 'Tyranny, Parody, and Ethnic Polarity: Ritual Engagements with the State in Northwestern Zimbabwe', *Journal of Southern African Studies*, 24, 3: 561–78.

World Bank (1981) *Accelerated Development in Sub Saharan Africa: an Agenda to Action*. Washington, DC: World Bank.

World Bank (1989) *Sub-Saharan Africa: From Crisis to Sustainable Growth: a Long Term Perspective Study*. Washington, DC: World Bank.

World Bank (1994a) *Adjustment in Africa: Reforms, Results and the Road Ahead*. Oxford: World Bank.

World Bank (1994b) *Governance: the World Bank's Experience*. Washington, DC: World Bank.

World Bank (2000) *African Development Indicators*. Washington, DC: World Bank.

Wright, G. (1997) *The Destruction of a Nation: United States' Policy Towards Angola since 1945*. London: Pluto.

Wuyts, M. (1991) 'Mozambique: Economic Management and Adjustment Policies', in Ghai, D. (ed.), *The IMF and the South: The Social Impact of Crisis and Adjustment*. London: Zed Press, 215–35.

Young, C. (1988) 'The African Colonial State and its Legacy', in Rothchild, D. and Chazan, N. (eds), *The Precarious Balance: State and Society in Africa*. Boulder, CO: Westview Press, 25–66.

Young, C. (1999) 'The Third Wave of Democratization in Africa: Ambiguities and Contradictions', in Joseph, R. (ed.), *State, Conflict, and Democracy in Africa*. Boulder, CO and London: Lynne Rienner: 15–39.

Young, T. (1993a) *Forcing Men to be Free? Making Sense of the West's Agenda in the Third World: the Case of Mozambique*, paper for 'Detraditionalization: Authority and Self in an Age of Uncertainty', Lancaster University, July.

Young, T. (1993b) 'Elections and Electoral Politics in Africa', *Africa*, 63, 3: 299–313.

Young, T. (1995) '"A Project Yet to Be Realised": Global Liberalism and Contemporary Africa', *Millennium: Journal of International Studies* 24, 3: 527–46.

Young, T. (1999) 'The State and Politics in Africa', *Journal of Southern African Studies*, 25, 1: 155–63.

Zack-Williams, A. (1990) 'Sierra Leone: Crisis and Despair', *Review of African Political Economy*, 17, 49: 22–33.

Zack-Williams, A. (2000) 'Social Consequences of Structural Adjustment', in Mohan, G., Brown, E., Milward, B. and Zack-Williams, A., *Structural Adjustment: Theory Practice, and Impacts*. London: Routledge, 59–74.

Index